PLUNDER OF THE ANCIENTS

*A True Story of Betrayal, Redemption, and an Undercover
Quest to Recover Sacred Native American Artifacts*

LUCINDA DELANEY SCHROEDER

*Foreword by Ben Nighthorse Campbell,
Retired US Senator from Colorado and
Member of the Cheyenne Tribe*

LYONS PRESS
Guilford, Connecticut
Helena, Montana
An imprint of Rowman & Littlefield

An imprint of Rowman & Littlefield

Distributed by NATIONAL BOOK NETWORK

Copyright © 2014 by Lucinda Delaney Schroeder

British Library Cataloguing-in-Publication Information available

Library of Congress Cataloging-in-Publication Data available

ISBN 978-0-7627-9633-5 (hardcover)

♾™ The paper used in this publication meets the minimum requirements of American National Standard for Information Sciences—Permanence of Paper for Printed Library Materials, ANSI/NISO Z39.48-1992.

In memory of National Park Service special agent Susan Morton (05/14/52–03/18/10), whose dedication to the preservation of Native American culture was a gift to all

While pursuing monsters, be wary of not becoming the monster you wish to slay.

—WISDOM OF MONSTER SLAYER,
AN ANCIENT NAVAJO DEITY

CONTENTS

Foreword

During my tenure in the United States Congress, I supported the passage of a federal law titled The Native American Graves Protection and Repatriation Act (NAGPRA). The purpose of NAGPRA is to address the rights of lineal descendants of Native American tribes to their sacred items, objects of cultural patrimony, and human remains.

During the 1970s the FBI and the National Park Service developed evidence that Native American artifacts of cultural significance were being commercially exploited. Collectors and museum curators from the United States and all over the world had created a lucrative market for items of cultural significance to Native Americans. The trafficking of these items resulted in tribes being robbed of many of their precious artifacts, used in ceremonies that served to enrich the spiritual lives of Native Americans. Sadly, such thefts contributed to the abandonment of a number of ceremonial rites that had been conducted for centuries.

Plunder of the Ancients is a true account of how an undercover sting operation was conducted by three federal agencies to enforce the provisions of NAGPRA. During this investigation criminals were caught working underground trafficking in nearly one million dollars' worth of Native American artifacts. Readers will become acutely aware of the detrimental spiritual impact on Native American tribes, but will also rejoice in the repatriation of artifacts critical to expressing their ancient and sacred spiritual beliefs.

—Ben Nighthorse Campbell

Ben Nighthorse Campbell represented Colorado's 3rd District in the US House of Representatives from 1987 to 1993 and served the state as a US senator from 1993 to 2005. He is currently a member of the Council of Chiefs for the Northern Cheyenne Tribe.

INTRODUCTION

This book is a true account of an undercover investigation in which I was the lead investigator while I was a special agent for the US Fish and Wildlife Service, Division of Law Enforcement. Most of the names of the people that were involved have been changed (indicated by an asterisk). Their names are of no importance, but the exploitation of Native American spirituality is.

The defendants in this case, out of their purported love for Native American culture, spent decades trying to eradicate a spiritual lineage that had buoyed the massive migration of a human race into North America dating back thousands of years. Motivated by pure greed, these men stole, bought, and sold sacred artifacts that are still used to bring life and meaning to Native Americans in the American Southwest. With the spiritual lives of the Indian people at stake, the investigation I had embarked upon had much to lose and had to be won.

Like many complex undercover investigations, Operation Monster Slayer was fraught with challenges. None was worse, however, than the operation's betrayal by two federal agents, both of whom I regarded as beyond reproach. Even as my personal safety was seriously compromised, I fought to win justice for the Indian people, although it did not come about as anyone expected.

Throughout this investigation I was given privileged and unprecedented access to Native American spiritual and ceremonial items. Out of respect to Native Americans I have described only those artifacts for which I was given permission by the respective tribal spiritual leaders. In one example, however, I have described a corn mother that is widely described in Southwestern anthropological literature. I would like to acknowledge and thank the *hataalii*, shamans, and priests who crossed cultural boundaries to work with me to ensure that their sacred objects were returned to them in a respectful manner.

Finally, I had no idea that in the process of repatriating sacred artifacts to the Navajos, the Hopis, the Zunis, and the Pueblo Indians I would find a deeper meaning to my own inner being. With supreme gentleness, I would rise to find a place more peaceful than I'd ever imagined.

CHAPTER ONE

September 1994. Richard Crow,* a trader of antique Indian goods such as nineteenth-century beaded moccasins and beaded vests, nearly blew the clutch out of his Jeep Cherokee as he sped along the washboard roads inside the Navajo reservation. Driving from Carefree, Arizona, he wasn't late for anything, but he still drove like a man running from the law. And in a way he was. If a Navajo spotted a *bilagáana* stranger visiting the recent widow of a well-known heart healer the Navajos called a *hataalii*, they would have every reason to suspect that the stranger was up to no good. He was determined to get to his destination. He knew that time was of the essence.

Finally the Cherokee slid to a stop at a hogan in an isolated area where the land was dotted with prickly pear cactus and mesquite that cast a feeble shade in the desert sun. Heat waves shimmered off the tires of the bloodred Jeep as the trader followed a dusty trail to the hogan, the traditional eight-sided wooden structure that was still home to many Navajos. On this day the widow—a whisper of a woman who took up less room than her own shadow—sat quietly in the doorway. Beneath her were several lamb's-wool Navajo rugs woven by her own hands. The faint scent of sheep still drifted in the air. Every morning at the break of dawn the widow's late husband had stood within that east-facing doorway and offered a morning chant to welcome the coming day.

From here Dawn comes
She comes upon me with blessing
Before her, from there,
Behind her, from there,
She comes upon me with blessing

* Names indicated by an asterisk have been changed.

The widow was in the stage of life called "old age going." This meant that as she neared the end of her life on Mother Earth, she spent her days resting her mind on good things. The expression on her face was one of contentment that could not be disturbed.

The fiftyish, tall, lanky trader, who wore a sweat-stained straw cowboy hat, noticed that the widow hadn't changed much since he'd last seen her. Her muddy-colored hair, streaked with shiny strands of silver, was pulled back into a tight bun; the grooves on her face were like the dry arroyos of her homeland. The widow wore an indigo cotton dress drawn together at the waist with an exquisite silver concha belt. She also wore several Navajo-made silver and turquoise necklaces and a gaggle of silver bracelets around her frail wrists. Turquoise earrings from her youth dangled from her ears, and huge turquoise rings partly concealed her arthritic fingers. Anglo women coveted turquoise jewelry as a fashion statement; Navajo women wore it for divine protection.

The closest town to the widow's home was Lukachukai, near the base of the Chuska Mountains in northeastern Arizona—one of the wettest areas in Arizona, with enough rainfall to sustain a relatively lush forest of ponderosa pine trees. Created from uplifted volcanic and sedimentary rock, the mountains changed color with every movement of sunlight. In the valley various species of cactus and sagebrush dotted the rocky and sandy landscape. If you were lucky, you might see a Gila monster or a jackrabbit. At night coyotes ruled, while snakes slid from their homes dug beneath the rocks. Elf owls left their cactus burrows to forage for moths and other insects.

Navajo protocol dictated that a dead man's belongings be removed from the hogan and that his name never be spoken out loud again to prevent disturbing his spirit. The trader's long unannounced trip to talk to the widow about her husband came quickly on the heels of his death on August 22. The trader, whose skin looked like tanned leather from years in the sun, didn't care about the dead Indian's spirit, but he was intensely interested in the spiritual items the *hataalii* had left behind. Federal law enforcement officials had long suspected the trader of selling eagle feathers and protected sacred Indian artifacts in a lucrative black market.

"*Ya-ta-he*," said Crow to the old woman, mispronouncing the only Navajo word he knew.

She nodded her head and released a small smile. They chatted for a few minutes about the lack of rain and a Blessing Way ceremony that was coming up.

"Speaking of ceremonies," said Crow, "do you still have your husband's *jish*?"

The widow told him that she no longer had what non-Indians call a medicine bundle.

"Who did you give it to?" asked Crow as he took a deep breath trying to hide his disappointment.

After a few quiet moments, the old woman answered Crow by putting her finger to her lips and whispering, "Can't tell."

The trader knew that when a healer died, his widow was to pass his *jish* to someone in her clan, where it would be cleansed and used again, but he had been assured by a Navajo that she still had the *jish*. His journey had been too long and hot for him to be disappointed like this. He must have wondered if she passed it along in the proper way, or if she sold it. If the *jish* had been sold, it was probably sitting on the black market in Santa Fe, the capital of New Mexico and the hotbed of protected Indian artifacts. In Santa Fe the bundle would surely be taken apart, as its parts would be worth more than the entire piece. The trader removed his hat and fanned his face, thinking how he wanted to kick himself for not getting to this woman earlier. If another trader had the *jish*, he was probably raking in money by the bushel.

No one will ever know why the widow did what she did next, but she mentioned she had some *yei* masks. These masks, which were actually hoods, were worn by select members of the tribe to impersonate certain *yei* gods in Navajo ceremonies. The dealer gave the widow a measured smile to hide his excitement. Humility was essential among the Navajo.

He helped her off her blankets and asked her to show him the masks. She led him inside the hogan and pointed to a large flat box covered with goat hide. The trader picked up the box and set it on the floor. Not knowing exactly what to expect, he opened the box. It was all he could to do to hold back his overwhelming astonishment. There were twenty-four masks in all.

"These are very nice. Thank you for showing them to me," said Crow respectfully.

Crow had seen Navajo and Hopi masks in private collections. Most of these had been repainted by the hand of a white artist. But the masks he was looking at displayed the raw patina consistent with being hundreds of years old. The buck-hide disguises bore sacred symbols painted on the faces with dyes made from native plants. Eagle, wild turkey, and northern flicker feathers adorned the tops. Fox fur or a ring of evergreen branches made up the collars. On some of the hoods the eyes were cut in a triangle shape pointing toward the temples. Other hoods had small round holes for eyes. Simple slits created nose and mouth.

Sacred Indian artifacts had been hard to come by since the early 1900s when white anthropologists traded foodstuffs with the Indians for their spiritual secrets. After a few years of being drained of their religious artifacts, the spiritual leaders banned all anthropologists from the Navajo Nation. To protect their culture, their spiritual beliefs withdrew into an atmosphere of deep secrecy, and their most important accoutrements were kept in ceremonial hogans.

The sheer rawness of the masks made the trader feel ravenousness to have them. These masks represented some of the rarest North American anthropological materials he'd ever come across. Crow began his pitch to the *hataalii*'s widow: "If you allow me to take these precious things, I promise to take care of them. This will bring many good blessing to you and your people."

She nodded as if to say, *Go on.*

"I'll give you ten thousand dollars, which will support you for the rest of your life. Your husband protected these masks for decades. It's only right for the deities to take care of you now."

Before the old woman could respond, Crow once again uttered his condolences over the death of her husband. As he spoke, he pressed his hand to his heart and told her of the great respect he held for Navajo culture. If she would give him the masks, he promised to keep them "home"—within the four sacred mountains of the Navajo Nation. As a

Navajo would, he pointed his chin to the four sacred mountains: Mount Blanca (near Alamosa, Colorado), mountain of the East; Mount Taylor (near Grants, New Mexico), mountain of the South; the San Francisco Peaks (near Flagstaff, Arizona), mountains of the West; and Mount Hesperus (Big Sheep Mountain, near Durango, Colorado), mountain of the North.

As if he didn't want the widow to see him tell a lie, he covered his mouth with his hand when he vowed that he would pass the collection on to a worthy practitioner. He promised that the paraphernalia would continue to be used for the benefit of the Navajo people. Finally, he argued that he would be doing her a favor by removing the burden of her having to make the contentious decision regarding the disposition of the masks. He assumed she was being pressured by the tribal elders to do what was proper. Her husband and the other chanters would have insisted that the masks remain with the Navajo Nation. Surely the trader's promises were of some comfort to her.

While he waited for her reply, the trader's thoughts drifted across the desert as he fantasized how these ceremonial masks would turn antique Indian art dealers into sharks vying for the bait. The trader didn't stop to think that his actions were a violation of federal cultural patrimony laws, as well as time-honored Navajo decrees. He reasoned that this transaction would be handled discreetly between him and the elderly widow. Later he would take the masks to a confidential trading post in Santa Fe that had a list of clients who would pay more than a hundred thousand dollars for a set of masks like this one. If the masks were sold individually, the take could be even higher, but so would be the risks.

Meanwhile the widow went back to her blankets and sat in silent contemplation as if waiting for the holy wind to speak to her with words of guidance. Crow knew that this was the time when he had to keep his mouth shut, for patience was considered one of the greatest of Navajo virtues. Even though he was definitely pushing the edge of breaking the law, he would sit all day and all night to get what he was after. As the shadows began to lengthen and great castlelike clouds formed thunderheads in the sky, the widow stood up unsteadily, her left hand bracing her aching back. Her only word was "Okay."

The swindler didn't dare leap for joy over his good fortune. Moving slowly, he placed the masks in a semicircle around the old woman and, before she realized it, he took a quick snapshot of her sitting with her gods. This would serve as the iron-clad provenance that any high-end collector would demand. With that, the penniless widow took the money and the trader loaded the masks into his Jeep. He had just violated numerous federal laws and Indian creeds, which would create a tide of evil that would affect many lives—including mine.

CHAPTER TWO

April 1995. After twenty-one years working as special agent for the US Fish and Wildlife Service, I was promoted to a supervisory position in Albuquerque, New Mexico. I loved the years I spent as a field agent making cases against wildlife poachers, smugglers, and people who exploited wildlife for huge sums of money. Fighting for wildlife was my life, and, best of all, I felt my work was meaningful.

As a supervisor I wasn't allowed to carry a case load. My responsibility was to oversee the work of five other agents as they investigated wildlife crimes. It was difficult for me to live vicariously through the successes of other agents. I wanted to be in the middle of the action. I wanted to sniff out the bad guys who were smuggling rare $10,000 star tortoises from Indonesia. I wanted to catch them in the act as they picked up their cargo at a major airport in the United States. I wanted to arrest the greedy smugglers and bring them to justice. Most of all, I wanted to take the tortoises home where they'd be released back to the wild in some faraway land. As a supervisor I couldn't do this. All I could do was to oversee operations like this one and read about them in dry and tedious case reports.

My workplace in Albuquerque was a crumbling disappointment. The main office space, which I nicknamed "the bunker," was no more than a cinderblock room without windows. It was connected to two garages that housed boats, a four-wheeler, an unmarked Camaro, and a white van. My clerk, Miss Nedra,* was a woman who stood only four feet eleven inches. Normally she was very sweet, but when crossed she could display the temperament of a viper. The two of us made a formidable front against five alpha-male agents who were stationed throughout New Mexico and West Texas.

Huddled in the bunker, I reviewed open cases left by agents that had moved on to other stations. It was now my responsibility to finish these cases and close them out. One of them was a case file titled "East-West Trading Post." In its pages I was introduced to an Indian trader from

Arizona named Richard Crow and Mrs. Fannie Winnie, the widow of a well-respected Navajo *hataalii* named Ray Winnie. The report chronicled the illegal sale of spiritual masks and eagle feathers by Mrs. Winnie to Richard Crow. From the first page, I felt as if I was in the middle of a Tony Hillerman mystery.

After the sale, Richard Crow took the masks to the East-West Trading Post in Santa Fe and left them there with his friend who owned the business. The friend, Bo Jenkins,* couldn't believe his good fortune. These masks were worth a bundle of money, and all he had to do was find a wealthy and discreet buyer. Jenkins wanted to move the masks as quickly as he could. If he got caught with them, he could end up in jail. The problem was, he didn't have a suitable buyer in mind, so he visited Mark Middleton,* one of his best confidants in the world of Indian artifacts.

Middleton was astonished that a collection so rare had suddenly popped up on the market. The photograph that Richard Crow had taken of Mrs. Winnie with the masks was a bonus, as it established rock-solid proof that the masks were an authentic collection of Navajo spiritual objects. For a generous commission, he agreed to help Bo find a buyer.

According to notes that accompanied the report, Mark later told investigators that he soon regretted his decision to help his friend. In the middle of the night he woke up with sweat streaming down his face. He'd dreamt that he'd died in the Navajo desert and ravens had plucked out his eyes. He snapped on a light, rubbed his eyes, and then looked at his hands for blood. To his immense relief his hands were clean, but his dream reminded him of the power of Indian curses. He was convinced that if he got involved in selling the deeply spiritual Indian masks, he would be cast into a den of devils for eternity. Desperation consumed him, and he decided to do anything to save his skin.

The morning after his nightmare Mark Middleton got up, took a cold shower, and put on the same clothes he'd worn the day before: jeans and a gray T-shirt with a Kokopelli on it. Climbing into his aging Datsun, he drove to downtown Albuquerque practically in a daze. He pulled into a parking spot in front of the Bureau of Indian Affairs (BIA) office and went inside. With nerves crackling, he asked the receptionist if he could see the BIA law enforcement agent, someone he'd never met.

"Sure," she said politely. She led him through a maze of cubicles until she stopped at one and introduced him to BIA special agent John McKinney.*

Mark shook his hand, mumbled his name, and fell into a wooden chair. Handing a manila envelope to McKinney, he said, "Sir, uh, I'd like you to take a look at this picture. I know who has them."

Agent McKinney, who was half Acoma Indian, half Irish and had been a federal investigator for over twenty years, was stunned when he saw the picture. Without a word he studied it for nearly a minute. He recognized several of the *yei* such as Fringemouth God, Talking God, and Monster Slayer. As a non-Navajo it was taboo for him to even look at sacred objects from another tribe, but he was also a federal agent and knew a crime when he saw one.

Meanwhile Mark sat on his quivering hands and, in what seemed like torture, spilled out what he knew. McKinney's mind spun with options until he settled on what he thought would be the most effective in catching the crooks.

The BIA agent pulled a chair close to Mark's so he wouldn't miss a word. Speaking in a low voice tinged with concern, he said, "Look, guy, you're the only one who can rescue the masks. That means you've got to help us set up Bo. Are you willing to do this?"

Mark shrieked, "Rat on my best friend! No way! I'm just giving you the picture—then I'm outta here! You figure it out!"

The BIA agent drew upon his wisdom and put his hand on Mark's shoulder as a father would. "It's not that simple. You're already involved. Right now you're at a fork in the road, and now it's a matter of which road you take. I'm offering you the opportunity to do the right thing."

Mark's voice weakened. "Bo was just trying to get me in on a deal that would make me money. He's not a criminal."

McKinney had heard this line before and already had a comeback. "Would a real friend drag evil and disharmony into your life? There's not enough money in the world to get you out of the trouble these spiritual deities could bring you. Have you considered that?"

Mark chewed on the agent's words and finally realized that McKinney was right. If he didn't work as an informant in the investigation, he'd be jinxed by spitting-mad Indian spirits for the rest of his life. He had no choice. He had to cooperate—it was the only way to save his soul.

- ⚊ ⚊

Barely a week later, agents from the FBI, the US Fish and Wildlife Service, and the National Park Service met to put their plan to rescue the Navajo masks into action. Oddly, BIA agent McKinney was noticeably absent due to a "scheduling conflict." Agents would learn later that McKinney, the only Native American on the team, had deliberately avoided being exposed to the masks because he too considered them to be conduits of spiritual dissonance. The other agents resented McKinney for backing out. After all, he had brought Mark into the case and had now abandoned him. Mark was left to place his trust in agents he didn't even know.

"Uh, guys, I'm not sure about this. I don't think I can go through with it. . . . I mean, I just don't think I'm your guy," grunted Mark during the meeting.

"You can't back out," said Park Service agent Phil Young sternly. "You've already signed a legal agreement with agent Grant. You're committed, my friend."

Now in his late forties, special agent Young was an affable man who was slightly taller than six feet. He kept in shape by playing tennis on a regular basis. His face was smooth and his cheeks showed a natural blush probably of Western European origin. He was dressed in brown slacks and a cream sweater. Like all federal agents, he didn't wear a uniform.

Agent Young paired Mark with with an undercover agent, Park Service agent/supervisor Bill Tanner, who had extensive knowledge of southwestern Indian ceremonial objects. Older than agent Young, he too was dressed casually. His penetrating brown eyes were partially covered by his bushy graying eyebrows. He liked to smoke a pipe, which made him look like the quintessential professor from an Ivy League school.

Tanner's job was to convince Bo Jenkins that he was a wealthy collector of Indian paraphernalia and was a legitimate buyer. Tanner's assumed identity was Dr. Richardson, a hand surgeon from Chicago. His story was that he'd been in Albuquerque attending a medical conference. Such a flimsy cover could have been easily debunked by Bo, but as it would turn out, greed made him blind to any dangers.

Also present at the planning meeting was special agent John Neal of the US Fish and Wildlife Service. John would write detailed reports that would document the case in its entirety and would be referred to for years to come.

Mark Middleton and "Dr. Richardson" drove to the East-West Trading Post in Santa Fe, where Dr. Richardson walked around the shop examining ornately beaded leggings, vests, and moccasins. To seal his credibility as an experienced collector, he verbally identified which of the tribes these items originated from as he looked them over carefully.

Twenty minutes later Bo Jenkins revealed the Navajo masks to the "doctor," who reacted with unbridled enthusiasm—which of course was part of the act. After some bartering, Dr. Richardson agreed to the purchase price of $170,000. Then he said, "I have to leave and call my broker about the money."

Within seconds, four federal agents flooded the showroom, responding to the preplanned code that signaled that the agents surrounding the trading post could now conduct their raid. Bo Jenkins was read the Miranda warning, taken into custody, and transported to the United States Courthouse, where he was arraigned before a federal magistrate. Charges filed against him included the possession and the offer to buy and sell Native American items of cultural patrimony protected under the Native American Graves Protection and Repatriation Act (NAGPRA), as well as the illegal possession and offer to buy and sell eagle feathers and other migratory bird feathers protected under the Bald and Golden Eagle Protection Act and the Migratory Bird Treaty Act.

In the end, the masks and other illegal Indian ceremonial items were seized by the federal agents. At about the same time, Richard Crow was arrested in Arizona. He was later sentenced to five years' probation. Bo Jenkins paid a small fine and went to jail for several months. Busted and broken, the East-West Trading Post was forced to close its doors.

In the back of the case file prepared by agent Neal, I found a statement by Navajo *hataalii* Alfred Yazzie explaining the significance of masks to the Navajo people:

The Navajo belief is that when a yei impersonator puts on the hood representing a deity such as Fringemouth God, Black God, Talking God or Monster Slayer, the impersonator becomes that deity. The yei masks are essential to the spiritual enrichment of every Navajo and must be returned to protect the integrity of Navajo culture. Without our spirits we lose our culture and will suffer depression and dreadful illnesses.

It saddened me that Yazzie had to make such a personal statement about his tribe in order to prove that under a white man's law the masks were sacred to Native Americans. In spite of Yazzie's urgent appeal to get the masks repatriated, the government paperwork needed to release the masks was still being processed by the National Park Service's repatriation office in Washington, DC. It was now my job to move this along. I had no idea that it would take several bureaucratic lifetimes.

CHAPTER THREE

June 1996. I was well entrenched in supervising agents, going to meetings, writing reports about what my agents were doing—all the while hating it. It was as if the marrow of my bones had been sucked dry and only a superficial part of me remained, acting out my role like a robot. While I did what I was supposed to do, I wasn't doing anything for the natural resources I loved. But change was in the air.

One morning as I was "grading" case reports, Park Service special agent Young dropped by the bunker. Since Phil Young had been one of the lead agents in the East-West Trading Post investigation, I had great respect for him, as his dedication to his job was as strong as ever.

Speaking with urgency, he explained that he had been receiving complaints of sacred items "disappearing" from the Navajo Nation. The main market for these items was in Santa Fe, so that would be the obvious starting point. Agent Young said he had a strong feeling that an unidentified individual was stealing artifacts from the kivas and society houses of the regional pueblos and tribes and was running them to discreet dealers in Santa Fe for huge profits.

Referring to the East-West Trading Post investigation, I said, "So, this is the same song, second verse."

"Unfortunately," said Young. "I believe there's one main rez runner at the center of the current trafficking. This little shit is out there profiting from the spiritual lives of Native Americans. Ever since the East-West Trading Post investigation, he's been supplying other dealers willing to take the risk." Agent Young shook his head. "The FBI and I have beat our heads against the wall trying to figure out who this guy is. We can't set up another undercover sting. Every crook in town knows who we are. But you can. Anyone who can bust an illegal Alaskan hunting camp and survive can get to the bottom of this."

"Sure," I said, smiling. "And Alaska was such a snap!"

Agent Young gave me some notes outlining an undercover operation starring me. In a near-pleading voice he asked if I'd find the rez runner and the participating crooks and shut down the illegal trading of Indian spirituality forever.

What a dreamer, I thought, but my words were "Nothing is forever. Besides, your whole plan only takes up one paragraph—I guess I'm supposed to turn it into a book."

I immediately regretted my words. To agent Young I was the only logical choice to take a run at these felons. I had much more experience doing undercover work than most agents, and as I was a supervisor, the crooks didn't know me. After all, I was sequestered inside a cement bunker day after day.

While agent Young continued talking, my undercover mind started snapping with ideas. It didn't matter what the crime was, most criminals operated in ways that were fairly predictable. For a brief moment I fantasized about catching them, which is why I couldn't believe my own words when I turned him down. I never turned down anything. Crossing my legs, I told the already frustrated agent that I was swamped with supervising five male agents, attending meetings at the US Attorney's Office, and maintaining a face for the US Fish and Wildlife Service within the local federal law enforcement community. I simply could not take on an undercover investigation. Plus, I was sure that my supervisor wouldn't approve it.

As agent Young got ready to leave, I could barely look at the disappointment that dripped from his face. As if it were a consolation prize, I said, "Come back if you come up with a solid lead on the rez runner. One of my agents might be able to help."

After Young closed the door behind him, I went to the restroom and looked into the mirror at my lying face. I hadn't told Young that I'd already jumped into another covert investigation like a duck to water.

CHAPTER FOUR

A few weeks earlier I had received a call from a tipster reporting a possible parrot smuggler. I had begged my supervisor to let me take a shot at this case that required undercover work. The agents who worked for me were too well known in the area to go undercover—and on top of that, they were not cut out for covert work. I'd done undercover work for two decades and loved catching bad guys when they were at their worst and thought no one was looking.

For two months now I'd been attending meetings of the New Mexico Bird Club under my assumed name Jayne Dyer. I had plenty of identification cards in her name—including a hard-to-get social security card. My target was the club's president, Reuben Harris,* who was highly suspected of smuggling wild parrots and macaws from the rainforests of South America into the United States to sell. Illegal drugs were often smuggled with exotic birds. According to an informant, Reuben had often bragged that he couldn't be caught. A bad guy who thinks he can't be caught rises to the top of any agent's list.

Reuben had an aviary to cover his illegal smuggling operation. At one of the bird club meetings I'd talked Reuben into letting me work at his aviary in exchange for an African Grey parrot. He thought this was a great idea and wanted me to start working the next day. So every afternoon around three-thirty, I drove the white panel van to Reuben's aviary, which was really a house he'd had converted. Cages flowed from inside the house out to the former backyard. I parked the van on the street and let myself into the aviary through the front door. My job was to process raw vegetables through a commercial-grade food processor and feed them to the birds. My other *job* was to wait for a shipment of smuggled Yellow-Naped Amazon parrots Reuben was expecting any day. These birds sold for about $8,000 each.

Also working at the aviary were twenty-something Paco and Raul, who only spoke Spanish. I never let them know that I understood every word they said. I noticed they were jittery around me and found out why. I checked them out with the US Immigration and Naturalization Service and found out they were in the country illegally.

Working inside the guts of a criminal enterprise made me feel alive again. In just a few weeks I'd developed evidence that Reuben was evading taxes, was a bookie, and was operating an illegal chop shop. On top of this, the illegal parrots would be arriving any day. The thrill of the kill was so near. Even so, I took the risks I was exposed to very seriously. Reuben had been busted before, and he wouldn't go down a second time very easily. I carried a 9mm Smith and Wesson semiautomatic in the small of my back every day, and I was accomplished at shooting it.

One day, Miss Nedra told me that my boss had been talking about my undercover work so much that it was now a major topic of the rumor mill at the US Fish and Wildlife Service's regional office. She said clerks and others were asking her about it, when they weren't supposed to know a thing. I was stunned to hear that people in my own agency would put me in such jeopardy. This leak would spread to other offices, and then it'd be out on the street like a virus. The worst part was, there was nothing I could do to stop it.

Then one afternoon I heard the Mexicans chattering in Spanish about how they were going to subdue and rape me in a shed behind the aviary. I was stunned and began mentally preparing myself to shoot them if necessary to defend myself. I'd fire two quick shots to the chest and once in the head. In the meantime I resolved to stay clear of them the best I could.

But the final straw came when some bad-boy bikers stomped into the shop and accused me of being a cop. They were some of Reuben's chop-shop clients and were suspicious of me just because I was a new person on the scene. While I was able to talk my way past their accusations, I didn't want them checking me out. Most crooks had a contact with a police dispatcher who could run license plates. A check on my van's plate would come up as "Not on File"—a dead giveaway for an undercover police vehicle.

The overall situation was becoming too dangerous. One of the three threats would get me: the rampant rumors, the Mexicans, or the bikers. I thought about the risks I was taking, and then I thought about my family. I wasn't being fair to them. Quickly I wrote Reuben a short note saying that I had to quit because my "sons" needed me at home. When I walked out the door of the aviary, I felt both relief and frustration. I was glad I was safe, but I was devastated that I couldn't catch an everyday wildlife crook like Reuben smuggling parrots.

CHAPTER FIVE

The next morning at the bunker I called my boss and told him why I'd quit my job at the aviary. Hardly sympathetic, he began chastising me for being so reckless that I couldn't even catch a common bird smuggler. I was despondent to the bone, so I just listened and said little to defend myself. Sure, there were serious factors that made me back out, but I still wondered if I was losing my snap. Were my undercover tactics getting rusty? I nearly went crazy with the idea that I wasn't up to undercover work anymore. My cover had never been compromised this seriously before.

Now I was stuck back in a windowless cinderblock office, being a mother/supervisor to complaining agents. I was indescribably miserable, and it wasn't long before an agent colleague told me that I looked lower than whale shit going to the bottom of the ocean. I had to find another way to escape the bunker, but I didn't know how. Meanwhile I still had Alfred Yazzie breathing down my neck. He wanted to get inside the FBI's evidence room to bless the sacred masks. I was certain the FBI would have no part of this, but I decided to try.

On a Friday afternoon I sat in the waiting room of the FBI office in Albuquerque, New Mexico. It was exactly one o'clock. FBI special agent Dave Foley* appeared through the door wearing a dark blue suit, a white shirt, and a red, white, and blue tie—the FBI uniform. I had specifically worn a well-tailored Talbot's suit to meet the dress code.

Agent Foley began our conversation by saying that no one other than the assigned evidence custodian could enter the barricaded evidence room. Only other agents could check out evidence for forensic examination, or lawyers who needed the evidence for trial. Having unauthorized personnel like Yazzie inside the room would violate the chain-of-custody rules.

"I don't agree," I replied. "Mr. Yazzie just wants to take a peek at what rightly belongs to his tribe. He's not going take the masks anywhere. He just wants to see them—to make sure they're okay."

"They're just fine," grunted Foley. "Yazzie's presence in the evidence room will taint all the other evidence. A defense attorney could throw a legal fit arguing that Yazzie had the opportunity to manipulate or even steal evidence. I can't take that chance. I will not let him in!"

Technically agent Foley was right. Access to evidence had to be tightly controlled. Just then Foley and I turned at the sound of a buzzer. The security guard had let in Jonathon Jordan,* an assistant US attorney (AUSA) whom I'd called about the situation. Basically, he was my personal cavalry.

AUSA Jordan was a quiet man whose obvious intellect radiated everywhere. He was a Bostonian who had ended up in New Mexico for reasons even he couldn't explain. His handsome boyish face contrasted uniquely with hair as white as a Persian cat's fur. His eyes were a gorgeous blue. Any woman would be drawn to him. AUSA Jordan didn't know much about Native American issues except for the American Indian Religious Freedom Act, for which he held a high respect with a dash of fear. No attorney wanted to end up on the wrong side of a freedom of religion issue, especially when it involved Native Americans.

Agent Foley led AUSA Jordan and me to the evidence room. There was a lobby area and then a locked half-door with a counter on it. The counter was for signing chain-of-custody forms. Foley unlocked the half-door and closed it and stood solidly behind it like a Marine guard.

AUSA Jordan explained to agent Foley that viewing the masks fell within Mr. Yazzie's religious rights. Foley made his argument about the chain of custody, but it was clear that the Department of Justice had ruled against him. Yazzie would be allowed the freedom to exercise his religious rights. The door to the lobby swung open and Alfred Yazzie, dressed in jeans and a western shirt and wrapped in a Navajo blanket, walked in. He also wore an off-white headband. His black and gray hair was braided imperfectly down his back. The creases in his face flowed like rivers of wisdom. Even I hoped to age that way.

"Hello, Alfred, we've been waiting for you," I said.

Yazzie looked over his shoulder and said, "Come on in. It's okay."

"*What?*"

Behind Yazzie were three more *hataalii* dressed much like Yazzie. The three were noticeably nervous being in the white man's world and followed Yazzie's every step.

"Alfred," I said. "I thought only you were coming. Who are these guys and what are they doing here?"

Yazzie stood before me solid as a rock. "Agent Lucinda, the prayers we offer today must come from the cardinal directions. It takes four healers to do this."

"Of course," I lied. "I think you mentioned this."

AUSA Jordan smiled and nodded to Foley to open the fortress gate. As we all filed into the evidence room, I wished I could gloat a bit. Instead I maintained a demeanor of profound deference to what was about to happen.

Foley delivered the box that contained the masks and placed them on a large table. The *hataalii* crowded around the box, which was still covered with a goat hide. Yazzie protested when Foley tried to open the box. Only a Navajo *hataalii* could do this. This must have irritated the FBI agent even more.

Alfred raised the lid of the box, and when the masks came into view, all four medicine men gasped as if someone close to them had been horribly offended. Yazzie removed the masks one by one from the box. As quick as lightning, the four men rearranged the masks in a certain order.

I had done some research on *yei* masks and learned that each mask represented a deity that helped the Navajo people live. For example, Fringemouth God was the god of the harvest, and in ceremonies he was asked for good crops. Talking God taught the people how to be compassionate. He also had dominion over corn, game, the eastern sky, and dawn. Monster Slayer's mask was black. The top was tufted with horsehair and a turkey feather. A white lightning streak ran down the right side of his face. His image was terrifying, which I guessed was the point. He was the deity who fought off evil forces. I was beginning to see that deep faith and belief by the people formed the energy that gave the deities their life force. To most Native Americans the universe was an orderly system of interrelated elements of both good and evil.

Without prelude, the ceremony began. The healers took their positions: east, west, north, and south. All at once they exploded into a chorus of chants that had a drumbeat to them. Their feet bounced subtly as they stretched their arms over the masks and allowed their hands to tremble. The hand-trembling looked as if an otherworldly presence was taking over the bodies of the tremblers. It didn't look natural at all.

As the chanting continued, a spiritual force seemed to resonate through the chanters. Yazzie was sweating profusely as he dusted each mask with corn pollen that he kept in a leather pouch around his neck. The run of emotions was so high, I expected that one of the men might collapse. I didn't move, but whatever energy I had drained from my body. My heart pounded and my muscles melted like butter. A wonderment I'd never felt before consumed me. I pushed away a nagging question: *Is there really something to this?* Agent Foley looked too afraid to even speak. AUSA Jordan was stoic, as if he'd put up a barrier that refused to reveal his true reaction.

Meanwhile the chanters screamed primordial sounds that made the whole room vibrate. After about fifteen minutes Alfred Yazzie signaled the end to the rite. Coming out of his frenzied abstraction, he had a profound look of satisfaction on his face.

"Everything is okay now," he said. "Okay, let's go."

But before leaving he said that we *bilagáana* had to be cleansed. Reaching inside the old leather pouch hanging from his neck, he retrieved yellow corn pollen and held it tightly between his thumb and fingers. He told Foley, Jordan, and me to form a line and then approached each one of us and daubed corn pollen on our foreheads while chanting vowels and consonants that made no sense.

When he was done, he said, "There, no evil can harm you now."

The experience left me with an eerie, whole-body itch. I wondered if it had something to do with the deity Monster Slayer. After all, he was the destroyer of evil spirits, while I stopped lawbreakers. I wanted to know all I could about him.

CHAPTER SIX

After the ceremony in the FBI evidence room, I was unsettled. I couldn't focus and felt jittery all over. I blamed everything on the masks and the energy I felt during the hand trembling and chanting. I decided I needed the masks off my plate. For the next month I pestered the Park Service's Repatriation Office with constant phone calls and e-mails. I had become so irritating that the staff person I was working with finally provided the official release of the masks.

I called Yazzie and gave him the good news, but his reaction was a flat "Well, it's about time."

I was disappointed that he wasn't happier, but I understood. It was time. In a move that surprised me, he invited me to a *Yei'i bicheii* ceremony that would be done to welcome the Navajo deities home.

"Are you sure it's proper for me to be there?" I asked.

"Yes. Because I'm inviting you, you will be welcomed."

I accepted the invitation to be polite, but I was worried that I'd be haunted again.

The ceremony lasted nine nights, and I showed up on the last night. I climbed a hill in the Chuska Mountains of Arizona to the light of a bonfire whose flames roared into the sky. It was only late September, but the air was chilly enough to warrant a winter coat. I was underdressed but decided to stick it out.

Three pueblo-style drums pounded so hard that they sounded like the heartbeats of giants. The booming drums, the persistent chanting of primordial sounds, the fire flashing against the pitch-black sky, and Indians wrapped in blankets milling about all made me feel uneasy, as if I'd stepped back in time.

Finally Yazzie's form materialized through the smoke like an appari-tion. He rushed toward me and grabbed both of my hands and kissed my fingertips. "Thank you, thank you for coming," he said.

"I feel very privileged to be here. But, what is this all about? I'm confused."

Gently Yazzie guided me through the night to another, smaller fire where a young woman stood among thick vegetation that had been torn away, giving her a small protected space where she could do her work. In her hand she held one of the masks I recognized from the East-West Trading Post investigation. Yazzie told me it was the mask of Talking God. When the woman saw me, she reared back and looked at me with eyes that screamed, *Hey, white woman, you're not supposed to see this!* I felt that my presence offended her in the strongest way possible. The woman was using a plant-based dye to paint the leather hood white. Using dark ink, she refreshed a drawing of a corn stalk that went from the mouth of the mask to the forehead. A fringe made from straw that was dyed red ran from ear to ear. On the top of his head were five eagle feathers spread like a fan. The woman was performing a sacred ritual, and she was right, I had no business being there. Just the wild look in her eyes told me to run.

After a minute or two, Yazzie gently guided me around to different campfires where other women were freshening up masks. Between camp-fires he talked about the ceremony that was about to begin. "We Navajos believe that a person who walks in beauty is aligned perfectly with the forces of earth and sky."

I assumed that the balance he was talking about had to do with good versus evil. It was as if the balance of the mind and body meant keeping evil in check. I found it fascinating that evil forces were identified and action was taken by the tribe to get rid of it. For example, if a person acted with self-gratification and selfishness, a rite had to be performed to put the person on the correct path. Yazzie explained to me that much of the community participated in these elaborate ceremonies, which had to be done with exact precision. The chanters and dancers spent the greater part of their lives learning and memorizing the rituals. Not everyone had the mental capacity to do this, but those who did were recognized and revered by the tribe.

I asked Yazzie how long these ceremonies had been conducted. He looked at me like I was an ignorant tourist. "Long, long ago," he said, "since time beyond memory."

His words "since time beyond memory" stuck with me. He was saying that the *Yei'i bicheii* dated back to when the ancients first settled in this place—maybe even as long as ten thousand years ago.

Yazzie guided me to a traditional hogan and invited me inside, where several Navajos greeted me with supreme grace. I sat down to a customary meal of mutton stew and fry bread. While I was chewing on my stew, an elderly Navajo woman approached me, placed her gnarled arthritic hands into mine, and spoke to me in her native tongue.

I had no idea what she was saying, but I replied, "I'm so happy to be here. Thank you so much."

She left me with an endearing, warm smile on her face. I could actually sense the beauty she had bestowed on me with only her mind. This woman had crossed the line of cultural antipathy, and for the first time I understood the leper who had been heartened by the touch of another caring person.

The woman went outside and sat on the ground with other Navajos. I too moved to sit among them. Soon cold crept out of the ground, and I began to shiver. As I moved closer to the fire, I could feel the vibrations of drumbeats coming from every direction. Without warning, the *yei* impersonators burst from a nearby sweat lodge where they had been cleansed. Their dancing and chanting to thunderous drumbeats overpowered all of my senses. These deities were the personification of great power, spreading blessings and demolishing evil. Even as an outsider, it was hard to believe anything else.

At one point, Monster Slayer stood in front of me and quivered until he reached a near frenzy. His mask was all black with black messy hair on top. Small holes created his eyes and mouth, and the hide of a red fox was draped around his neck. Parts of his arms and chest were streaked with a white chalky substance, and his chest was laden with silver and turquoise jewelry. He shrieked like an angry cat, as if he was trying to scare me out of my wits. I held my ground and looked him straight in the eye. He moved closer to me and, as hard as it was, I gripped the grass and didn't back away.

Although we lived in different worlds, I was intrigued with the idea that Monster Slayer and I had the same missions of righting what was wrong. When he went on to dance around the circle, I felt he'd left me with a visceral message of some kind. But I couldn't begin to decipher it. I took a deep breath; I had just met Monster Slayer, a spirit that would resonate with me for a long time.

CHAPTER SEVEN

For days my mind was consumed with smoke, fires, and images of the *Yei'i bicheii* ceremony—especially Monster Slayer. The experience left me with spiritual stirrings I couldn't ignore but didn't dare talk about. Who would believe my reaction to Indian gods that most whites felt were phony? Meanwhile I still loathed everything about my work. I wasn't helping wildlife; I wasn't helping anything. I remembered Yazzie saying that the *Yei'i bicheii* was supposed to bring about an enlightened consciousness. Perhaps that's why I was feeling so restless. I needed more. All I could think about was Monster Slayer and the strange intimation I picked up from him. I decided I needed to get back to work. I needed some criminals in my life.

Later that week I picked up the phone and called Matt Miller, who was the chief of the Special Operations Unit in Washington, DC. He oversaw multiple covert investigations that were being conducted all over the country. I briefed him on the information I had from the National Park Service regarding the black market trafficking of Indian sacred items and eagle parts. I pointed out that every time a sacred item was taken off reservation lands, the piece and its accompanying eagle feathers had to be replaced. The need for eagle feathers fueled yet another crime where eagles were either trapped or shot out of the sky and their feathers sold. The criminal activity was concentrated in the Southwest, which held the greatest number of intact Indian tribes that still practiced rites from ancient times. I said the criminals were operating almost exclusively in the Southwest, which of course was my backyard.

"I think I can infiltrate this crowd and stop them," I said confidently.

Matt immediately countered with "Even after the aviary fiasco? You were damn lucky you weren't hurt on that one."

I sighed. "I have to admit, that was a close one, but I got out in time."

Miller found a quick way to reject my plan by saying his special operations unit lacked the funds to conduct such a complex investigation, which required making expensive purchases that would become evidence. I knew this was coming and told him that I'd already discussed the project with the Park Service and the FBI. They had legal jurisdiction and money. A pool of money cobbled together from other agencies would provide enough cash to at least get started. I proposed that I open an undercover business to buy and sell legal artifacts with the idea of generating funds for the investigation. To save money, I even offered to use a guest bedroom in my own home to serve as my office. Undercover agents never did something so irresponsible, yet I had no choice but to throw it on the table as a way to cut costs.

Matt was still in mode negative. "Can't you make this case from your own field station? You don't have to transfer to Special Operations."

"Matt, I'm a supervisor and can't run a case at the same time. And frankly, I couldn't control the leaks in my parrot investigation. Rumors got out of control, and soon everyone knew what I was doing. I don't want to go through that again. The Special Operations Unit at least understands what it means to keep things secret."

Then I changed the subject to something all supervisors are sensitive to: "Look at it this way: An Indian case would make you look good with the 'superiors at Interior.' I can't imagine them not liking a case that benefited the Indians."

Matt knew that the US Department of the Interior had recently listed Native Americans as one of its primary constituents and had mandated that its agencies develop programs to promote Indian causes. To the Division of Law Enforcement this translated into making cases that would benefit the tribes. I hated that I was making a political pitch instead of one based on the facts of rampant lawbreaking. I wanted to catch criminals who were exploiting wildlife and a native culture out of sheer greed.

"How truly interested is the FBI in joining forces with the US Fish and Wildlife Service?" asked Matt.

This was a legitimate question. Why would a giant agency with 15,000 criminal investigators want to dance with an agency of only 220 wildlife crime fighters? It made no sense until I explained that the Santa Fe FBI office ended up with kudos from headquarters over their work on the East-West Trading Post. Since then, they had made it known that they wanted more cases in Indian Country. On top of this, the FBI had just come off a lousy decade of Waco, Ruby Ridge, the Boston mafia fiasco, and the disaster in the Four Corners area where they bungled a search for three men who shot and killed a sheriff's deputy.

"Shit, I really don't want to do this," moaned Matt. "We've never done a case like this, and you can be a loose cannon—not to mention a pain in the butt."

"I'll try and be a small pain," I said, laughing.

"But you have a point. A good Indian case isn't something that comes around very often, and you seem to have enough intel to grab onto. Just promise you won't screw up. I don't need the hassles."

"I promise to be a good Girl Scout and follow the rules."

"Yeah, right," said Matt sarcastically. "But seriously, I can't commit more undercovers to this, so you'll be on your own."

What's new? I thought.

It was just a matter of paperwork to change my position to the Special Operations Unit. Matt Miller would be my new supervisor, and he was far enough away that I could function without being under a microscope. I opened an official investigation and named it Operation Monster Slayer. Monster Slayer's image and his mission still echoed in my mind. He bushwhacked his way through mountains of evil forces as if they were mere anthills. Just the idea of having that kind of strength and perseverance was invigorating, and I yearned to feel his hatchet in my hand ready to do battle. No one else but me could understand this.

The first thing I did was to get a business permit in New Mexico under the name Dana Delaney Antique Indian Arts. I registered an unmarked government Camaro in the same name. My plan was to buy and sell legal

Indian items and hope to sneak in some illegal purchases of sacred arti-facts. As simple as that sounded, the reality was I had the enormous task of building an air-tight cover story that would lure in the bad guys like bear to a bait pile.

During my research at the University of New Mexico library, I learned that part of the international trade in Indian items took place among collectors in Germany. Every spring there was an Indian festival in Dresden, during which North American Indian dancers performed and enthusiasts gathered to trade Indian paraphernalia and to "play Indian." The gathering was called the Karl May Festival and had been a popular event for decades.

Karl May was a German writer who wrote popular books for children about the American West. His characters included Indians from various tribes and genuine cowboys who were tougher than steel. May had never traveled to the United States but had read enough that he was able to make his readers feel the spirit of the Old West and allow them to fanta-size about how it felt to be wild and free.

May's immensely popular bestsellers fueled an intense German interest in Native American culture. Over time Germans flocked to the Southwest to buy rare and expensive regalia for their personal collections at home. The US Fish and Wildlife Service already had plenty of intel-ligence indicating that eagle feather fans and headdresses were part of the exodus of Native American paraphernalia. Eagle and all migratory bird feathers are protected under federal law and cannot be possessed, bought, sold, or exported. To date, no German citizen had been caught doing this, but the vast number of Indian collections in Germany that contained eagle feathers left many questions.

My undercover plan included attending the Karl May Festival and "working" the crowd to learn anything I could about the international trade in Indian goods. I also wanted to attempt to document the ille-gal trade of eagle feathers by finding out if the American Indians who danced at the German festival were supplying feathers to the European wannabe Indians.

In addition I'd try and develop fake German "clients" who I could use as fake legitimate clients back in the States. Under this guise I'd try and buy black market Indian items, which of course would never go to my fake clients. This plan followed my basic rule in developing a covert operation: Find out what the bad guys wanted and give it to them. I knew my targets would want a safe place to sell their illegal artifacts, so offering them the opportunity to sell to foreign clients would be easy. I wanted dealers Stateside to feel safe from legal scrutiny.

On paper, my proposal sounded very doable, and I was eager to be back into the game of chase. I was packing my bags to travel to Dresden when I got a call from a desk agent in Washington, DC, who explained that the German government would not allow me to work in an under-cover capacity in their country. I could attend the festival, but only when accompanied by a plainclothes German police officer.

I felt like I'd been hit with a front-end loader! How could I roam the festival collecting intelligence with a police officer attached to my hip? The Washington desk officer was convinced the trip would be a waste of time and money. Eventually I persuaded him that I'd wring something out of the trip and it was critically important as part of my backstory. As for the plainclothes police officer, I'd act as if he was simply a companion. A German guard dog companion.

CHAPTER EIGHT

On April Fools' Day 1998, I took the long and tedious flight to Dresden in the former East Germany. At the airport I grabbed a cab and handed the driver the name and address of my hotel. He took me there and fortunately the desk clerk spoke English well enough to check me in. My room was austere, with a single bed, no TV, and few furnishings. At least it came with hot water, for which I was very grateful. Within minutes of settling in I took a long look outside my hotel room and was immediately astounded. Hundreds of buildings lay in total disarray as if frozen in time after the devastating bombing of Dresden by the Royal Air Force and its allies during 1944–45.

From high school history classes I remembered that Dresden was an important military target due to its vast train system and munitions factories. Sir Winston Churchill had made the decision to ruthlessly bomb Dresden, destroying much of it and killing some 25,000 people. It was horrifying to see how much of the city remained in rubble.

I spent much of the day in my hotel room in bed trying to recuperate from jet lag. Around eight p.m. I was starving and ventured out into my new neighborhood looking for a restaurant. At the first corner, I passed a Lutheran church that had been destroyed during the bombing. Its bricks were stacked neatly in a square. The only surviving feature was a statue of Martin Luther. I was saddened to think that after all these decades there hadn't been funds to reconstruct the church. The delineation between war and peace was marked by a wide cobblestoned street that I'd crossed to sit down at a chic café with outdoor seating. Luckily a woman who spoke some English brought me a glass of water.

After ordering my meal while speaking the worst German possible, I put down the menu and eyed my waitress, who I considered might have been alive during World War II. It took me a second to build up the nerve to ask what I knew would be a sensitive question.

"Why is it taking so long to repair these buildings?" I asked.

Her eyes squinted as if I'd offended her in the worst way. She pointed a kinked finger at me and scolded, "The destruction in our city is a reminder that . . . well, never again. Don't be surprised when you see this—everything remains in ruins so that we are reminded every day of that horror of war."

It was only then that I understood.

— ~

At ten the next morning Detective Dietrich Schmidt* of the Dresden police department picked me up at my hotel. If I had to describe what a German police officer looked like, Schmidt would have been the blueprint. From the perspective of my five-foot-three-inch frame, I was sure he was over six feet tall. He had the broad chest and shoulders of an NFL linebacker, and his dense, silvery-streaked black hair matched a dark bushy mustache that suggested no flippancy. He spoke excellent English, which was a great relief to me—but probably not to him. As a series of coughs erupted from deep inside his chest, he moaned, "I was sent because I speak the best English. I should be home in bed."

This was the first good sign of a bad day.

Schmidt's "plain clothes" consisted of dark dress pants with a seam pressed sharp enough to cut ham and a tan turtleneck sweater finished off with a corduroy jacket. But his real fashion statement was his massive grips. I couldn't see anyone getting beyond those. In contrast to this lion, I looked like the original flower child from San Francisco. I wore a brightly colored tiered skirt that flirted with my ankles. My carefully crafted southwestern American look was enhanced by handfuls of mismatched drugstore Indian turquoise jewelry. Most of all, I struggled to maintain the whimsical smile of a harmless girl.

As the German plainclothesman and I strolled through the growing crowd, he told me that his orders were to make sure I didn't make any investigative contacts at the festival. I could observe, but nothing else. Unfortunately, he knew my history. After my Alaskan case I'd applied for a visa to travel in Germany in order to interview a German citizen who had poached a moose and a Dall's sheep while I was with him in the Brooks Range. Later he was charged with violations of federal hunting laws, which were felonies. The US Department of Justice had given me permission to travel to Germany to get a written affidavit from the German poacher. I assumed that a German officer similar to a conservation officer in the United States would find this guy and help me get the affidavit. Instead, an English-speaking diplomat from the German ministry in Berlin called me to advise that my German target was too important and too busy to be bothered by a measly wildlife investigator. The diplomat assured me that if I appeared at the German border, I'd be arrested.

None of the supervisors at FWS Washington headquarters knew what to make of this turn of events. Normally a request like mine was a routine matter. Foreign wildlife agencies were usually eager to cooperate in apprehending wildlife thugs—no matter how much money they had in the bank. Looking back, I can only assume that the US-indicted German big-game poacher had political connections that went way beyond the powers of the US Fish and Wildlife Service.

Just inside the entrance to the Karl May Festival flew a red banner that marked the popular Karl May Museum, a mecca to Indian lovers throughout Europe. I wanted to go inside and asked permission of my German police escort. To my surprise he allowed me to venture inside alone while he stayed outside. I couldn't believe this . . . then I realized he wanted to smoke.

The museum was built like an old western wooden cabin with an authentic totem-pole greeter at the front door. I'd been to Indian museums all over the United States and didn't expect much here. After paying for my ticket, I was immediately pulled back in time by panoramic exhibits of life-like scenes of North American Indians who lived more than a century ago.

A ruddy-skinned Apache glared straight ahead wearing moccasins, leggings, and a shirt made from the hide of a brain-tanned doe deer. A leather breech with a six-inch fringe draped from his waist. His right hand grasped a bow made of willows, leather, and sinew. The quiver strung across his back was full of a half-dozen sturdy sticks embedded with hand-chinked stone points. The opposite ends were expertly fitted with the trimmed tail feathers of a red-shafted flicker.

Another Indian mannequin, dressed in Northern Plains regalia, stunned me with his full-length headdress of golden eagle feathers that cascaded along the length of his back to the floor. Generally speaking, Indians had always ascribed to eagles an ability to carry prayers to gods who lived in the sky. The Plains Indian's robes were made of dark blue felt that probably came from a trade with a white man. He wore a breastplate made of two rows of dozens of eagle wing bones, which offered protection from arrowheads. I studied the intricate beadwork that appeared on the band of the headdress and on the pipe holder and knife holder the Indian held. I recognized the glass beads, attached to a doe hide with sinew in a lazy stitch, as Venetian beads that were heavily traded for in the late 1800s and early 1900s. This regalia represented a supreme masterpiece that paid the highest tribute to Native American culture.

The museum was also full of eagle feather prayer fans along with pipestone pipes whose handles were hung with eagle and hawk feathers. Hides from mink were everywhere. Oglala-Lakota Sioux buffalo hides draped over period furniture along with old Navajo *yei* blankets. The collection data displayed with the items showed they'd been collected in the late 1800s, which was consistent with the times when American and European anthropologists scoured Indian Country for anything of ethnographic value. Money, liquor, and foodstuffs were traded as items of fair value for rare and sacred artifacts. As a result, a fascinated few acquired huge collections of memorabilia to be hung on wall or kept in glass cases.

The displays continued with fantastic exemplars of Tlingit art, leather dresses dotted with elk teeth, fully beaded dresses, ornate vests, and intricately beaded moccasins. In one case I saw finely beaded children's outfits and baby bonnets—most likely beaded for white children, since Indian children weren't dressed this way.

Finally, there was a section reserved for the sacred. Kachina dolls, fetishes, and ritualistic masks from the Hopis, Navajos, and Apaches were literally stacked upon one another. I even caught a glimpse of what looked like a couple of *yei* masks that I'd recently come to know. The ghostly renderings of ceremonial entities born of nature and spirit poured from their leather bundles still yellowed from corn pollen dustings. At that point my mind screamed, *Robbed! My country has been robbed of its cultural heritage!* I wanted everything in the museum to go home.

〜〜

After an hour I stumbled into the bright sunlight of the festival grounds. I found Schmidt sitting on a bench, coughing and rubbing his tired eyes. I thought for sure he'd been napping. When he saw me, I'm sure he was glad that I hadn't run off. He glanced at his watch but didn't say anything. He stood up and silently we blended in with the buzz of people exploring the festival.

"Having fun?" I asked.

No answer.

The crowd was growing with tourists and people dressed up in Indian or mountain man outfits. Moving at a snail's pace, it seemed like Schmidt was trying to kill as much of the afternoon as possible. After all, my plane back to the States was for the following morning and I would be on it. Schmidt instructed me that I could take pictures only with his permission. Although my ball and chain dragged, I managed to take about a dozen offhanded pictures without him noticing. Still, I held the realistic dread that my camera could be confiscated.

I stopped and said hello to a group of dancers from the Muscogee tribe in Oklahoma. Even though Schmidt had given the nod for me to speak to these guys, I knew I had to be careful. There were five young men dressed in fancy-dance regalia of their own design, made of modern fabrics, machined beadwork, and colored turkey feathers. One man in the group stood out because of his Brillo pad orange hair. Joking, I asked him how he ended up with hair so hot looking it could light a prairie fire. He ran both of his hands through it, saying that it was a tribute to his great-grandfather who was a French Canadian trapper. It was a good story, even if his hair looked as though it had been spray painted.

"So you guys came all the way over here from Oklahoma? That's a long trip."

"Yeah, but it's worth it. These people are crazy about us and they pay us real good."

"You get paid to dance!" I said, laughing. "How do I get a job like that?"

My nonthreatening humor was loosening things up bit, so I continued, "What other tribes are here besides you?"

"There's some Navajo, Cherokee, and Sioux over there on the other side. Otherwise it's mostly Germans dressed up like Indians."

Politely I asked my minder if he'd take a snapshot of me with the Muscogee tribal member who introduced himself as Quinn. I was surprised when Schmidt dropped his guard a bit and took the picture. I hardly knew what to say when the German policeman asked me to take a picture of him with the Indian. Not even the stoical Schmidt could resist trying to connect with an aboriginal culture light-years from his.

A thousand questions for Quinn piled up in my mind. If the German hadn't been on my tail, I would have developed Quinn into an informant and worked him like a June bug on a string. Eventually I'd uncover enough information to reveal illegal schemes designed to exploit Native American heritage around the world. Yes, I was a big thinker.

Meanwhile I wanted to melt ambiguously into the air so that Schmidt wouldn't even notice me scheming. I imagined that I was a red-tailed hawk, motionless and invisible in the jess, watching and waiting. In the midst of deafening drumbeats and chants, and still within earshot of a Sioux Indian rendering the story of the Sun Dance, I murmured: "Who's selling Indian stuff here?"

The Muscogeean gazed at his hands and spoke barely above his breath. "Luke over there. He's a hoop dancer."

"Halt!" barked Schmidt, his eyes burning at me with outrage. "You no ask questions!"

For the rest of the day I watched my words, and when Schmidt dropped me off at my hotel, there was no warm display of international cooperation or world peace.

CHAPTER NINE

Before the wheels of my United Airlines flight touched the ground on US soil, chills and coughs consumed me, and I immediately named my cold "Schmidt's Crud." Back in my home office in Albuquerque, my boss Matt Miller put me on a conference call with his boss Special Agent in Charge (SAC) Tom Sneed. With two supervisors on the line, my case of the crud didn't seem so bad.

In a voice that sounded like a foghorn, I gave a short briefing on my trip.

Miller spoke up first. "I thought you'd come up with more than this."

"I tried," I said. "But it was tough with a personal German guard."

"I figured you'd get around him somehow and get some dirt on at least a few people."

"But you told me to play it straight."

"I've seen you work like a damn wrecking ball—"

"Look," I interrupted, "I have pictures that will solidify my backstory. I can say that I've been to the festival and that I'm a dealer with German clients. As for intelligence, I didn't get squat. It was impossible."

Then SAC Sneed spouted, "You should never have let her out of town, Miller. I'm the Chief of Investigations and have to report this fiasco to the Chief of Law Enforcement. He's not going to enjoy what I have to report."

Matt backed me up. "Hey, what happened in Germany is not Schroeder's fault. Her information about the illegal trafficking of eagle feathers and artifacts in Germany is probably good—we just can't prove it yet. I'm just worried about the cost of jumping into a black market no one knows much about. Undercover investigations have a bad habit of going over budget anyway. These illegal artifacts are ridiculously expensive."

"I'll watch the money and let you know about every nickel I spend," I said, using my own hot air to keep my case in the air.

I floated a plan in which I'd concentrate on finding the mystery rez runner. If I found him, that would make my supervisors feel a lot better about moving forward. I surmised that he hung out with the antique Indian dealers. After all, he had to sell what he was stealing.

"Let me try and find this one guy and take him out of the picture. Then we can go from there if we want to."

"Sounds reasonable," SAC Sneed said. "Go for it, Dana."

"Wait . . . a . . . minute!" I said sharply.

"W-what's the matter?"

"Don't *ever* call me by my undercover name."

"I was just joking—what the hell is wrong with you?"

"Only the bad guys call me Dana. The good guys call me by my real name. Otherwise I get confused. It's not a joke—"

Matt Miller cut me off. "Don't worry about it, Tom, it's psychological stuff. But she's right. We teach all of our covert operatives not to use their undercover name unless they're in role. It helps to prevent slip-ups."

I was so glad that Matt was able to say something to an upper-level supervisor that I couldn't. I tried to end the conversation. "Sorry, I flipped off. I've got the crud and everything is rubbing me wrong."

Matt meted out the final word. "I'm not crazy about you working undercover so close to where you live. That may have been part of why you went under in the parrot case. If I ever tell you to get out, don't give me any crap, just cut and run. There's plenty of crime out there for you to work on."

CHAPTER TEN

I had chosen Dana Delaney for my undercover name because Delaney is my maiden name and it hadn't been whispered by me or anyone else in nearly three decades. Dana Delany is also a living movie star. I thought the name would be easily remembered by the crooks and offered a shimmer of glamour doused with the smell of money. I wore the same southwestern skirt I wore to the German Indian festival, the same black blouse, but this time I was loaded with antique Indian-made silver and turquoise bracelets, necklaces, and earrings. All of my jewelry was made prior to 1940—which was one of the subtle signatures of a serious Indian artifact dealer. The pieces I wore came from government inventories of property seized by the IRS and the US Marshals Service. The jewelry had been purchased with ill-gotten money like illegal drug sales.

My look, my car, and my agenda were carefully put together to lure those greedy enough to steal, buy, and sell holy artifacts that gave air to the flame of an ancient culture. My challenge was to ferret out the bad guys and offer them exactly what they wanted.

I set myself up with a leather Franklin Planner stuffed with a calendar that confirmed phony appointments with clients, business cards of a dozen antique Indian art dealers, pictures from the Karl May Festival, and doctored receipts from Indian galleries reflecting huge purchases. These external trappings would help carry the day. But I also planned on mirroring the body language of my targets to gain rapport quickly, and using verbal tactics I been trained in to get to the truth.

I kept the government Camaro inside the bunker's garage, since I didn't want it seen in my home driveway. I had registered it earlier under the name Dana Delaney. The car actually bothered me a lot. New Mexico

State Police officers drove white Camaros that were clearly marked with state law enforcement insignias. They were built with an oversized engine to accommodate "in pursuit" situations. My Camaro was simply an unmarked red State Police car. A routine plate check would not come up as "Not on File."

I had a lot to learn fast, so I hit the Coronado Room at the University of New Mexico's library. This room held the best collection of books regarding Southwest Indian culture going back to the earliest records. It was here I would learn how to identify sacred Indian artifacts. Feather identification was easy for me, as I'd been thoroughly trained in this. Very few people knew how to identify bird feathers, and I would play this up as much as I could. Giving expert Indian traders the impression that I knew more than I really did was a dangerous game

I'd studied the history of beadwork and learned to identify the colors of the tiny glass Venetian beads that were available during the high years (1800s–1920) of handmade Indian goods. If the beadwork wasn't right, then the piece was a fake or had been refurbished with new beads. Overall, I discovered that most of the people involved in the trading of Indian goods yearned to connect with the spirit of the Wild West and held a total appreciation for the mystery and beauty of Native American life. But everything has a dark side, and my business was to find it.

To document criminal activity, I carried a large black leather bag in which I'd concealed a mini-camera that was attached to a cassette recorder called a Z-Box. Since I was working alone, the movies I made would be my notes and witness. The recording equipment had listened to my heartbeat more than once during a tight situation. My only other partner was a 9mm SIG Sauer semiautomatic pistol that I could shoot with deadeye accuracy.

At the Ramada Inn in downtown Albuquerque, where an antique Indian art show was being held, I backed the Camaro into a space that was wide open. This was a standard police parking technique done in case I had to quickly find the car and flee the parking lot on two wheels. I always tried to prepare for unexpected contingencies.

In spite of the homework I'd done, I was aware that any new face on the block might generate attention. Staying safe was a matter of passing the waves of scrutiny that would surely come my way. After all, if I was such a productive businesswoman, where had I been all these years? I had to be prepared with an answer.

For three days I hung out watching buyers as they scoured the rooms of the hotel scouting for the perfect pair of nineteenth-century Sioux beaded moccasins or a Chippewa cradle board intricately beaded with thousands of beads into a floral design that captured nature at its best. A collector might pay up to $8,000 for the moccasins and $40,000 for the cradle board. Meanwhile thousands of incredible artifacts lay in between, priced to what the market would bear. These items were all a part of the legal antique Indian art market.

Whatever anxiety may have been felt by buyers was driven by the constant fear that the object of one's desire was stolen, was a fake, or was illegal to sell. To remain legal, a collector had to have a shrewd eye for anything that was considered sacred or contained eagle or other migratory bird feathers. My strategy at the hotel was simple—spread my business card around, meet a few of the dealers, and soft-pedal my way through. While it was too soon to do any serious business, I was open to making small purchases called "confidence buys."

On the third day I began by visiting the rooms that took up the mezzanine level overlooking the pool and a small waterfall. The sound of water helped to dissipate my nerves as I crossed the threshold into a small corner of the world I'd never been in before. Although every "store" was different, the general layout consisted of mostly Anglo dealers who spread their wares across the top of the bed and on every other vacant surface. Leather dresses and beaded vests hung in the closet and fine Navajo blankets hung over the door of the bathroom.

I'd gone through ten rooms before I entered room 150. The dealer introduced himself as Burt Simmons.* He was a man in his mid-fifties who wore a CHIP ball cap, blue jeans, and a polo shirt. He made sure that I knew he was a retired California Highway Patrol officer, and I made sure that he knew I represented discriminating German clients willing to pay plenty for what he had. I also floated the story of the German writer Karl May. Since no one had heard of him, his story helped give me the in-depth credibility that any undercover agent strived for.

Inside room 150 I fingered a small beaded leather knife case and said, "This is something I could send to Germany easy enough."

Simmons took the bait. "It's a great piece from the 1870s and was carried around by a warrior from the Northern Ute tribe. It's only three seventy-five, but I bet you could get double that, especially in Germany."

I gave him a knowledgeable smile and said, "You may be right. In fact, I just got back from over there." I took a minute to show him my mini-album that contained the pictures of the German festival.

"Do you always take such crooked pictures?"

Ouch. I felt like I'd been picked off by a shrike and properly impaled on a barb-wire fence. I should have caught this. I'd taken these pictures on the sly without the benefit of a viewfinder. Quickly I closed the album and said, "I have some better pictures at home, but I'm not showing them around right now—if you get my drift." I hoped this comment would give him a slight whiff of someone who had something to hide.

Even though I had no confidence in Burt's spoken provenance of the knife, I opened my cash-ready wallet and peeled off $400. He quickly pocketed the cash and then bent down on one knee and pulled a small item wrapped in tissue paper from beneath his bed. I perked up, as it appeared that Burt felt I was good for more. Carefully unfolding the tissue from the fragile item, I discovered that it was an eagle feather fan, carried by Native Americans in ceremonial events and during powwows.

"Wow!" I gasped, acting how I thought Dana would. "These feathers are in perfect condition. And look at the beadwork!"

"Yeah, but don't tell the feds about the feathers. They act like real assholes when it comes to feathers. I don't get it personally, and frankly I could care less. Just because it's a law doesn't mean it makes sense."

Apparently Burt felt that his background as a cop gave him the rationale for breaking laws he didn't agree with. I didn't tell him that the fan had probably been made during the sixties or seventies and the feathers were relatively fresh. The smell of mothballs to curtail feather mites was a dead giveaway that this piece had been in a white man's hands. Indians didn't use offensive chemicals on anything of spiritual significance.

The fan was a perfect example of modern paraphernalia made by Indians or non-Indians in which eagle feathers were needed. People like me who were willing to pay for items like this only fueled the trade. I paid the ex–highway patrolman $750 for the fan knowing that Mr. CHIP, like so many other petty violators, had to be stopped. (Months later Simmons would receive citations in the mail and would pay fines of over $2,000. According to an agent who interviewed him, Simmons assumed that the woman he sold to was also cited for violating federal laws.)

Moving to room 203, which coincidentally was my badge number, I adjusted my tinted glasses on my nose and eased closer to an exquisite polychrome pot sitting on a bedside table.

"Where is it from?" I asked the man, who was in his early thirties.

"The Acoma Pueblo, an hour west of Albuquerque," the seller said. "It was used by women to carry water up the old stone steps to the mesa. It's about four hundred years old. I just heard about it yesterday. It's very fresh."

The word "fresh" is code language for something that has just been acquired. Maybe the pot had just been stolen. I couldn't imagine someone selling such an old piece. People had lived at the Acoma Pueblo for the past five hundred years, so it was entirely possible that the pot was as old as the seller claimed. In fact, much of the pueblo remained as it had always been. Low-slung adobe homes that still didn't have electricity or plumbing dotted the top of a 365-foot-high mesa. The doors of the homes were painted turquoise, the color of protection.

As if not to disturb the spirits held in the pot, I spoke in a raspy, low voice. "I've never seen anything like it."

I retrieved a magnifying glass from the large black leather bag I was carrying. The glass was 3.5 inches in diameter and was supported by a sturdy handle. This was my primary prop that made me appear to be a collector concerned with authenticity.

Even though I had no basis, I said, "The patina seems consistent with having been used as a household item for hundreds of years, yet it's still in remarkable condition."

The seller puffed his chest out a bit. "Yep, you won't find another one."

"It's fabulous," I said with amazement. "How much?"

"I need eight thousand. It's one of a kind, of course."

"Can I hold it?"

"Sure, just be careful."

I took off my heavy Navajo-made silver bracelet decorated with red spiny oyster shell and laid it on the bed in the hotel room, hoping that the seller would notice it for its obvious value. I lifted the pot and turned it slowly to drive up the seller's anticipation of making a sale.

As I set it back down on the table, I sighed. "I'm just not sure."

The pitch in the seller's voice shot up a notch. "I swear it's totally authentic. I bought it off an old woman who said that it's been in her family forever."

When I heard this, the image of slimy Richard Crow, bilking an elderly Navajo woman out of the most precious things she had, crept into my mind. I could almost see this guy inside one of the ancient adobe homes of the pueblo, his hands pressed against his heart to vouch for his so-called sincerity as he promised to give the pot a good home. But I still thought it was stolen.

Like a low-level trader on the streets of Tangier, he kept up his schmooze. "You see, I have connections with all the Indians around here. They let me into their homes during feast days, and I bring them things from the city. I'm part Jicarilla Apache on my mother's side, so they trust me."

"You're very interesting," I said, egging him on. "I suppose you can get more fabulous items like this?"

"Absolutely, and I'm the only one around here who can. I can go any-where—the Hopi, the Jemez, even the Isleta." Then he added, laughing, "My girlfriend is Navajo, so I really have an 'in' there."

The boastful nature of this man did not fit the general Indian char-acter, which demanded humility in all matters. I took a careful moment to look him over. His black hair was pulled back into a braid that ran halfway down his back, where I noticed a few silver strands intertwined. He wasn't a kid. A copious mustache curled just over his lips. He wore a Navajo-made silver earring in his right ear, a Zia Pueblo T-shirt, faded jeans, and high-top leather moccasins with hard soles. To me his outfit looked as if it had been conjured up in a drugstore on Route 66.

"So what about the pot?" prompted the seller. "Can I sell it to you?"

"Hmmmm, will you take six thousand?"

He broke eye contact and crossed his arms. "I don't think I can go that low. I had to pay a lot for this pot, but I'll take seven and a quarter."

I maintained eye contact and kept my arms open. "I'll give you seven thousand dollars even."

"Okay, deal," he said as he dropped his arms.

"Deal," I said, smiling. "Can I write a check?"

"Uh . . . I normally don't take checks. Do you have cash?"

"Not seven thousand. Listen, I live in Albuquerque, my check is good."

"Are you sure?"

"Don't insult me."

"Okay, I'll take a check this time."

"So, who do I make it out to?"

"Tony Lorenzo.*"

I felt a surge of excitement—I had finally come across a hot suspect. So far he had all the elements. Even so, I pressed my lips tight to keep from laughing. A half Jicarilla Apache man with an Italian name was a first for me. While I wasn't sure about Lorenzo's authenticity as a Native American, I felt strongly that the pot was genuine. My guess was that the widow Lorenzo spoke of had died and he had lowballed her family for the pot. Or he had someone steal it for him. No Indian matriarch would let go of such a significant household piece that had been handed down for generations. No way.

Lorenzo's next move made me jumpy. He closed the door of the hotel room. I was suddenly alone with a man I didn't know but suspected was a crook. Cold sweat ran down my cleavage, stopping at the two-shot derringer that I'd stuffed in my bra. In my mind I rehearsed how I would retrieve the weapon and use it if I had to. Then I remembered my 9mm SIG Sauer in my bag. I'd shot it hundreds of times during training exercises, and my solid shooting scores reflected that I shot to kill. If for some reason Lorenzo jumped me, I hoped I could get to my lifesavers soon enough. There was no reason that he would. But he could.

Lorenzo pulled some brown wrapping paper from beneath the bed and then disappeared into the bathroom. My heart rate spiked again. As a rule I never let the bad guy out of my sight. Bizarre things could happen in just a few unguarded seconds, and the feeling of vulnerability felt like crap. As it turned out, Tony came out of the bathroom with nothing more than an empty box. While my heart beat slowed, I still didn't take my eyes off of him.

He carefully packed the pot in the box, using copious amounts of tissue paper. "It'll be a long time before I get another pot like this one," he said. "This is your lucky day."

I maintained a gratuitous smile as I handed him my check along with my business card. He took the check and the card and studied them both carefully.

"Oh, you're an Indian art dealer. I didn't realize that," he said, looking up at me.

"Yes. I sell mostly to Germans. I've established a lucrative client base in Germany. As you may know, German collectors have been interested in Native American culture for over a hundred years."

Lorenzo nodded as if he already knew this.

"It all started with the writer Karl May," I explained.

"I think I've heard of him," said Tony, who I suspected was bluffing.

"Oh, I'm sure you have. He's the very reason there's such a hot market for Indian material in Germany today. But it has to be old."

"You mean pre-1940."

"At least."

"What's this on your card? Is it German?"

"Yes. *Gerade vom Indianerreservat in den Vereinigten Staaten.* It means, 'Direct from Indian reservation in the United States.' I assume I can honestly say that this pot came direct from the reservation."

"Absolutely. I wouldn't tell you that if it wasn't true. So, you already have a buyer in Germany?"

"Most likely. I'll e-mail my client tonight. If he wants it, I'll fly it over myself. It's far too valuable to ship."

"I agree, but you have to be really careful. Don't tell Customs what it is—I don't think they let real Indian stuff out of the country."

"I take artifacts out all the time. I know what to do."

"Uh-huh. Good." Lorenzo pulled a business card from his wallet and handed to me. "You know, I might be able to get more stuff for you. Call me sometime."

"Let me find out if my client wants anything else. I'll let you know."

"Okay, but you'd better make it quick. I get new material all the time, and I have to get rid of it as fast as I can."

"I'm sure we'll be able to work together," I said with a reassuring smile.

Lorenzo picked up my bracelet from the bed and eyed it. "Hey, don't forget this. It's an antique, isn't it?"

"Yes, an old Navajo piece," I said as I slid it onto my wrist. "I love it."

"By the way," said Tony. "Where have you been? I haven't seen you around."

"I've spent the last few years selling off a huge estate. It's gone now, so I'm on my own."

"Oh yeah, that makes sense."

Lorenzo lifted the large box that now contained the priceless Acoma water jug and carried it to the parking lot where I had parked my red car.

"Wow, you drive a Camaro?"

"Yes, I call it my Crimson Rose." My subtle strategy was for Tony to relate to the car as a rose and not an unmarked police rig. Admittedly it wasn't the sharpest idea I'd ever had, but I still hoped it would divert his mind from state police cars.

"'Crimson Rose,' I like that," Lorenzo said, grinning. He set the box on the narrow backseat of the Camaro. I got into the front seat and pulled in my ankle-length Santa Fe–style skirt. As I drove away, I fluttered my manicured nails and said, "See you later, Tony."

——◆——

Back at my house, I plugged the Z-Box into a TV monitor and watched every contact I'd made that day at the hotel. To my surprise, I found something I'd forgotten about. It was a statement Lorenzo made justifying the sale of Indian artifacts to white people:

"I'm telling you that collectors are the only ones who can preserve Native American culture. The Indians don't care about their stuff. Collectors are chomping at the bit to get more and more stuff so they can save it for future generations."

This statement would go into my case report. If I could prove that the pot had been stolen or otherwise removed from tribal lands illegally, he'd hear these words again in court. His justification wouldn't go over well with any judge or jury or especially any Native American.

CHAPTER ELEVEN

On Wednesday morning of the following week, I drove my official tan Dodge Ramcharger into the heavy commuter traffic that was traveling north from Albuquerque to Santa Fe. The traffic was further impeded by an obstacle course of orange barrels that marked the never-ending roadwork being done on I-25. In New Mexico spring and summer were considered "orange barrel" seasons, which came and went like the regular ones. My four-wheel-drive vehicle was overkill for the interstate, and its heavy-duty tires made for annoying road noise. I tried to drown it out by listening to the romancing guitar strings of Ottmar Liebert playing his lovely "Barcelona Nights."

Once I broke away from the orange barrels, I took in the fabulous scenery. Open spaces stretched as far as I could see, dotted with sagebrush, piñon pines, Utah junipers, and outcroppings of volcanic rock. Extinct volcano cones stood like sentries to time and eternity. The whole landscape spoke of an ancient silence never to be broken.

As opposed to many roads in New Mexico, this route wasn't lined with fast food restaurants, shopping centers, or housing projects. The land was owned by four different Indian pueblos that kept it for their people, wildlife, and plants. According to pueblo traditions the good of the people revolved around being good to the land, which in turn created harmony within the universe. Ancient dogma dictated that the land and its people were inextricably connected and any harm done to the land would disrupt the balance of life. It was a philosophy that I'd read about in one of my books on Native Americans and one that I totally embraced.

Twenty minutes later I drove up La Bajada, a rocky, steep hill that historically marked a critical obstacle for horse-drawn caravans traveling between Albuquerque and Santa Fe. As I cruised up the incline, I thought about how in the old days getting over La Bajada was a major feat. There were many stories of horses, wagons, and stagecoaches that spent days bogged down on this hill. But less than a hundred years later, I buzzed over it in less than a minute. Once in Santa Fe, I made my way through circuitous and narrow streets alleged to have been built over old cow trails made during cattle drives. It was hard to believe anything else.

Finally I located the US Post Office building, which housed the FBI field office for northern New Mexico. I took the stairs to the third floor, turned left, and encountered an office where a bulletproof window protected the receptionist from suspects, lawyers, and agents. Special agent Scott Wilson* was waiting for me behind the receptionist's desk and spoke through an intercom.

From my perspective his boyish face almost made him look too young to carry a badge and a gun. But he wasn't that young; in fact he was almost thirty years old. He stood about five-ten, with light hair that blended in with his fair completion. While he was pleasant looking, he didn't have the stereotypical hard look of a federal agent. Of course, I had the same problem.

"Hi there, you're right on time." Wilson pushed a button that sounded a buzzer signaling the heavy door was open.

I entered an office compound that appeared rather pedestrian due to a worn carpet and a decorating scheme of surplus government furniture built with no design in mind.

"Come on," said Wilson, "I want you to meet some folks."

My chest tightened. I had just begun an undercover investigation and hated being paraded around, even in places that were supposed to be safe. Suddenly laughter and chatter burst from a conference room and made me even more wary.

"Say, Scott, if you don't mind, I'd like to skip the social bit and get to our meeting. My time is a little tight."

Scott's face stiffened, like he'd been snubbed. "Sure, follow me."

As we passed through the office, a man in his mid-fifties came out of the conference room. "There you are, Scotty, I was wondering where you went."

"Hi, Garry, sorry I cut out, I've got a meeting with US Fish and Wildlife. This is agent Schroeder from Albuquerque."

Then Scott turned to me. "This is Garry Sullivan*; he's retiring as of today. He's been an FBI agent for twenty-five years. That's pretty impressive in my book."

"It sure is," I said, as I shook Sullivan's hand. "Congratulations."

"Thanks. So you're with the Coot and Carp Club, eh? No offense, of course, that's what us old-timers call you guys. Are you working with my buddy Scotty on that Indian stuff?"

I kept it simple. "We have something going."

"Well, hurry up and get it done so Scotty can get back to cases that will protect our flag, constitution, and the American way of life. Indian cases don't cut it." Then Sullivan slapped Scott Wilson on the back. "Catch you later, buddy. Watch your back with fin 'n' feathers. I hear they can be pretty wild. Get it? Ha!"

I gave Scott the stink eye. "He knows about our case?"

Scott's shoulders turned in slightly as he thrust his hands in his pockets. "Well, not everything."

"Scott, I don't like this. We agreed to keep this case on a need-to-know basis. It's obvious he knows about the case and doesn't even think the FBI should be involved."

Straightening up a bit, Wilson tugged on his tie to loosen it. "He's okay. He just thinks the FBI is all about bank robberies. That's old hat, of course. Besides, he might be an old fart, but he's really a good guy. In fact, he's helping me build a patio onto my house. He built his own house. He's got an unbelievable collection of antiques, you should see it."

I forced a blank stare to show I just didn't care. The good-old-boy system had been a thorn in my side since the day I was hired. In this case Garry-the-buddy trumped my safety, and I was not happy about it.

Scott and I walked inside Burt Weisenhunt's* office. Weisenhunt was the Special Agent in Charge for New Mexico. He wasn't in his office, but I could hear what I thought was him in the hallway dousing more atta-boys on the retiring agent. While Scott and I made ourselves comfortable at the large conference table, I looked around. All of the furniture was made of matching dark mahogany—a definite upgrade from the rest of the office. Along with dozens of awards there were pictures with Weisenhunt with the directors of the FBI and CIA and the senior US senator for New Mexico. My snap judgment of the man was that he was a political hack who had kissed butt on his way up the bureaucratic food chain. He probably had plans to go even higher.

Just then Weisenhunt, a barrel of a man who topped six feet three and was built like a 250-pound silverback gorilla, barged into his lair. "Sorry I'm late—had to give Garry a good send-off. I'm sure gonna miss that guy, he's funny as hell."

Having never met the man, I was rocked back by the intensity of Weisenhunt's deep-set steel-blue eyes. His square face and jaw were rigid, as if they'd been that way since birth. I figured he had the flexibility of steel-reinforced concrete—which set my instincts up for battle. This guy was going to be trouble.

I took a deep breath and began the meeting by saying, "Last Saturday I made a covert contact with a man I believe might be an active rez runner. He claims to have access to just about anything Indian and he's selling to the art galleries in Santa Fe. Anyone seeking authentic ceremonial Native American material knows that the best stuff is in Santa Fe. All we have to do is find out which Indian art dealer he's selling to."

SAC Weisenhunt immediately launched an attack. "Are you aware, agent Schroeder, that there are two hundred and fifty art dealers in Santa Fe? That's more art dealers per capita than there are in New York City!"

"Yes, sir, that's true."

"And how are you going to narrow the scope? We can't target hundreds of people, you know."

"I believe that this rez runner will lead me to the primary suspect, or suspects. I made a confidence buy from him yesterday."

"What did you buy?" he said, narrowing his eyes.

"An old Acoma pot. He either stole it or paid a pathetically low price for it."

"How much of our buy money did this cost?"

"Seven thousand dollars."

Weisenhunt reacted by jumping out of his chair and stomping around the office. "You spent seven thousand dollars of FBI money on a goddamn pot!"

I shot back, "The entire budget is fifty thousand and it comes from three agencies, not just the FBI," reminding him of the agreement the FBI had with the National Park Service and the US Fish and Wildlife Service. I was getting steamed myself. His rant was not about the money, it was about being large and in charge. Regardless, I continued with my justification.

"Now this guy, Tony is his name, thinks I'm good for buying high-quality merchandise. I'll probably make another confidence buy from him, maybe something of lesser value. Then I'll start asking him for something that's illegal. Eventually he'll start coughing up who he deals with in Santa Fe."

Weisenhunt liked to be in charge. "Why in the hell would he reveal who he sells to? That makes no sense! You could bypass him and start buying from the art dealers directly. There's no way he's going to reveal his buyers. He's gonna want to keep you all to himself."

Weisenhunt had a point, but I stood my ground. "Lorenzo's ego is all tied up in the big-name art dealers he sells to. Eventually he'll brag to me about them. Besides, I'm posing as a dealer who wants to buy low and sell high. Why would I go to anyone else but Lorenzo? I won't get a low price from a retail dealer."

"I agree with her," mumbled Scott, apparently too timid to say much more.

Weisenhunt sat back down, looked at Scott, and spoke as if I wasn't even in the room. "You know I ordinarily wouldn't want Fish involved in FBI matters. But FBI headquarters insists on more cases from Indian County. Scott, I want you more involved. Get a handle on what she's doing. What the hell are we going to do with this pot, for God's sake?"

"Yes sir," mumbled the agent. "But if this pot is used in ceremonies, then it would be a good case for us under NAGPRA."

"Another thing, I don't give a hoot about eagle feathers." Weisenhunt scowled. "Don't bring me any feathers cases, they're—"

Before I blew up, I had to interrupt. "Did you know that NAGPRA violations are misdemeanors, whereas the sale of eagle feathers is a felony?"

"Is that right, Wilson? Are these Indian cases just misdemeanors?"

"I believe so," replied Scott, sounding uncertain himself.

"So you see," I said, speaking like a lawyer, "adding eagle feather charges against whoever is selling sacred artifacts will add significantly to the penalties we can press for."

"I can't believe this shit," moaned Weisenhunt. "I still don't give a squat about eagle feathers, and this case isn't about feathers. I want to get to the bottom of the artifact black market, or whatever you call it. When do you think you can wrap this up?"

"I'm actually just getting started. It's taken me two months to find Lorenzo, and he just fell into my lap. If he's a key player, I'll find out. But I'm going to need some flexibility on the time."

Weisenhunt spouted, "I need a deadline. Headquarters isn't going to put up with a bunch of never-ending amateur crap."

I was on the verge of pounding my fist on the table. How dare Weisenhunt refer to my work as "amateur crap"? I was the only person actually doing anything. But then Weisenhunt broke eye contact. I knew something bad was coming.

"I'll give you guys three months to make some significant progress. If there is none, then I'm pulling the money."

His words felt like a kick in the gut. The money that the FBI giant had committed now had conditions attached to it. Money, and lots of it, was the only way to lure in the crooks who were selling off Indian culture for hundreds of thousands of dollars. As it was, the project was already badly underfunded. I could ask for more funds later only if I had solid justification. That meant I'd need to develop more defendants. I tried hard not to react to the blow Weisenhunt had dealt. I didn't want to say something that would make him even more irate.

I looked at Scott and faked a bit of confidence. "We'll get there—I'll get us there."

"Good enough, now you two get out of here. I've got work to do. Keep me posted, Wilson. I want everything on 302s, I've haven't seen shit from you yet."

"Yes sir."

Agent Wilson had been submitting my reports covered with an FBI cover sheet, which is actually what I'd recommended. If Wilson started generating case reports that differed in the slightest from mine, a defense attorney would use them against us in court. Besides, Wilson wasn't the undercover agent and wasn't even a witness. What could he possibly report?

Agent Wilson and I walked out of the office into the hallway, where I hoped to have a one-on-one talk with Wilson. But first I had to get

Weisenhunt out my system. "Your boss is quite the jerk. What the hell's the matter with him?"

Rubbing the carpet with the toe of one shoe, Wilson looked like he was trying to eliminate an imaginary stain. Maybe the spot was a symbolic bloodstain from the wounds his boss had just inflicted.

I wished agent Wilson would reveal his true feelings, but he didn't. "It's just his personality, don't worry about him." Then, in true government style, Wilson changed the subject. "Hey, I just thought of something. I asked BIA agent John McKinney to meet with us today, but he said he was busy. I got the feeling he just didn't want to show up."

"That's right. Don't count on him. He's not going to help us."

"Why not? He's Indian, isn't he? I'd think he'd care about this stuff."

"Part Indian. His mother is from the Acoma Pueblo, which means he doesn't want to get involved with artifacts from other tribes because of what might happen to him spiritually. If we were dealing with a murder, it'd be different."

"You're joking."

"No, I'm serious. Messing with foreign tribal artifacts could cause him a spiritual sickness. McKinney is just trying to protect himself."

"Great. So the BIA is out."

"I'm afraid so."

"What about Park?"

"They're in, but they only have one agent, and he's pretty busy."

Wilson sighed. "I'll try and support you the best I can, but I gotta tell you, I think you're crazy to be working undercover within fifty miles of Albuquerque. You could get burned faster than a pig in a pit."

Spare me, I thought, but I let it go.

"I've worked undercover alone before," I said, "and I don't like it either. It's obvious I'm going to have to expose myself even more to keep the case rolling. Believe it or not, I'm more worried about the Indians. If we don't start catching some bad guys, all hell is going to break loose on the reservations."

"Like how?"

"I've spoken to a Navajo chanter, and he told me there's been a rash of *jish* thefts, right from the hogans where they do their ceremonies.

Someone is getting to the medicine bundles and selling the smaller stuff that's in them. These things are like diamonds—easy to conceal and easy to move."

"What should we be looking for?"

"I don't know exactly, they won't tell me, so I'm still trying to figure it out on my own. I just know that when the right ceremonies can't be done, the Indians get a spiritual sickness that leads to depression and all sorts of bad things."

Wilson rolled his eyes. "You're starting to sound a little spooky."

Just then the elevator door opened and released a small band of bureaucrats returning to their pigeon coops. The extra few seconds gave me enough time vent my irritation. "Knock it off, Scott. I'm serious about this."

"Okay, so what's your point?"

"In some ways this case is like investigating a murder where understanding victimology can be critical. The Indians are clearly the victims, and understanding how they use these artifacts will help us understand why they are so significant."

Even I was just warming up to my own idea.

Wilson started rubbing the rug again with the toe of his shoe. "I don't understand . . . but I guess that's because I'm from Alabama. All we have are voodoo witches."

When the elevator door opened again I was on it, even though it was going up instead of down.

CHAPTER TWELVE

So, the FBI supervisor had increased the pressure and I wasn't sure I could make significant progress within his arbitrary timeline. I had to figure out a way to get things moving quickly. It was true that I could identify antique Indian objects like parfleches and pots and possible bags, but my knowledge of sacred Indian artifacts was woefully inadequate. I had learned about *Yei'i bicheii* masks from the East-West Trading Post investigation, but if I was going to recover other sacred items, I'd have to dig deeper for secrets I wasn't meant to know.

I'd read that when the Catholic Spaniards discovered the Southwest Indians during their quest for gold during the 1500s, they tried to crush all aspects of Indian deities and their ceremonial life. I learned that these extremely spiritual peoples saw no separation between everyday life and what was sacred. Every meal, every undertaking, every relationship held a sacred place in their cultural sphere. Each person's goal was to constantly maintain perfect harmony between what was good and what was bad. Any incongruences had to be overcome by healing rites that were performed continually over the millennia with great precision. There were rites to initiate the young, and rites filled with blessings and magic intended to spiritually rejuvenate the person in spiritual jeopardy. The key component to maintaining the potency of these rites was to keep the chants, dance, and every symbolic aspect of the ceremonies cloistered in deep secrecy. Intruding outsiders only served to undermine the holiness of everyday Native American life.

Secluded in a quiet corner in the Coronado Room at the University of New Mexico, I spent days looking for anything that would give me insight into the sacred objects that would be pertinent to my investigation. I read the chronicles of turn-of-the-century anthropologists who made contacts with the Navajos, Hopis, and Puebloans. To this day, Navajo and Hopi historians gnaw over the fact that much of what was sacred to the people was traded to anthropologists for mere sacks of flour.

Finally I stumbled upon a book that provided a thorough introduction to the Navajo *jish*. *Navajo Medicine Bundles or Jish* was a thick volume with a red cover, written by Charlotte J. Frisbie, Ph.D. A large doeskin bag, the *jish* holds the sacred medicinal tools used by chanters to heal the Navajo people, both physically and spiritually. The book described in detail the dozens of implements found in the *jish* that practicing chanters used in conjunction with song and deep meditation to bring about the desired effect. I learned that following the dictates of the ancients was paramount to maintaining the essential balance between earth and sky. According to Navajo doctrine, imbalance in a person manifests itself in disease, crankiness, depression, and the inability to be reasonable. Restoring a person to beauty is an expensive, difficult, and dangerous psychophysical procedure.

I was totally fascinated, but I couldn't begin to understand all the mysteries of the *jish*, so I focused on talking prayer sticks. One set of talking prayer sticks was part and parcel of every *jish*, and replacing them took enormous time and ceremony.

Talking prayer sticks are two flat sticks wrapped together with grasses or string. Each stick has a face on it, and together they represent the inseparable hero twins who appear in the Navajo creation story, the sons of White Shell Woman. The first twin was *Nayenizgani*, also called Monster Slayer, for he was the stronger one and the slayer of alien gods. Monster Slayer's brother *Tobadzaschaina*, or Born for Water, helped Monster Slayer by warning him when trouble loomed and made sure his brother didn't overuse his powers.

According to Navajo mythology, in the beginning the earth was infested with giants, foreign gods, and man-eating birds, who were destroying the people. Monster Slayer slew these monsters of evil with his hatchet and supernatural bows and arrows. The remains of these slain giants can be seen in the huge rock formations in Monument Valley, Arizona.

I didn't take mythology lightly. Every culture I could think of had its own mythology as a way of explaining how the culture came to be. Myth was the key to explaining the logic of almost all things, especially things in the spiritual world.

Monster Slayer is still called upon today to ward off evil. While his role in the creation story is complex, the hero twins are nevertheless very important for the wisdom they provide. Together the brothers offer guidance to the spiritual leaders who meditate and pray over them. I found it especially fascinating that Monster Slayer created the first moral code for the earth people to follow. He established the distinction between good and evil, which the Navajos follow to this day. Once again I found myself drawn to Monster Slayer. I liked everything about him.

I was further amazed at the strict protocol that remains in place for the construction and usage of ceremonial objects. The Indians themselves opined that the same primordial dogmas had been repeated with perfection as far back as ten thousand years ago—or, as Yazzie had put it, "since time beyond memory." Watching a ceremony today would be like getting a snapshot of human activity as it occurred during ancient times. It would be like traveling in a time machine; the whole idea was spellbinding.

Today it remains incumbent upon the chanters of all the native tribes to reproduce every word sung, every movement made, and every object incorporated into the various rites. The amount of memorization and practice involved is mind-boggling, and for this reason not all chanters can sing for every ceremony. Alone in my corner at the library, I devoured books that contained precious few pictures of ancient ceremonial objects. These pictures, taken in the late 1800s and early 1900s, were of poor quality but provided indisputable proof of Native American ceremonialism. Finally I had an idea of what to look for on the Indian black market, and I was more anxious than ever to get on with the hunt.

CHAPTER THIRTEEN

August 1998. Posing as Dana Delaney, I gazed up a steep, ancient staircase to the Spirit Bear Gallery, an upscale Indian art gallery located in the heart of Santa Fe. I was wearing my quintessential southwestern tiered skirt with colorful floral designs. My purse was the same leather bag I carried when I met Tony Lorenzo. The Z-Box was loaded with fresh film and was already rolling.

The Spirit Bear was one in about a dozen galleries I'd visited covertly trying to sniff out suspects. While I didn't expect the hunt to be easy, I was becoming discouraged. So far none of the galleries on the famous Canyon Road showed any hint of dealing in illegal sacred material. The German-client bait I'd thrown out was of no interest to anyone. I'd probably have to make a number of visits to these galleries and make confidence buys before anyone would trust me enough to show me what they had hidden in their back rooms. Thanks to the FBI, I didn't have this kind of time.

The Spirit Bear Gallery was not on Canyon Road but was located near what had been the cultural center of Santa Fe for centuries, the Plaza. It was the place where Mexican folk dances took place, art festivals were held, and Indians sat on blankets selling their handmade jewelry. The main building on the north side was the Palace of the Governors, established in the early seventeenth century as Spain's seat of government. Today it serves as a museum of New Mexico's history beginning with the Native Americans, the Spanish, the Mexicans, and finally the westward-bound US pioneers.

The gallery took up space on the second floor of a centuries-old brick building on Palace Avenue. As I climbed the narrow wooden staircase, I focused on pacing my breathing. Gasping for air at the top wouldn't set the tone I wanted. At the top of the stairs I pointed my camera in the direction of a wooden table bearing an old drum covered in rawhide. The drumhead had a ferretlike mammal painted in red and black on it. Next to it was an armless wooden figurine with an all-white face and brown body. Hanging on the wall behind the table was a red-black-and-gray-striped

Navajo-woven rug that bore a $78,000 price tag. Just the price tag told me the type of neighborhood I was in.

As I turned the corner to enter the main part of the gallery, I nearly gasped at an incredible beaded Shoshone cradle board, circa 1885. The top of the cradle board was done with a background of sky-blue turquoise beads and red geometric designs. A dark-blue beaded outline around the board offset the designs beautifully. The price tag read $85,000.

The gallery's few pieces of southwestern-style furniture were used to display a tasteful array of Indian art such as old pots, baskets, and arrow sticks. Even though by now I'd been in dozens of galleries, I'd never seen anything like these arrow sticks. One end of each stick was hand-carved to look like mesas with three steps leading to a flat top. The faded turquoise color was barely discernible. Sitting on a mantel, they held the appeal of something significant from another culture. As simple-looking as they were, I assumed they had a remarkable story at the cost of $8,000 each.

My attention shifted to a pair of simply carved wooden parrots displayed on a low table. Once again, I was set back by the outrageous $30,000 price tag. Both parrots were wearing necklaces made from the short wing feathers of an Amazon parrot. After my experiences at Reuben's aviary, I was very certain about the identity of the feathers. Then connections flashed through my mind. I had read that parrots carried from the south had been incorporated into Native American spiritual life. It was hard to believe that these birds were so special. They weren't like eye-catching artwork or even an unusual decoration. Anyone would have walked right past them—especially for $30,000. Then I considered that a high price tag would attract wealthy collectors who believed that the more something cost, the rarer it had to be.

What I noticed about the parrots was that they showed no wear. Collectors loved to opine about patina—that is, the wear an object shows as a result of handling or exposure to the elements. If a particular piece showed patina to be two or three hundred years old, it could still be a newly made fake. Woodworkers could make things look deceptively old. Or, if a piece was falling apart, it wasn't collectable. When I was evaluating an antiquity, I often referred to the patina as being either consistent or inconsistent with its age—even though I had no idea. All collectors and dealers talked about patina, so I used the term to bolster my contrived credibility.

That said, the parrots looked old, but not worn. They were extremely smooth and didn't show the slightest damage. Displayed in the gallery, their simplicity offered a sense of elegance that came from deep within. I had a heartened feeling that I was onto something.

I was beginning to understand why tracing items sacred to Native Americans was so difficult: For the most part, no one knew what they looked like. Only a handful of people thoroughly schooled in the anthropology of Southwest Indian culture would know where to begin. It would be easy if I could find an expert who could render an opinion as to which of the tribes these birds came from, but I didn't dare take the risk of talking to anyone. I had to figure out as much as I could on my own and then reach out to the tribes later. This was the backward way of doing things.

Even though I felt like I was the only person in the gallery, I knew I wasn't. A densely woven Mexican-made Indian blanket covered the door that led to a back room. As I secretly filmed the gallery, I wondered who might be watching me. While I tried to stay as quiet as possible, my footsteps echoed between the wooden floor and the high ceiling. Finally a woman appeared from behind the Indian blanket.

"Hello, might I help you with anything?" she asked.

I turned and pointed the camera lens slightly upward to get a good picture. She was as beautiful as a model in a magazine—dressed in a sleeveless sweater and faux leather skirt brought together with a large trendy belt. Her hair color was not natural, but the deep-red shade complemented her olive complexion well. Large hoop earrings dangled nearly to her shoulders. She added a definite shine to an already classy business.

"I'm just looking," I said, smiling. "I've never been in here before. What a fascinating gallery. Some of the ethnographic material here looks extremely rare."

"Yes, Mr. DeVries* is a discerning dealer. You won't find material like his anywhere."

"Where does he get them? Collectors today want to know the exact provenance of what they buy."

The woman didn't miss a beat. "Mostly from estates," she said. "People die and he buys up what they leave behind." She waved her arm around the room. "Some of these things have been in private collections for decades. But each piece comes with a precise provenance."

Nice company line. Artifacts that had been in a closet for decades suddenly appeared on the market through estate sales. Even I had used that lie.

"I'm Dana Delaney, and you're . . . ?"

"Mona. I help Mr. DeVries at the gallery three days a week."

"It's so nice to meet you. Is he here today?"

"No, he's meeting with one of his important clients. He'll be back soon, though. Is there something you're interested in?"

I assumed she was trying to give me the impression that her boss was a big deal. I handed Mona my Dana Delaney business card and said, "Yes, I have a collection, but I mainly buy for clients in Europe."

Mona paused a moment and with heightened interest said, "Oh, really? I'm sure Mr. DeVries would like to meet you. Can I make an appointment for you to meet with him?"

"I would like that."

Mona disappeared into the back room and came back out with a calendar. Perusing the calendar, she said, "He's available next Wednesday around two p.m. Can you make that?"

"Sure," I said, nodding. "I'll be here. Thank you so much for your help."

"No problem," she said, smiling.

"See you then."

I turned and gripped the wooden rail for my uneven trip back down the stairs that were once dusted by petticoats.

Out on Palace Avenue I reached inside my bag and turned off my third eye. I thought the contact at the Spirit Bear Gallery had gone perfectly. There were even a couple of things that bore checking out—the parrots and the strange-looking sticks. They made me suspicious.

My spirits were high when I thought about Mona telling DeVries about me. She'd probably tell him how nice and honest I seemed. She'd recount how impressed I was with his collection and how I had a cadre of clients ready to spend. She would build me up, saving me the trouble of having to establish my own credibility. After listening to Mona, I was sure DeVries would be receptive toward me.

I blew to the air a cheery "Thank you, Mona!"

CHAPTER FOURTEEN

September 1998. With the FBI still breathing down my neck, I needed to generate income to make meaningful buys—especially if I was going to deal with DeVries. I attended a little-advertised antique Indian art auction at a hotel in Eau Claire, Wisconsin, hoping to buy merchandise at reasonable prices to sell later at a profit.

At the show I was amazed to find scores of authentic antique Indian items displayed on auction tables inside a conference room. "Stores" were opened in some of the rooms, and I pursued them like a shark on the hunt for something special for my so-called German clients. Some of the sellers recognized me from other shows I'd attended and even remembered my name Dana. Perfect. The word was spreading that I was who I said I was, and I was becoming more confident in my role.

No one was in room 118 when I sauntered inside looking over the various Indian items for sale. The inventory consisted of old kachina dolls, jewelry, beaded leggings, moccasins, vests, rugs, baskets, and miscellaneous antique clothing worn by Indians, soldiers, and cowboys in the early twentieth century. Everything looked normal.

A tall woman with long, stringy, mousy gray hair walked in sipping iced coffee from a tall plastic cup. She wore snug western jeans, a concha belt, and a very nice western button-up blouse with tasteful Indian designs on it. Even her gaudy glasses from the sixties gave her the perfect look for a dealer in antiques.

But her first words nearly knocked me over. "Hi . . . haven't I seen you somewhere before?"

I gulped and took another look. "No, I don't think so." I struggled to place her. But then she did it for me.

"About seven years ago, some Fish and Wildlife agents raided my shop in Albuquerque and seized a bunch of really old kachina dolls."

"Why would the government take a bunch of kachina dolls? They're everywhere," I said, as my voice grew weaker and I felt like I was moving in slow motion.

Everything clicked as I recognized Charlotte Small. I had been one of the agents in her shop, but there were about six agents there that day. I didn't live in Albuquerque at the time and had been shipped in for the assignment. But I was the only woman there, and I probably stood out.

"The feds claimed that the dolls had eagle and owl feathers on them. They *could* have just taken the feathers, but no! The assholes seized sixteen very valuable dolls. You look like one of the agents. In fact, you were the only woman."

"God, I have no idea what you're talking about," I said, barely stuttering. I couldn't give in, no matter what, so I shot back, "And I don't think you do either."

"Yes I do. I remember every minute of that awful day. You know, I had to pay the collectors back, and they were so pissed they'll never do business with me again. I almost had to shut down, but enough people had faith in me and my merchandise that I'm still kicking."

"What a bummer," I muttered. But she was right—I had been in the shop the day it was raided. She was selling feathered items right and left, including some not-so-old lances that had commercially loomed beadwork near the spearhead and fresh eagle feathers attached with leather laces. The lances represented part of the trade of cheap Indian trinkets that were decorated with eagle feathers acquired from eagles killed in the Jemez Mountains. I remembered that on the day of the raid, Charlotte had fully confessed to one of the agents that she knew it was illegal to sell eagle feathers but minimized her crimes by saying, "Everybody does it—you should go after the big boys and leave us little dealers alone." She became so belligerent that she was nearly arrested for obstruction of justice.

My mind flashed back to the day in Alaska when the accusation of a big-game skinner made me feel like I was the one being fleshed out instead of a grizzly bear hide. The skinner had said, "I think you could be a government plant put in here to catch us." My world started to fall apart like a low-flying Super Cub that had just lost its lift. Amazingly, quick thinking saved me then. But would it save me now?

"Look, Charlotte, you've got me pegged all wrong. Here, look at these pictures of me at the Karl May Festival in Germany. I scout shows for good stuff for my German clients. Some of these people are really loaded."

As I flipped through the pictures I'd taken in Germany, Charlotte tried to get a good look but I didn't want to give her too much time.

"Stop," she insisted. "Let me see that picture again."

Instead of letting her see the photo, I folded the album and stowed it in my black bag.

"Why did you close the album so quickly?"

"There's nothing else to show . . . that's all." Charlotte almost had me. In the album I'd inserted an evidence photograph of a genuine Sioux shield with eagle feathers on it. One look at the picture of an illegal item might convince her that I really was an agent—given her history with the law. My hairline burst into beads of sweat while Charlotte continued her methodical dismemberment of me.

"You sure closed the album fast, like you didn't want me to see something. And you're acting very nervous."

Ouch! I was definitely experiencing the fight-or-flight syndrome common to officers facing a shoot-out. This woman was on the verge of impaling me, and I had to get out of her sights.

"I'm not nervous," I whimpered. "I'm having a diabetic reaction. Right now I feel like I'm going to faint." This wasn't much of an act for me. I'd grown up with two diabetic brothers and knew what an insulin reaction looked like.

Suddenly Charlotte actually sounded concerned. "Can I do anything?" *Was she falling for this?*

I tried to look as green as I could. "I have to eat a glucose bar . . . like right now. I'll catch up with you later." With that, I simply walked out of her room, kicking my own butt all the way.

I went to my room and collapsed on my bed, rolling back and forth, groaning. My body shook, but not from a diabetic reaction. Undercover work could catch you up in a thousand ways that you could never see coming. If Charlotte started flaming rumors about my true identity, people might believe her. Then I'd have no choice but to simply disappear—I'd be finished. But then I thought about Monster Slayer. He was strong and never gave up, not even in the most dire circumstances.

I decided to face the music and see what would happen next, no matter how much it hurt.

—◦—

The next morning I felt like crap over my bungling, but I knew I had to head back to the auction. While getting ready, I did a lot of self-talking: Dana Delaney had to go back into the lion's den and keep her game face going. The truth was, Charlotte didn't have anything solid on me. My best hope was that she was second-guessing herself and was realizing that she could be wrong. If she did attack, I'd firmly remind her that mistaken identities happen all the time and that she'd better leave me alone.

As I'd taught hundreds of agents before me, never admit to being an agent. It was possible that if Charlotte started a story, it would sound so incredible that no one would believe her. Charlotte already had a sketchy reputation among dealers in western memorabilia. For years she'd battled rumors that she'd pilfered old western badges from a show and then sold them in her shop in Albuquerque. The incident tainted her credibility, and I could use that against her. I looked at myself in the mirror and smiled. Who would believe that a sweet-looking woman like Dana was really a gun-toting federal agent?

—◦—

As it turned out, the auction was very poorly attended and the bidding was slow. This wasn't good for Paul Axel,* the man sponsoring the auction. Seated at the head table, Axel was a big man who wore fine Tony Lama boots and a Stetson hat. While I signed the roster, Mr. Axel told me that his vision for the auction was for it to make him a big player in the cowboy and Indian memorabilia trade. To my surprise, he shared with me his worry that the low turnout might ruin him.

The room was set for 150 people, but there were only about 35 in attendance. I had my bidding card ready for action, but I didn't dare bid on anything illegal if I saw anything. I had to act like a bidder interested in a few quality items and not like an agent trying to gather evidence. Meanwhile Charlotte stood quietly in the back of the room with arms folded, like a wooden Indian.

By that afternoon I had acquired a fabulous Indian woman's red woolen dress with the front randomly patterned with the ivory incisors of ten bull elk. (Many Indian experts think that the teeth were worn by wives to honor their husbands' proficiency as hunters.) I paid $2,000 for this dress, which was easily worth much more. Someone like DeVries would sell it for an outrageous $25,000. To build my inventory, I proceeded to fill my basket with old knives, Indian beaded clutches made for a white woman, leather leggings, a bow and arrow set, and trinkets. My new collection was totally authentic, and I'd acquired it for far less than what it was worth.

During the three-day auction, not one other person challenged me about being an agent. I enjoyed friendly conversations with dealers who were history buffs. They taught me nearly everything I needed to know about the trade, along with the fascinating history behind Indian memorabilia. Even though I was working, I was engaged in an absorbing topic. The storytellers at the antique Indian art show made Native American history come alive for me. Meanwhile Mr. Axel looked like a drowning man, with a lovely Filipino wife who pampered him all day with whiskey and aspirin.

I packed my new collection and boarded a plane to Albuquerque. Charlotte was on the same plane, and it was obvious to me that I'd always have her lurking behind my back. I still worried that she might cause a stink. Between Charlotte Small and the FBI and their arbitrary timeline, I was feeling a lot of pressure. I had no idea that these were the good times.

CHAPTER FIFTEEN

That night when I got home to Albuquerque, I spent the evening alone with my husband, Lonnie. We caught up on the past few days' events as I adjusted to an environment that was reality. Home reminded me that I wasn't really Dana Delaney, a woman running around catching bad guys. In so many ways I was like a lot of women who worked and had a family. But the 1990s society hadn't caught up to women in law enforcement, and if it weren't for my husband, a devoted friend and a wonderful father to our daughter, I couldn't have done my job. I had heard my male colleagues comment that they wouldn't *let* their wives work in law enforcement. Well, maybe these women didn't want to. It wasn't for everyone. But I met several wives who felt they were being held back by their spouses for one reason or another. Not in my life.

The transition from undercover work to home life didn't come easy, as I could never let my guard down completely. In this case, Operation Monster Slayer was becoming a bigger part of me as I became more determined to get to the bottom of the illegal artifact trade and the desecration of the Indian spirituality. But I had to be careful about letting the case consume me. My family came first, even if I had to stop and remind myself.

I had to admit that jumping in and out of roles sometimes made me irritable. At home I was saddled with housework, grocery shopping, doing laundry, and cooking dinner. There was never enough time to get everything done. Work was much more exciting when I was plotting against the bad guys and making cases. But it had its stressors, like the nights I spent transcribing tapes and writing case reports. On weekends I filled out travel vouchers and accounted for every nickel I spent out of undercover funds. Because of my trip to Wisconsin, I now had to inventory property and enter these items into a database. I could legally sell these items and wasn't required to make a profit. I hoped my reasonable prices would attract buyers, giving me the opportunity to dig deeper into the Indian antique market.

⹌⹌

The wooden parrots I'd seen at the Spirit Bear Gallery continued to nag me. I wasn't sure, but I felt they had to be spiritually significant to an Indian tribe somewhere. In just a few days I was going back, and I wanted to have my act together. I still didn't know anyone I could safely talk to, so I headed back to the Coronado Room to get lost in more history. The large tables were mostly vacant, but the Xerox machine hummed almost constantly as there was always a line of people waiting to use it. The library's warden kept a close eye on the rare book collection to make sure none of the books grew legs and left the room.

I went to my favorite corner and dug in. My reference books were the ones written by anthropologists who tried to decode the Indian view of the universe. It was difficult, dry reading, as the mythology and explanation of ceremonies were complex and confusing—nothing similar to the Hansel and Gretel fables of my childhood. No wonder social scientists spent decades trying to decipher it all. It was also no wonder shamans and chanters spent their entire lives learning every minutia of what the ancients taught to them since the beginning. As for the Indian peoples, none of this could be lost.

I was reading so much about mythology, I had trouble finding anything that was pertinent to my investigation. In this respect a stolen art case seemed like a snap. After hours of poring over books, some of which I'd already looked at, a grainy black-and-gray picture caught my attention. It showed an underground altar consisting of carved stone figurines, sticks with eagle feathers, bundles of wild turkey feathers, rocks, and assorted items taken from nature. Amid this group were two wooden parrots mounted on sticks. They looked exactly like the ones displayed in DeVries's gallery, except they lacked the Amazon parrot feather necklaces. I suspected the necklaces had been added by DeVries to make them more attractive. If these were the same parrots DeVries was selling for $30,000, how on earth did he get them? The harder question was, how was I going to get my hands on them? The parrots were clearly sacred and were a violation of NAGPRA. I couldn't buy them, as this would bust my budget. I wanted to seize them with a search warrant, but it was too early in the investigation to be serving warrants. My best strategy was to wait and get him to show me other sacred objects he probably had, and later seize everything at once. But I couldn't wait too long. Someone might come along and actually purchase the parrots.

In other books I learned that parrots were birds of the sun that worked with the germinating forces held beneath the earth. These two forces were responsible for the sprouting of seeds that produced food such as corn, squash, and beans. Foodstuffs were a sacred gift that provided subsistence for the people. Whatever sprouted from the earth could do so only by the supreme intervention of the sun. Parrots were believed to soar beneath the sun and help deliver its rays to the fertile earth. I could totally understand why the early peoples would have considered the food that sustained them to be sacrosanct, and it seemed that parrots were paramount in the life-giving play between earth and sky.

I studied the grainy photograph and read that I was looking at a sacred altar that had been constructed with exactness hundreds or even thousands of years ago. Every item and its placement represented something spiritual that was vital to the spiritual leader's persistence in guarding the life-path of his people. The objects had probably been refreshed over time, but their placement was the same. When anthropologists first discovered these underground altars, they became ecstatic. Discovering items never seen before enhanced their academic stature and made them famous. But in the process they looted and destroyed what they had found, and caused a deep spiritual sickness within an enduring culture. Now I had a chance to return these parrots to their sacred home.

The picture also identified the tribe to which the shrine and the parrots belonged, but I kept this very quiet for a very long time.

━━━━

The following morning, after seeing my biologist husband off to the wilds, I went into my home office and saw that there was a message light on my undercover answering machine. I prayed it wasn't Charlotte. She could have gotten my phone number from Paul Axel at the auction. Was she calling to harass or even threaten me? To my relief it was Tony Lorenzo, whose message was to the point.

"Dana, call me. I have some goodies you might be interested in."

The fact that Tony called me was a good sign. If he was running the reservations for merchandise, he needed buyers. I wanted to be one of the last ones he would ever have. I took the tape with Tony's message out of the recorder, tagged it, and placed it inside a gun case that filled half of the closet. I placed a fresh tape in the recorder and gave the normal preamble: "This call is being made to Tony Lorenzo at (505) 347-2953. Time: 8:04 a.m."

As I listened to phone dialing, I wrote "Dana" on a yellow pad, so I wouldn't slip up and use my real name. I always did this. Then I scribbled a few notes reminding me of the points I wanted to cover.

After several rings I heard, "Hey, Tony here."

I had to clear my throat before getting the first word out. This was a sure sign of nerves, and I hated it. "Hi, Tony, this is Dana."

For the next few moments there was silence, and I thought I'd been cut off—or maybe he was plugging in *his* recorder. Then Tony spoke. "Oh, it's you. How are ya?"

"I'm great, Tony, never been better."

"Good," said Tony. "Listen, the next time you're in Santa Fe, I'd like to show you my collection at my house. You might find something you can't live without."

"I'm sure I could," I said, chuckling.

"Yeah, my collection is unbelievable. In fact, I don't show it to most of my customers."

"I'm glad you're being careful, but I'd love to see some of your stuff. I'm looking at my calendar now. How are you set for the day after tomorrow?"

"I won't be here. I'm going out to the Navajo to see my girlfriend. But you can come tomorrow morning if you want."

I scribbled "tomorrow morning" on the yellow pad. "That would work. What time?"

"Is ten in the morning too early?"

"It's just right. The traffic will be better by the time I leave Albuquerque at nine."

"I hear the traffic is a real pain because of all the orange barrels."

"Yes," I said lightly, "it's the season, you know. Can I photograph some items that my clients might be interested in?"

"No, I'm nervous about pictures. They could get around . . . if you know what I mean."

"Sure, I understand. See you tomorrow."

As I hung up the phone, I realized I shouldn't have said anything about taking pictures. It obviously made Tony edgy. But I'd still be filming him, so nothing would be lost. He was clearly still making his mind up about me, but my perceived money and hungry clients were keeping him interested. Eventually I would want to know where Tony was getting his material, and who he sold to. I sat back in my chair and rehearsed some verbal scenarios in my mind. I wanted to be prepared for what I'd say when I crossed the threshold into Tony Lorenzo's Indian Country.

CHAPTER SIXTEEN

Just before turning onto Piedra Lane in Santa Fe, I plugged my Z-Box into the battery pack and felt the recorder for the slight vibration that indicated the tape was running. Satisfied, I felt the middle of my bra for the lump of my derringer that I kept close for extreme emergencies. I reminded myself that the weapon was best fired within close range and preferably if the target didn't know it was coming. Fortunately, I'd never had to use it. I pulled the Camaro just past Tony's driveway and then backed into it. This was in case I had to make an unexpected but quick getaway, which I was fairly confident wouldn't happen.

Tony was standing behind his screen door. "Hi, Dana, come on in."

Right away I noticed that he was dressed in his Santa Fe best: a Hawaiian shirt, Levis, athletic shoes, a leather belt with a not-too-cheap turquoise and silver buckle. A four-inch knife in an old beaded leather case hung comfortably on his hip. Knives bothered me more than guns. A close encounter with a blade could inflict severe bodily damage in less time than it took to slice up an onion. I knew he didn't have it to skin a deer.

"Have a seat," said Tony, pointing to a double bed covered with modern Navajo blankets. I was loath to sit on Tony's bed and asked if I could sit on a vinyl-covered kitchen chair similar to one my mother had in the 1960s.

"Sure. Can I get you something to drink?"

"Water would be fine," I said as I quickly scanned the living room.

Tony came back from his kitchenette with a glass of lukewarm water, which I decided was the best this bachelor could do.

"So, Dana, didn't you tell me once that you'd actually been to Germany?"

"Yes, I've been there several times to recruit clients. Last year I went to the Karl May Festival in Dresden. It's all about North American Indians. I have pictures if you want to see them."

Tony took the album and flipped through the pictures until he stopped at one of me and Schmidt together.

"Oh, that's Mr. Moog," I said. "He's one of my best buyers. Rich, too."

Tony laughed. "Is his name really Moog?"

"Yep. I laughed the first time I heard it, too."

While we talked, I kept my eyes moving. The efficiency apartment consisted of two rooms: a combination living room and bedroom and a tiny kitchen stuffed in a corner. Tony was certainly living on the cheap. Most of his mismatched furniture carried a light layer of dust. Except for a spot where he had recently removed an object with a round bottom. Right away I suspected that he'd put away something that he didn't want me to see.

Nearly twenty ceremonial rattles hung from his ceiling. Old wooden bookcases were loaded with Indian books. Painted kachina dolls, turquoise-painted leather dance armbands, tin rattles, baskets, and prehistoric-looking cooking pots were scattered everywhere.

Tony trotted out his back door and returned with a *tablita* like the ones I'd seen in historical photographs. The one Tony held was not new, as evidenced by its peeling paint. The lightning designs on it strongly implied power. To come off like an expert, Tony explained what was completely obvious.

"This *tablita* symbolizes the power of lightning," he said. "You can tell by these zigzag sticks on the side. See the arrow points on top? I think it used to be black—the color of the north direction where the storms come from."

"Makes sense to me," I said.

"They're very hard to get."

"So, who gets these for you?"

"One of my best scavengers is Alfonso* from the Isleta Pueblo. He comes up with great pieces. They're okay, because they aren't being used anymore, and he knows where to look for the old ones. Here, look at this warrior hair tie, now this is really special."

Tony handed me an eight-inch arrow stick with feathers of a red-tailed hawk, an eagle, and a parrot attached with wraps of common packaging string. The stick had been painted turquoise and outlined in white.

"These are what the Jemez warriors wore when they went out for battle. They wore them for protection." Tony's chest puffed up as he continued to educate me. "Hair ties are very powerful to the men. A friend of mine got this one from a society house on one of the pueblos."

I glanced at my watch and sweat immediately erupted around my neck. "Can I use your restroom?"

"Sure," said Tony somewhat hesitantly. "I hope it's not too messy."

As expected, Tony's bathroom was a certified cesspool. I didn't dare touch anything for fear of becoming seriously infected. I was only there to change out the tape on the Z-Box, as it was running short. Defense attorneys loved it when the prosecution presented a conversation that was only partially recorded. The lawyers could claim that important information was deliberately left out . . . just like in the Nixon tapes of 1973, which were partially responsible for the fall of a president.

Back in Tony's main living space, he continued to pontificate about his ability to travel the Indian reservations and buy what no one else could. Once again he claimed he was a quarter Apache, when in reality he looked like the quintessential cardboard pizza boy set up in front of a pizza restaurant. Still, he boasted that the Indians loved him and often invited him into their homes during feast days.

"So, do you see anything your German clients might want?" he asked with hopeful eyes.

"I have one client I'll be talking to tonight. He's especially interested in anything that's used in ceremonies. The *tablitas* are good, but this one is a little large to ship. What do you have that's small?"

From a drawer Tony pulled out some old leather pouches that he said were filled with the ashes of trees struck by lightning. Then he showed me something I'd seen at the Spirit Bear Gallery—a Navajo bullroarer. Bingo! I knew both the pouches and the bullroarer came from a *jish*.

"You won't find bullroarers anywhere. In fact, I'm the only one who can get them."

As I fingered the artifact I put up some resistance. "How do I explain what it is and its authenticity?"

"Easy, easy," said Tony. "They come from Navajo medicine bundles. The black pitch on them is from a tree that has been struck by lightning.

That makes them very powerful to the medicine man. He swings them above his head to call in the gods. I'm only showing them to you because they're leaving the country. Right?"

"Absolutely—look, I'm as safe as a baby in bed. I just want to make sure these are real. Okay, so how much?"

"A thousand dollars."

"No way, Tony. I'll give you seven hundred and then charge my client a thousand."

"Come on, Dana, these are very hard to get."

"So are rich clients."

"Okay, deal. But I'll need more the next time you buy from me."

I winked at him and said, "Not to worry, it'll all work out. By the way, is this all you do?"

"Well, professionally I'm a drummer, but I do this for now. I'm building a nest egg for later on in life. You know, for when I want to take it easy."

"Good thinking," I said. "Say, I've got to get going. Here's my check, and I'll let you know how it goes."

"What about the pot I sold you? Did you ever send it over?"

"No. Like I told you, it's too fragile. I have a buyer, and I'll fly it over in a month or so."

—◦—

As I drove back to Albuquerque, I felt very satisfied with the way things were going. Tony had to be the surreptitious rez runner I was looking for, and he was quickly becoming one of my primary targets. Eventually we would become such tight amigos that he'd begin to confide in me about his Indian contacts. I wasn't worried that he'd hit on me. After all, I was fifteen years older than Tony, and I was armed. My plan was to keep him slightly off balance, never giving him the satisfaction of thinking that I was his client exclusively. On occasion he might wonder about my legitimacy, but his greediness would dispel any qualms he might have about me. There was no one like me in his inner circle. While part of him might want him to keep his distance from me, he wouldn't be able to resist what I had to offer—security, confidentiality, and money.

Tony was hardly the sophisticated Indian antique dealer I'd met in other places, but he had sacred artifacts that few people dared to deal in. His collection even smelled different, probably from the sacred corn pollen that permeated everything. Tony reminded me of a drug smuggler, whose clandestine suppliers were willing to risk their very souls to keep in the favor of the ever-moneyed Tony.

While Tony's freelance business seemed to be headed for the jet stream, he had to have known that it wouldn't last forever. He was putting aside money for the future, which meant that he expected he might get caught someday. In fact, the bullroarer he sold me was already enough for me to get a search warrant, though I wanted to work him just a little longer. I wondered what would happen to Tony in the long run. According to what I'd read about Monster Slayer, drifting to the dark side in Indian matters often resulted in lives becoming infested with unrelenting evil. Tony's life was going to be an interesting one to watch.

CHAPTER SEVENTEEN

October 1998. It was the time of year when the tourists were gone, and folks kept a sharp eye out for celebrities strolling along the streets of Santa Fe. An hour before my undercover contact with Dirk DeVries, I decided to kill some time by browsing through several shops along the square and past the row of Native American marketers on the north side of the Plaza. As I passed by a gelato shop, I overheard someone talking about Shirley MacLaine, who had apparently passed by wearing large sunglasses and her trademark hat with a huge brim to protect her from the sun and people.

Finally I reached the Double Rainbow, a trinket shop located just off the Plaza on the north side and across the street from the Spirit Bear Gallery. The Double Rainbow satisfied the need for unique souvenirs that consisted of an eclectic array of new artistic kachina dolls, inexpensive Navajo rugs, and Navajo folk art. The folk art was a relatively recent art form consisting of hand-carved sheep, cattle, and chickens.

The Double Rainbow also carried an extensive inventory of two-to-three-inch skeletons that were used during El Dia de los Muertos, also known as the Day of the Dead. This is a Mexican tradition where on November first (All Saints Day) families honor those who passed before them. The tradition calls for decorating the home with miniature dressed-up skeletons that strum guitars, play the piano, or cook in a mini-kitchen. These creepy little boned people gave me the shivers. That was saying a lot for someone who had been shot at. There were hundreds of them, making simple browsing a ghoulish experience and not the right thing to do just before crossing the street to where I was about to make a recorded undercover contact.

—◆—

Still shaking off the bones, I nearly stepped into the path of a BMW driving down Palace Avenue. Waving apologetically, I trotted to the other side of the street and walked to the ladderlike stairs that led to the Spirit Bear Gallery. Reaching inside my bag, I turned on the Z-Box and headed up. By the time I got to the top, my quadriceps burned like they had been barbecued. Once inside the gallery, it took only half a second for a man to appear from behind the Indian blanket curtain.

"Hi, you must be Dana," said the man. "I'm Dirk DeVries. Mona just reminded me that we have an appointment this afternoon. Please come on back."

One look at the man said *Dutch*. I already knew he was a US citizen, but I couldn't tell from his driver's license picture that he had a distinctly European look about him. His hair was thin and pale yellow, combed forward over the top of his head. He wore frameless glasses that almost blended into his face, but his diamond-studded Rolex was very prominent. His attire was chic, with beige linen pants and an expensive off-white shirt with the sleeves rolled up.

Dirk led me behind the Mexican rug to a room full of stacked boxes, interesting art displays, and an antique wooden desk. I expected Dirk to have an alluring and exotic accent, but he didn't. His tongue was solid Californian, which is where his background check said he was from.

"This is a little workroom I use for shipping out orders and for some storage," he said almost apologetically.

Slowly I moved my bag around, hoping to capture part of the scene: a postage meter and scale on a large table along with packing supplies like bubble wrap and brokendown boxes. A metal file cabinet probably held his business records. The records were something I'd remember to seize whenever I was ready to apply for a search warrant.

While Dirk was digging through a drawer for a business card, I noticed a book titled *Navajo Medicine Bundles or Jish*, a thick volume with a red cover, written by Charlotte J. Frisbie. This was the same book I'd been studying at the University of New Mexico to learn about the hundreds of objects contained in a *jish*. Dirk DeVries probably used this book to identify the sacred items he was selling as Indian "art." The book was also proof that he had knowledge he was selling sacred material that was against the law. This would be very important when we got to court—if we ever got there.

Eying the rest of the area, I noticed displays of hundred-year-old animal fetishes that appeared to be authentic and pieces of thousand-year-old pottery, no doubt dug from Indian sites. I spotted a hand-woven basket filled with prayer sticks and eagle feathers, probably taken from an outdoor Indian shrine. Where was he getting this stuff? I also noticed a white box set on a shelf with a handwritten note on it that read "To be repatriated to the Navajos." Later I'd put this in my case report. He probably had *jish* items in this very box, and I was already salivating to get a search warrant.

The top of his desk was littered with a few files and an artistic array of several flat kachina dolls, a type not seen on the legal market because they were used in Indian homes for religious purposes. I looked for pictures of family and saw none. His background check indicated he was married with a daughter and a son of high school age. A family man would have pictures of them. I glanced at my watch to keep track of the time. I had forty-five minutes left.

"Well," said Dirk, settling into his chair. "Mona tells me that you have some clients who are looking for rare Indian material."

Thanks to Mona's prep job, getting into my business model was easy. I explained that I had German clients ravenous for authentic Native American artifacts.

"It's amazing what they're interested in. I sent over a pueblo drum just last week."

Dirk was now paying attention. "Really? A big one?"

"Big as a coffee table—it cost a fortune to send it," I said, laughing. "You should have seen the box I sent it in!"

"That's funny! So, do you go to Germany often?"

"I don't really have to. I make most of my deals online," I said. "But I try and go once a year."

I reached into my bag, pulled out my mini-album, and handed it to Dirk. "These pictures were taken at the Karl May Festival in Dresden. I was there meeting and soliciting clients. There are pictures of me with some of my clients toward the back."

He thumbed through a few of the photographs and returned the album. "Very interesting."

"As you may know, Germans have a special fascination with North American Indians—their regalia and ceremonial items. I look everywhere I can for hard-to-get material."

Dirk rubbed his chin. "To tell you the truth, I've never seriously considered the foreign market. Although I have a pretty good client base in the US, I can always use more clients."

"I think there's a lot of potential with foreign buyers. The collectors I've encountered are well educated and know how to spot fakes, so I'm very concerned about authenticity and provenance."

"I can sure understand that."

Dirk seemed to be relaxing a bit. Quite unexpectedly he launched into a well-rehearsed discourse about Southwest Indian culture and how it has managed to remain intact, unlike other North American Indian tribes. This made the authentication of sensitive material easier, he said, because much of it was still being used today. He said that when artifacts come off Indian lands, they come with a rich history behind them, which only adds to their value.

"Domain, provenance, and appraisals are my specialty," he added with a winning grin.

There was something dead wrong about his bravado. I already knew that DeVries had been denied membership in the highly reputable Antique Tribal Art Dealers Association. ATADA is very strict, admitting only dealers who are known for their integrity and for the authenticity of their trade goods. Every prospective member is carefully vetted by a board of experienced collectors. DeVries didn't make the cut. He was an outcast among his own colleagues because they didn't like the kind of business he ran. Also, I'd never heard a dealer use the term "sensitive material," which is code language for anything illegal.

"You must have an excellent reservation resource," I said.

Dirk hesitated but said, "I have several sources, which I keep confidential, of course. I use old photographs and descriptions from early anthropologists to establish what is genuine. I've been hanging out with the Indians around here since the 1960s and have been in business for decades."

He handed me a copy of a glossy magazine called *American Indian Art*. I thumbed through it until I came to Dirk's full-page ad on black slick paper with the name Spirit Bear Gallery artistically scribed across the page. His name and address appeared at the bottom. The subliminal message was that if you didn't buy from Dirk DeVries, you weren't serious about buying truly authentic Indian art.

"Yes, I've seen this," I said, not lying for once. "I especially liked your article on ledger drawings."

"I get ledgers occasionally," he said. "I'm one of the few who can appraise them."

"What do you have now that I could interest a client in?"

Dirk leaned back in chair and put his hands behind his head. He was in his comfortable salesman mode now.

"When it comes to owning Indian material, an old Navajo weaving is one of the most valuable assets you can have. As you can see from the walls in my gallery, I have some of everything: rugs, serapes, shawls, blankets."

Dirk pointed to a dark blue weaving with alternating zigzag and straight lines done in reddish tones. "This is a Navajo Moki serape with three terraced geometric designs. It was woven in the 1870s after the Navajo incarceration at Bosque Redondo. The Navajos were looking at hard economic times, which led them to produce fine woven pieces for the marketplace."

All this rug talk was burning up tape, so I cut him off and said, "I'm so glad to finally meet you. Most people don't appreciate Indian material for the history that comes with it. I find you very refreshing."

Pleased with the compliment, he was only encouraged to talk more about blankets. He said that he'd just sold a First Phase Chief's blanket with Bayeta stripes for $90,000. I couldn't believe the prices. A dealer I met at a show complained that Dirk DeVries was *the* man responsible for inflating the cost of Navajo blankets. DeVries had even written and self-published historical anthologies about Navajo rugs, creating an image of himself as a highly regarded authenticator and appraiser of Navajo rugs. He had a motive, of course—run up the price of rugs so he could capitalize. I knew I had to start talking money. The truth was, compared to his real clients I was stone broke. But I had to give him the opposite impression.

I kept up my theme of potentiality. "I have a German client who has a lot of money, but getting him to part with it is difficult. I need to find something that is truly extraordinary."

DeVries led me into his main gallery, raving about his rare inventory of sacred Indian ghost shields, historical moccasins, baskets, and pots. He carried on to the point where I was becoming weary. Every time he launched into a story about which famous Indian possessed what, he moved his hands. I counted three positions: left hand covering lips, left hand rubbing off his chin, right hand pulling on his right earlobe. His made-up history continued to chew up my tape! I had to get him to say something about the parrots, which I already knew were sacred.

Dirk moved around the gallery and showed me a beautiful Navajo rug loaded with symbols and swastikas woven all around the blanket as a border. He explained what I already knew.

"Ancient native cultures, including American Indians and Far Eastern philosophies dating back thousands of years, used the swastika to represent the greatest power in the universe. The Navajos call it a rolling log, but the symbolism is the same—it represents the highest authority over everything. The Nazi party turned it forty-five degrees to make it their own. Hitler, as you know, wanted to be the superior leader of the world, so he used the swastika as his trademark."

"Yes," I said, "I've seen them on petroglyphs. The earliest peoples used the symbol to recognize the highest universal force."

Worried that my tape was going to stop, I turned and walked to where the carved parrots were on display. Dirk had been avoiding them, so I asked, "Are these birds special in some way?"

Dirk came closer to me and acted as if he were letting me in on a big secret. He said that these very parrots had been used in private ceremonies conducted by the women of the Jemez Pueblo. He went on to explain that the birds were put on sticks wrapped with ribbons. The ceremony is done only on a night when the moon is full, so the parrots can be presented properly. Only the Indians know about it.

Ridiculous, I thought. Dirk's fabrication about the parrots ticked me off. While he tried to come off as a person who respected Native Americans, he actually had no regard for them at all. His fine-tuned blab was designed to lure buyers into thinking they were getting something that was unequal to anything on the market. These parrots were not used by the Jemez people in secret ceremonies, and the rightful tribe might send DeVries straight to hell if they found out how he'd desecrated them.

I looked at DeVries and could hardly contain my disgust. His words defiled time-honored doctrines of another culture and sent a message of the deepest contempt. In my mind DeVries was a selfish lowlife—a self-made bullshitter who scammed people who trusted him. His clients paid him exceeding well for something they hoped would fill their souls and perhaps mend a hole in their hearts. Even for non-Indians, native spiritual connections offered something much deeper than Anglo organized religions that tended to the soul once a week.

"Well?" asked DeVries. "What do you think? These are one-of-a-kind artifacts. I only have one pair and don't see getting any more. They're that rare."

I believed this. The birds were used by the Parrot Clan of one particular tribe. They were rarer than rare. As much as I wanted to seize them on the spot, I couldn't, as I'd have to blow my cover. "They're very interesting," I said, still gazing at the carvings. "But I'll have to get back to you. Sorry I have to run, but I'm already late for another meeting. Nice meeting you; please keep my card. I'll be in touch."

As I scrambled down the wooden staircase, I gave the stairs an extra punch to cover the clicking sound of the Z-Box as it shut off. I didn't really have an appointment, of course, but I had a lot to think about. So much was going through my mind, I barely found the Camaro I'd parked in a public lot.

I cranked the engine and paid my way out of the parking lot. Soon I was weaving through Santa Fe to the I-25 south to Albuquerque. I began thinking like a criminal profiler. What made DeVries feel so driven to possess, profit from, and literally destroy objects that helped to define ancient societies? Clearly he felt satiated every time he acquired something no one else could and bragged about it endlessly. To me this was a sign of an underinflated ego. There was nothing I could do about that, but as with most criminals, DeVries's need for ego gratification would increase over time. He would always want the rarest, most spiritual, and most precious objects to keep him satisfied. These sacrosanct items helped to define morality, the sense of community, and the understanding of life itself within Indian societies. It was enough that he scammed buyers—he robbed ancient cultures that had endured since their arrival in North America some ten thousand years ago. DeVries would not stop until I stopped him. DeVries was now my number one target.

CHAPTER EIGHTEEN

I hadn't submitted an update to the FBI, the Park Service, or even my own agency, so there was no reason for them to complain. Also, I'd been burned by leaks so many times, I considered almost anyone capable of blowing my cover. The less they knew, the better. I cut them in when the time was right. In this situation only I knew what I had for evidence and what I needed to build a solid case against my suspects.

I resented the FBI time limit I was working under. I kept wondering why Weisenhunt had imposed a deadline. It made no sense. Regardless, I kept running and planned my investigation carefully. I didn't have much time left.

Everywhere I'd gone, my main story had stayed the same, but sometimes details would change according to the circumstances. I worried that eventually I'd get caught up in my incongruous lies. While I had developed several secondary suspects in the Santa Fe area selling sacred material, I didn't have the time to work them thoroughly. Tony Lorenzo and Dirk DeVries had floated to the top, so they were my focus. Tony Lorenzo was clearly a rez runner, and I cringed to think about the number of masks and other ceremonial accoutrements he'd ripped from the Indians. Tony made Richard Crow look like a novice who got lucky. While Crow was caught within a few weeks, I suspected Tony had avoided the trap for years. Meanwhile DeVries had cleverly positioned himself at the top of the antique Indian art dealer echelon—at least according to a few wealthy clients. He created the illusion of having exclusive access to the best and rarest of what the Indians used in their hallowed lives.

While neither DeVries nor Lorenzo had the intrinsic knowledge of Indian ways honest dealers usually had, they filled in the blanks with their own bizarre stories. Buyers and collectors seemed to believe every word. Unfortunately, these fabrications would float through time until they became forever inseparable from fact. For thousands of years the Indians of the Southwest had made maintaining their traditions and beliefs paramount. Now they were being ripped apart by greedy white people who saw an opportunity for easy money—which resulted in nothing short of cultural genocide.

Added to this damage was the slaughter of birds for their feathers. In the underground market of artifacts, eagle feathers on old objects were often replaced with feathers from freshly killed birds. Mountain bluebirds, red-shafted flickers, ravens, crows, red-tailed hawks, and wild turkeys were high among the favorite birds, but many songbirds were trapped for use on ceremonial objects. The Navajos, Hopis, and Pueblo Indians of New Mexico believed deeply in kachinas, whose powers were enhanced by migratory bird feathers. They appeared on every kachina doll.

Ideally, two undercover agents would be working Tony and Dirk separately. The two criminals were working at different levels of the trade and consequently would attract different types of buyers. Tony was the scrounger, selling low, and Dirk was the big-money guy. It didn't make sense for Dana Delaney to be buying from both of them. At this point they didn't know what I was up to, but when they caught on, their minds would start spinning with suspicion.

I decided to wrap up Tony by buying the Jemez hair ties that he claimed provided spiritual strength to warriors as they prepared for battle. The rest of his contraband I'd get with a search warrant. But search warrants had to be obtained and served within ten days of when the illegal items were seen by a law enforcement officer. This meant I'd have to get back into his house and do some more filming with the hope of coming up with several items that Tony possessed in violation of federal law.

Then I'd write an affidavit for a search warrant to be served on the Spirit Bear Gallery for the sacred parrots and other sacred items on display. The two warrants had to be served almost simultaneously. I'd have to pull in teams of agents and brief them on a unique trade they'd never heard of. This was a lot to do in ten days, and it wasn't even the deep cleaning job I wanted to do. I wanted sales records, hidden contraband, and lists of contacts. I wanted to bury these guys in evidence that would convict them in a heartbeat. But I also had to be realistic. With the little probable cause I had, I'd only be able to seize what I'd seen. Regardless, I thought I could do enough damage to stop them for a very long time and hopefully at the same time make others reconsider drifting into this type of crime. Because of the arrow sticks and bull roarers both crooks possessed, I was sure Tony was Dirk's supplier. Knocking both of them out at the same time would do a lot of good.

The next morning I made a cup of strong coffee and went to my office, which was just another room in my own home. I hooked up a recorder to the undercover phone and wrote Tony's cell number on a pad along with my fictitious name Dana.

On the first ring Tony picked up. "Tony here."

"Hi, Tony, this is Dana. I'm going to be in Santa Fe tomorrow around noon. Do you mind if I drop by?"

"No, sure, that would be fine. I was meaning to call you anyway."

"That must mean you have something I won't be able to resist," I said, inserting sunshine in my voice.

For the next few seconds there was silence, then he came back with, "I don't usually disappoint my people, so yeah, come take a look."

"Thanks, Tony. See you tomorrow . . . say, noonish."

This was great. Maybe Tony would show me more illegal material in the boxes he had stacked everywhere. This would surely give me legal justification to widen the search and pile up more evidence against him. I couldn't wait.

CHAPTER NINETEEN

Just before noon the next day, I took the turn onto Piedra Lane in Santa Fe and backed into the driveway, as a matter of habit. Tony was standing behind his screen door with his hands stuffed into the front pockets of his jeans.

I got out of the low-slung Camaro and waved.

"Come on in," said Tony as he held the door open.

Passing the bed, I settled into a plain wooden chair that had been painted black, yellow, red, and white. I recognized these as the four cardinal colors in the Native American circle of life. The Z-Box was running in the bag on my lap, and I hoped that the camera was capturing Tony in living color.

"So," I said with a relaxed sigh. "How the heck have you been?"

"Did you tell me that you'd actually been to Germany?"

I didn't like the fact that he had started out by questioning me about something he already knew, but I went along.

"Yes, I've been there several times to recruit clients. I told you that. In fact, last year I went to the Karl May Festival in Dresden. I have the pictures with me if you want to see them again."

"Not really," he replied. He was now sitting in a straight-back chair with his arms folded tightly across his chest. His eyes remained in a dead stare.

"What I'd really like to know is why you're poking around me. I never knew about you before, and suddenly you pop up like you've been big into Indian stuff forever."

I focused on sounding matter-of-fact. "Over the past few years I've been selling things from a very large collection—one piece at a time. This kept me in Albuquerque nearly full time. Now that the collection is gone, I have to hunt for more treasures to sell. That's why you're just seeing me," I explained.

I noticed that Tony's hands were still stuffed under his armpits. This was a defensive sign that was not good. I scanned his body for bulges in his clothing suggesting that he was packing. To my relief nothing stood out.

Tony's voice turned even colder. "To be honest, you don't act like a real Indian art dealer, and I'm just not sure about you. I've worked too hard and too long to do business with someone I can't trust."

I could feel sweat erupting under my shirt and was afraid it would show through. *Shit!*

"What on earth are you saying, Tony? There's no reason you can't trust me. Like I've told you, everything I get, I send straight out of the country. There's no documentation, no trail, no nothing." I was actually surprised at how convincing I sounded.

"You're good, Dana," said Tony, who was actually grinning, "but I still don't believe you."

I leaned over and rested my arms on my knees to keep them from bouncing. I was in trouble, but there was no way I was going to tell Tony who I was, even if I ended up dying as Dana Delaney.

He opened a drawer in his kitchen and pulled out a small leather mask. It was child-sized and was devoid of painted designs, beadwork, and feathers. He held it up and said, "If you want to do business with me, buy this. It's one of a kind for only twelve hundred dollars."

I came back strong. "I don't know where you're going with this, Tony, but that's a fake. Come on, stop this crap."

"Crap? So what do you think of this crap?" Tony's words coincided with his putting his hand on the handle of the four-inch hunting knife slung on his belt. I was acutely aware that if Tony went ballistic I was within seconds of being cut. A close encounter with a blade terrified me more than anything. Suddenly the kachina dolls and fetishes stacked around the room seemed to snarl at me. Somehow I had to calm Tony down or his aggression would only rise.

"Tony," I said calmly. "Just talk to me. What is wrong with you?"

My mind shifted to the SIG Sauer semiautomatic in my bag, but the level of threat hadn't reached the point where I'd be legally justified in using it. Once I revealed the gun, Tony would snap into survival mode and the game would change drastically.

Tony threw the leather mask down and started screaming. "Who are you, Dana? No one in the business has ever heard of you. I don't want anybody fucking with my life, no matter how many rich clients you claim you have."

Quickly I pulled out the card of another undercover agent in Arizona, who had agreed to vouch for me if I ever needed a backup. "Call this guy. He has a shop in Carefree and I deal with him a lot."

Tony took the card and put it on a table. His face held the pain of someone who had been gut-shot with a .22 rifle. It was the look of deep betrayal by someone he had begun to trust—me. His breathing was sharpening, and I wanted to bring it down.

"Tony," I pleaded. "Please calm down. What in the world is bothering you?"

Tony plopped back down in the wooden chair. "I don't know," he said, wiping his eyes. "I think it's time for me to get out of the business. You know, go do something else. I've still got my band."

I felt some relief. Tony's tears were a sign that he was physically releasing stress. This was not the time to disagree with him about anything.

"That's fine, Tony, if that's what you want to do. Maybe you handled something hot and it's getting to you. I'm talking about some kind of Indian curse, you know."

I hoped that blaming his stress on an Indian sickness would get his mind off me.

Staring straight ahead, he said, "One of my main suppliers just died, and I don't know if I can go on alone."

I didn't believe this, but I went along. "That's it. You're under a lot of pressure, that's understandable. Was it Alfonso? You told me he was diabetic."

"Yeah, he went into a coma and just never came out."

Tony was sniffling and blowing his nose. I had no idea if Alfonso had died, but that wasn't the point. Tony was super suspicious of me—I couldn't forget that. But it was clear he liked a part of me. Contrary to every instinct in my body, I approached Tony and put my hand on his shoulder as if to comfort him like a mother.

"Look, I'm leaving now. You need time to grieve for your friend. This is not a good time right now, so take however long it takes and call me when you're ready. And call my buddy. You'll feel better."

Finally Tony said, "Okay, Dana, thanks."

The air hung with things we both knew that, if spoken, could make an already precarious situation burst. I was sure Tony was confused. While I feigned a calm demeanor, I wondered if he was worried that I had a covey of backup agents ready to burst in to arrest him. With the immediate threat toned down, Tony's wild, fiery eyes softened. I prayed that Tony had the sense to know that hurting me or especially killing me would get him nowhere—except for years in prison. But that held little comfort, since I had no sure idea what was going through his mind. As I turned to leave, I prepared myself for the sting of his knife as it flipped through the air and into my back. Thinking the worst was not helping me, or maybe I'd seen this in too many movies. I had to get out before my fears took over. I opened the door and closed it quietly behind me. It was so hard not to look back. Once in the car, I cranked the engine, begging for it to start more quickly than ever before. Thankful that I'd parked it nose out, I punched the gas pedal for a fast getaway. Gripping the steering wheel, I took a deep breath. God, I was lucky. Tony had probably found out who I really was, yet he had let me go easily. I knew things could have been much worse, but that didn't change the fact that I'd be burned—seriously.

On my drive back to Albuquerque my mind was on autopilot, unaware of the traffic as it sped around me. My normally sharp mind had failed me, and I fell into a trap I never saw coming. Still reacting to the fear I'd experienced, the blood in my body was concentrated around my core to protect my organs. This was a primordial way of keeping me from bleeding out if I'd caught a serious injury in my limbs. I turned up the car's heater to force blood to the surface of my skin and calm the uncontrollable shivering.

I'd been on the road for forty-five minutes when Rich, my vouch in Arizona, called.

"Hey, some guy named Tony thinks you're a cop. I tried really hard to convince him that you're good. But he never sounded like he believed me.

I'm worried that whoever busted you is a very credible source—one that I couldn't overcome. Sorry, but I tried."

"That's okay, Rich, I appreciate what you did. I'm blown with this guy and another target associated with him."

"So what are you going to do?"

"I don't know yet. I just don't know."

"Look," said Rich, "if there's anything I can do, let me know."

"Thanks," I said as we hung up.

Even though my brain was barely functioning, one question consumed me. What went wrong? My look was good, my backstory was the best I'd ever developed, and I'd taken extra precautions to keep my investigation under wraps. But I wasn't stupid; my cover had been blown and I didn't dare walk the streets of Santa Fe again. How could this have happened?

Once in Albuquerque I drove to the bunker, backed out the Ramcharger, and put the Camaro in its place. With my constant vigilance, I was as sure as I could be that no one had followed me. Inside the bunker, I unlocked the evidence room door. I found the Acoma pot I'd bought from Tony and took the tissue paper off it. Ever so lightly I ran my fingers across the ancient images of parrots, rainbows, stepped forms, and dragonflies. These were the images that spoke of life-giving water, the earth and sky, and the inextricable interrelationship of all living things. I now felt certain the Indians would view this pot as a sacrosanct object. It was used to carry the greatest gift of life—water.

My new realization nearly kicked my feet out from under me. Why had I been so blind? The pot in my hand was covered with sacred symbols. I wondered if it was used as a centerpiece in family rituals and personal rites, as it had every blessed essential of life eloquently etched in it. I wondered who Tony had recruited to steal the pot. I couldn't imagine a tribal member parting with it willingly, especially to a white man. It was solid proof of Tony's profiteering from the Acoma Indians' deep reverence to all that was sacred to them. I rewrapped the precious vessel and set it back on the wooden shelf, its evidence tag declaring that it was government property. Someday I'd give the pot back to the Acoma, but due to unseen forces I had no control over, I'd never bring Tony fully to justice. He would continue to plunder the ancients and supply glutton-ous dealers like DeVries. These two men, out of their purported love for Native Americans, would conspire to eradicate a spiritual lineage that had buoyed the massive migration of the human race into North America. I had come close to stopping them, but now there was nothing I could do.

—◆—

I climbed into the Ramcharger. Lonnie was gone on a business trip, so I arrived to an empty house, which was good—I deserved solitary confine-ment. I poured myself a glass of wine and took the glass and bottle with me to the TV room. The first glass would act as a mild sedative, while I hoped that subsequent glasses would simply drown me. I'd lost my rudder and the fight was out of me. All I wanted was to feel my heart beat and breathe at a rate that would barely sustain me.

The feeling of a deep curse consumed me. How did Tony find about me? I began to speculate about Charlotte again. But she wasn't con-nected with the Santa Fe folks at all and had no credibility among serious dealers. I hadn't told the FBI or the Park Service about Tony or Dirk. Only two US Fish and Wildlife supervisors in Washington read my case reports. Regardless, this was the end of the road for me, and it made me sick. Finally, after too much wine and anguish, I ran to my bathroom and threw up.

CHAPTER TWENTY

The following morning I was still sprawled on my couch. Sleep had been fitful, but I never moved to my bed, as I didn't think I deserved the comfort. Somehow I'd screwed up, and I deserved to suffer mightily. But I was hungry and chomped down a bowl of crunchy cereal. The empty bowl went into the sink, and I moved to my office, where I set up a monitor on which I could review the tapes I'd cut with Tony, Dirk, Charlotte, and a couple of others. For hours I re-watched my taped contacts with these outlaws, paying particular attention as I worked Tony and Dirk like a shark on the hunt. Where had I slipped up? While I didn't cut myself any slack, I simply didn't detect any serious flaws. Sure, there were a few things I wished I'd said differently, but overall I looked, acted, and sounded like a woman who was as willing to break the law as they were.

I thought a lot about Charlotte Small. Although it was never spoken, we both knew she had pegged me as an agent. It didn't make sense for her to rat me out to other dealers, because it would be to her advantage as a legal dealer to have me bust the illegal dealers. Competing against dealers who broke the law only made it harder on her. Also, she'd already been in trouble with the government. I'm sure she wouldn't want to face an obstruction of justice charge by spreading the word on me. While she remained a possibility, I wasn't convinced.

Stripped of every morsel of self-esteem, I didn't shower or get dressed for two days. Microwaved burritos and more wine kept me alive as I sulked around the house on the brink of depression. I had had this feeling once before. It was in Alaska when a flying poacher dropped me off in the middle of the tundra without a word or reason. Alone in grizzly bear country, I wailed as I realized that there was too much working against me. My grandiose ideas of busting lawless big-game killers now seemed so trivial. Thoughts of not seeing my husband and child again had set in my mind like black dye. At least in Alaska I knew who my enemies were, but in New Mexico I didn't. Someone for sure knew I was a federal agent and was out to get me. This viper had to be found and dealt with. I cried out to Monster Slayer to help me.

——

Lonnie came home on Friday night, and as hard as I tried to buck up, he knew something was festering. "There's something's wrong, so why don't you just tell me?"

"Nothing," I mumbled. "I'm just preoccupied with a case I'm working. I think I've lost it. Someone knows who I am. I can't go on."

My husband had long before lost his patience with my obsession to catch crooks, and he let me know it.

"You get too involved in these cases of yours," he said. "Look at you. You look terrible. You act like cases are real-life cop shows. They aren't. No one really cares if you miss a couple of bad guys. But your family cares about you and needs you." He placed his hands squarely on my shoulders and looked me straight in the eye. "Come back to us. Your daughter and I need you."

Lonnie's words struck a lot of nerves, and while I had a hard time accepting what he was telling me, I knew he was right. The cupboards were nearly bare and the cobwebs were taking over the corners in my house. Dust was so deep on my coffee table you could write in it. I had been so busy keeping up with Dana and her quest, everything else had become secondary. I was clearly out of balance.

I'd invested everything in being Dana Delaney—a Joan of Arc figure who was determined to save the spiritual lives of the Indians. She was strong and fierce and even envisioned Monster Slayer at her side. But this wasn't reality. I had to face it. Dana was dead and I was mourning her loss. I could feel her soul withering within me. Who was I without her? Where would my drive and ambition come from? Dana thrived on adventure and the unknown. No one could ever understand how important she was to me.

Lonnie and I spent hours that weekend talking about our relationship and patching things up. We loved each other and had raised a secure and happy child who was now in college. Although I was still struggling with the idea of just being me, I knew I had to do something to regain balance within my life. I wasn't sure where to begin.

CHAPTER TWENTY-ONE

It was midnight when summer torrential rains and flash floods came together in the Albuquerque area. I was jerked awake by thunder and terrorizing pain in my gut. I shook my husband awake and begged him to get me to the hospital. Soon thereafter I was rolled into the emergency room at Lovelace Hospital. I gripped the rails of a gurney to steel myself against the agony I was in. Hot lights of an interrogation room bore down upon me, making my head pound.

In a hallway the attendant slammed the gurney over a door sill. "Augh!" I screamed. "You're killing me!"

"Sorry."

Suddenly the faces of strangers and unfamiliar voices hovered over me like a fog of gloom. My gut writhed in anger, and every touch to my abdomen felt like a newly devised torture technique. Tears poured from my eyes as I screamed for relief. A doctor named Martin gave me morphine, but not enough. Among other things, he ordered a CAT scan of my abdomen.

While still on the gurney, I thought about the close calls I'd experienced during my career. I'd walked away from several minor car wrecks, missed being shot just after sunset by a hunter who thought I was a wood duck, and come close to drowning after I fell out of a running johnboat. I'd been lucky, for sure, but this pain was the worst I'd ever felt.

A couple of hours later Dr. Martin showed me the contrast x-ray image of my lower colon, which was pockmarked with what that looked like #4 buckshot. Infected pockets had made a minefield out of the walls of my intestines, which normally should have been smooth. Dr. Martin said I had just suffered an attack of acute diverticulitis. As he explained it, I was hovering between the shadow of death and a stubbed toe. If one of the pustules in my gut erupted, my entire bloodstream would become infected, which could be fatal. But if administered quickly, antibiotics would save me.

Dr. Martin prescribed antibiotic pills the size of a .45 caliber bullet and narcotics to control the pain. He told me that I'd always have these small pouches in my colon called diverticuli and would probably suffer occasional flare-ups requiring narcotics. If I couldn't keep the condition under control, I'd have to have major surgery. I wasn't scared of surgery, but I was worried I wouldn't be able to pass my annual government-mandated physical examination. If I didn't pass my physical exam, I could be forced to take a medical retirement, which would result in a lot less money in my pension check. In just a few years, in January of 2004, I'd be eligible to retire with a full pension. I had to make it.

The doctor cautioned me that my diverticulosis had probably been exacerbated by stress and lack of fiber in my diet. I told him I was already eating cardboard cereal for breakfast but confessed that I'd never learned to manage stress—I just ate it morning, noon, and night. Working undercover always brought on extra stressors, but now I was in serious trouble over it. I didn't tell anyone what I was going through. I would add painkillers to my diet and would push through. I had to keep my new disorder a secret. I didn't want the bureaucracy to claim that I wasn't fit for duty. Lying in the emergency room all day gave me time to think. I still had time in my career to salvage my case and find the dirtbag who was trying to destroy it. Even to me, I sounded totally irrational.

CHAPTER TWENTY-TWO

By Monday my pain was gone. I felt shaken but otherwise normal when Matt Miller, my supervisor in Washington, called me. "Hey, girl, what have you been up to? I haven't heard from you in a while. You're okay, aren't you?"

"Things aren't going well," I mumbled.

For the next fifteen minutes I explained the progress I'd made with DeVries and Lorenzo. Then I confessed that Tony Lorenzo had suddenly become very suspicious of me.

"My cover has been compromised," I explained. "The worst part is that antique Indian art dealers are well connected. Tony has probably already spread the word about me."

Miller cut me off. "So you're done?"

"For sure," I said through clenched teeth.

Miller had every reason to be upset. "First of all, why in the hell didn't you report this right away? This happened over a week ago, and I'm just now finding out about it?"

"It's only been four days," I corrected. "I've been too sick to talk about it."

"That's bullshit! So what am I supposed to tell the chief? Our darling Dana fucked up and didn't have the nerve to report it. This is bad—very bad."

"I'm sorry, Matt, I just needed time to try and figure out what happened. I've looked at all the tapes to see what went wrong, and I can't figure it out. All my contacts went very well. I have enough information to get search warrants on two suspects, and I don't want to give them up. I just have to figure out how to keep the heat on these two guys."

"How are you going to do that? You can't possibly go back under-cover. Someone got to you. Who do you think it was?"

"I don't know yet. I'll find out, and when I do, I'll—"

Matt cut me off. "Didn't you tell me a woman from Albuquerque was at the auction in Wisconsin and pegged you right off?"

"Don't you think that I already thought of that? She never truly con-fronted me. But just to make sure, I convinced her that she was sadly mistaken about who she thought I was. She didn't say a word about me to anyone—otherwise I would have heard about it. It was to her advantage to stay quiet about me since my goal was to knock out the illegal competition. Besides, Charlotte Small doesn't deal with Santa Fe folks. They're completely out of her pedestrian league."

"I still think Charlotte could be the rat. I told you from the get-go that you were working too close to home. After all, you were a straight-out agent for years before you got into this. Have you informed the FBI and the Park Service about this?"

"No."

"Well, I strongly suggest you get that done. Tell them the whole sorry story, and then get back to me so we can close Operation Monster Slayer out. I never liked the name of it anyway. I'll be thinking of another assignment for you, but it won't be west of the Mississippi, I promise you that."

I hung up the phone feeling like I'd been slammed with a wrecking ball. I didn't expect sympathy or support, but Matt really pissed me off. He was someone who had never done one minute of undercover work. He didn't understand that big problems were common when trying to infiltrate a criminal enterprise. At least I didn't get hurt or killed, which in my book is a real accomplishment in itself. If undercover work was so easy, why wasn't he doing it? And why didn't he give me a partner or a pittance of help?

Leaning back in my chair, I thought about Monster Slayer who specialized in eradicating evil. Just as evil came in many disguises, there were many devices available to get rid of it. Monster Slayer was revered for his perseverance and his insistence that giving up was never an option. From out of nowhere, words I'd spoken at an undercover school popped up in my head. I'd always taught special agent trainees that if an undercover team gets burned, you should always insert another team, and do it quickly. Another team meant a different look, a changed backstory with a flawless approach.

As my fingers dove into my Rolodex, I thought that in times of trouble even Monster Slayer would recruit allies. Over the years, I had collected business cards and contact information like trinkets that someday might become useful. Another thing I'd taught my students was to be on the constant lookout for potential informants. While not every person would work in every situation, there were plenty of nuggets that could be dug up when the time was right.

Finally my fingers stopped at a long-forgotten nugget. He was a Norwegian police investigator named Peder Sandbakken.* I'd met him in Spain in 1995 while attending an international wildlife crime conference held in Madrid. During one of our breaks, he approached me and gave me his business card that identified him as the director of the National Authority for Investigation and Prosecution of Economic and Environmental Crime—ØKOKRIM. Then he handed me a coffee table book written in Norwegian and titled *Fauna Kriminalitet*. Thumbing through the pages, I could tell it was a thorough analysis of wildlife crime and the global efforts to stop it. One picture revealed endangered peregrine falcons being robbed from a nest in Alaska to be sold to a Saudi Arabian sheik for over $150,000. The book exposed everything from the blatant poaching of bear in Europe to the slaughtered faces of rhinoceros in Africa. Rhinos were killed simply for their horn, which was carved into a large handle to hold a traditional dagger awarded in the Middle East to young men coming of age.

Mr. Sandbakken had pointed to a picture on page 64 and asked, "Is this you?"

I thought he was surely joking, but when I examined the picture, I was stunned to see that it was me, dressed in camouflage sitting behind the illegal Dall's sheep I'd shot in Alaska. The sheep was used as evidence to convict the outfitter. Sandbakken said that the accompanying article related how wildlife agents in the United States sometimes worked undercover to catch wildlife criminals. I quickly explained that a crooked guide told me to shoot the sheep, which was inside a National Wildlife Refuge.

"To catch a crook, you sometimes are required to be like one," said Sandbakken with a knowing grin.

I remembered thinking that Peder would be the perfect person for a situation that required a high-class-looking man of the sort everyone wanted a piece of. After having dinner with him, I was impressed that for an administrator he still had a lot of street sense in him. This meant he could think on his feet and wasn't afraid. Half joking, I told him that someday I'd call him. Surely there'd be a time when he could help the US Fish and Wildlife Service with a complex investigation. He laughed and said that he'd be waiting for my call.

Now, years later, I nervously fingered his business card and wondered whether to ask permission to call him, or call him first and apologize later. I decided to make the call. After all, I couldn't be in more trouble with my supervisor than I already was. It took me three tries to get through, owing to my inexperience in placing international calls.

When a woman answered the phone in Norwegian, I was stumped as to what to even say, so I just kept repeating, "Peder Sandbakken, please. Peder Sandbakken?"

The woman finally echoed, "Peder Sandbakken?"

"Ya-ya," I spouted.

The line was silent until a deep-timbred voice with a British-inflected Scandinavian accent came on the line. "May I be of help?"

"Hi, Peder, this is Lucinda Schroeder calling from the United States. I'm with the US Fish and Wildlife Service. Do you remember me from the meeting in Madrid a few years ago?"

"Yes, of course. How are you?"

"I'm well, and you?"

"*Ja*, fine."

Then I got right to the point. "I have a favor to ask."

"Please then tell me," said the Norwegian.

During the next five minutes I spoke slowly as I explained the situation regarding the Indians and their ceremonial objects that were stolen and illegally sold in Santa Fe. My question fired off like a shot. "Would you be willing to come to New Mexico and pose as a wealthy collector of antique Indian art? I need to find the criminals who are on the selling end."

Peder's response surprised me: He tried to convince me that he'd be a good pick. "I'm quite good at cultural heritage cases. We have them here, you know. With the Viking graves that everyone tries to dig into."

"That's so good," I said while letting out two lungfuls of air. "So you'd be willing to come?"

"*Ja*, shorr."

Over the next few minutes we discussed the logistics of his crossing the ocean to act as an informant for the US government. He reminded me that he had been in law enforcement for more than twenty years. I thought his experience coupled with a cool head and European origin made him the perfect missile that Tony and Dirk would never see coming.

I told Sandbakken that I might need him fairly soon. I wanted to give him a flash roll that would knock Dirk and Tony off their feet. Sandbakken cautioned that he still needed to check with his local federal prosecutor to make sure he wasn't violating Norwegian laws. But barring any resistance, Sandbakken said he was on board.

I hung up the phone and for a few moments basked in the knowledge that, with Peder on the case, there was still light on the wall.

CHAPTER TWENTY-THREE

Monster Slayer had clearly been working behind the scenes, I thought when I learned that FBI supervisor Weisenhunt had been transferred to Washington, DC. Suddenly he was out of my life forever. Although the deadline he'd set was now moot, I found out that he'd created it so he could put the Indian case on his resume before he got transferred. Now I could meet with FBI field agent Scott Wilson and National Park Service agent Phil Young to devise a new plan.

It was the late winter of 1998 when we met in Phil's adobe-style office in Santa Fe. Interesting prehistoric Indian artifacts gave the office the feel of a small museum. Phil's Smokey Bear hat from his younger Park Ranger years hung proudly on one wall like a trophy. FBI special agent Wilson was the youngest of the three of us. His blue eyes sparkled with the anticipation of getting involved in something exciting. I was especially drawn to his deep southern accent, bred in the heart of Alabama where my own mother was born and raised.

Seated at a small conference table, I explained to the two agents that my cover had been irrevocably damaged and I had to drop out. I told them that I had my suspicions and asked agent Young if he thought Charlotte Small could have been the snitch.

"Naw," said Young. "She's a weak sister if I ever saw one. US Fish scared her to death in the 'ninety-six raid—I don't think she'd have the guts to say anything, even if she was sure about you."

FBI agent Wilson's reaction was mild. "Well, you tried. I don't know of anyone who would have gone out on a limb like you did. Do you suppose the case is over?"

Quickly I outlined a new approach to infiltrating the Indian black market by using Peder Sandbakken, a Norwegian police supervisor. I made Peder look like Thor, the greatest of the Norwegian gods.

"All we have to do is tell Peder who to contact and educate him on what to look for. He'll have both Tony and Dirk eating out of his hands."

Both agents agreed that using Peder was a stellar idea—one that they'd have little trouble getting past their supervisors.

"Wait a minute," blurted agent Young. "Didn't an undercover FBI agent work on a stolen artifact case here in Santa Fe? It's been a few years, but I still remember it."

"Well, old man, you've been in Santa Fe the longest. You should know," teased agent Wilson.

I loved deep memories. Federal agents were transferred so often that the torch was rarely properly passed. A veteran agent like Young could yield a trove of great information. "Yeah," said Young. "The Peruvian government filed an official complaint saying that thousand-year-old tombs in their remote countryside had been robbed. Gold funerary figurines were somewhere on the antiquities market. The Peruvians had information that these little guys ended up in the US—after all, that's where the money is. An armchair anthropologist from Santa Fe called the FBI and reported that he'd seen these gold figurines right in the window of a jewelry store in town. All he really said is that they didn't look right."

"Then what happened?" asked Wilson, wide-eyed.

"An agent from FBI's art theft unit flew out here and made a covert purchase." Young snapped his fingers and said, "Just like that."

"What happened to the jewelry store owner?" I asked.

"The owner claimed he didn't know that the figurines were items of cultural patrimony, so there was little the US Attorney's Office could do to prosecute. You know, the 'lack of knowledge loophole.' But the funerary objects were seized, and as I remember, the shop owner cooperated by telling the FBI who he'd purchased the figurines from. These guys were big-league international smugglers and money launderers, so it turned out to be a good pinch."

"What are funerary objects?" asked agent Wilson.

Agent Young filled him in. "In this case they were golden figurines buried with an ancient Peruvian king or queen or other important figure to help out in the afterlife. They're considered objects of cultural patrimony and are protected. Just like our Native American sacred artifacts."

Agent Wilson was writing some notes. "Okay, I get it. You know, I think . . . I think our undercover agent and Pedro might make a great team."

"His name is Peder," I corrected.

"Sorry."

Agent Young went on to say that the FBI agent's undercover name was Wally Shumaker* and he worked out of the Philadelphia office. He worked stolen art cases and had a great track record.

"He shouldn't be too hard to find, Scott," said Phil. "See if you can dig him up. I think US Fish is right. A completely different look might work. This duo sounds better than Batman and Robin!"

I cringed at the thought of inserting an FBI agent into my case. While I had worked with many fine FBI agents over the years, my recent experience had been mixed. I had confidence in Peder, but the FBI agent was definitely an unknown, which made me nervous. Still, I had to admit that Peder deserved a partner and that a two-man team made for a safer operation.

With renewed energy I said, "This is great! I'll write up a proposal introducing the new operational plan and send it to both of you. Add what you want and we'll send it in to our sups. Scott, your job is to find FBI Wally. Let's get this rolling!"

"What about the Swedish guy?" asked Scott. "How long will it take to get him over?"

"He's Norwegian, Scott. Peder Sandbakken is from Norway," I said, sounding like a schoolteacher. "I've already called him, and he'll come whenever I ask him to."

Scott looked incredulous. "Is it that easy? The FBI would have to spend months getting approval from the State Department to bring over a foreign cooperator. Even then, they probably wouldn't approve it."

I winked at Scott. "That's the beauty of being the smallest fish in the sea. No one in the big government's ocean of agencies even knows we exist. Sometimes we can get away with a lot more than the big boys can."

"I guess so," said Scott. "I wish the FBI could be that flexible."

"Wait, there's one more thing," said agent Young. "The best time to do this is during the Santa Fe Antique Indian & Ethnographic Art Show. Everybody will be out selling Indian stuff, and buyers will be all over the place. In fact, the market drew a hundred and fifty thousand people last year. The Chamber of Commerce loves it."

The excitement of taking another run at Tony and Dirk was making me giddy. "That's a great idea, Phil! When are the exact dates?"

"Third weekend in August; it never changes."

"Okay," I said to finalize things. "The FBI's art theft undercover agent will pose as a broker for his Norwegian client, Peder. Tony and Dirk will be so greedy they won't suspect a thing. Even though Peder will be wired, every criminal act will be witnessed by a federal FBI agent. Peder has no actual authority in the US, but I'll get him signed up as a confidential informant, which will allow him to work under the color of law in the United States. If he violates any laws in connection with the case, he'll be protected from prosecution. Wally already has this protection."

"So," chirped Phil, "these guys can't go off and rob a bank on their own."

"Nope . . . not unless they get a permit."

Together we laughed. Suddenly we were filled with the renewed hope of catching outlaws who thought they'd long ago won the West and could run with impunity.

—◆—

It took nearly a week for my boss, Special Agent in Charge Matt Miller, to call me from his desk in DC. He got right to the point. "This proposal the Feebs and US Park put together is pretty good. I like it a lot." Matt didn't mention my contribution to the proposal, which didn't surprise me.

"Using a foreign informant—now that's a damn good idea," said Matt. "I have a buddy from Germany who would love an assignment like this. In fact, I told him if I could ever get him over here, I would."

I felt totally blindsided. I couldn't stand the thought of seeing this assignment go to one of Matt's friends.

"Personally," I argued, "I would have more faith in someone I know. His name is Peder Sandbakken. I talked to him for a long time at the wildlife conference in Madrid. He told me that he helped recover the famous painting *The Scream* when it was stolen the first time. He also investigates Viking grave robberies. I think he's a perfect fit."

"I know Peder too," said Matt. "I met him a few years ago at a conference in Budapest. He's a good man and a good pick. But I've got an obligation to my German buddy." Matt's voice cut to laughter. "When it comes to margaritas, he's an absolute sponge. He'd fit right in the Santa Fe scene. Besides, we go way back and I'd like to do him a favor."

I felt desperate to turn this around. "Has your contact done any undercover work?"

"No, but how much is there to it? He'll change his name, of course."

"Matt, I understand where you're coming from, but this case is very complex. I need someone with experience."

Matt's voice was tinged with sarcasm. "Give me a break. You don't have to be an Einstein to work undercover. My guy will be fine. Or, if you'd prefer, we just won't do anything. I've wanted to close this case anyway. It's been to hell and back . . . as you know."

"Matt, we're close to making something happen here. This could be a huge case."

Matt replied flatly, "Look, this job is not just about cases."

His comment truly shocked me. I must have had it all wrong. I thought my job was about stopping wildlife crime and protecting cultural heritage. According to my own boss, this job was apparently about administrative reports and gossiping with desk jockeys with important titles about other people who had even more important titles. The good-old-boy system was well oiled and working. As much as I wanted to scream down Matt's throat, I forced myself to settle down and start talking *his* language.

"I agree with you, but we can't let two other federal agencies down! They've already agreed to the plan you have in your hand."

"Wait a minute. Have you contacted Peder already?"

"Yes. But it was just to ask how Norway handles cultural heritage crimes. After I was busted, I needed to talk to someone who's actually made these kinds of cases. I just wanted some advice."

"Damn it anyway! You were supposed to get my approval first. You're always doing this kind of crap! Not only can you not supervise, you can't *be* supervised!"

Gripping the phone handle, I thought, *Help me, Monster Slayer. I'm in deep shit here!* "Matt," I said, "I wasn't trying to undermine you. I'm really sorry if you feel that way. Look, I've already told the bad guys that Germans love our Indian stuff. If we need another client, we'll bring in your guy. He'd be perfect. Let this proposed team get the first crack. Your guy can come in later and actually have some fun with it."

I could hear a sigh of impatience, or else it was getting close to lunchtime. "All right," he said. "But don't forget about my guy."

"I won't . . . promise."

I hung up the phone and quickly realized what a lousy thing I'd done. Matt had told me what he wanted and I told him what he wanted to hear. This was standard strategy I'd used many times against the bad guys, but never with my own people. The truth was that I had no intentions of using a German officer.

CHAPTER TWENTY-FOUR

August 1999. I stood outside Gate A-12 at the Albuquerque Sunport anxiously awaiting the arrival of the Northwest Airlines flight from Minneapolis. According to my calculations Peder Sandbakken had left Oslo nearly twenty-three hours ago.

My heart was still pounding from just having let my black bag, with my firearm inside, go through the security X-ray machine without declaring it. I didn't mean for this to happen, but I was in a hurry and wasn't thinking. When I retrieved my bag, its lead weight reminded me that my 9mm SIG Sauer revolver was still in it. My gut flipped. The airport security screeners had surely seen it and would detain me. First they'd ream me out, then they'd call in the supervisor and hammer me for breaking some very serious security rules. If I had presented my badge and declared my weapon in the first place, they would have let me through, no questions asked. I could see myself in a back room trying to talk my way out of legal trouble with airport security while my Norwegian informant wandered around the airport looking for his contact. Oh my God!

I continued to walk briskly, listening for the security officers screaming at me to return to the checkpoint. But they never did. I snuck a glance at the three officers on duty and heard them chattering in Spanish. They didn't know it, but they had just let a loaded firearm get past them—so much for national security. The scare made me reach for painkillers for my gut, which suddenly felt as if fireflies had just invaded it.

As the Northwest Airlines aircraft pulled up to the gate, my mind was fixated on Peder and nothing else. Like a nervous bride approaching the altar, I started having second thoughts. What if Peder Sandbakken didn't have the nerves it takes to do undercover work? What if he made a mistake that placed him in danger? What if the entire plan failed? What if he wasn't even on the plane? At times like this I wondered if all my motivation wasn't just a curse that led me straight to trouble. This wasn't fun and games—this was the real deal, and I felt oddly suspended between anticipation and dread.

Intently I scrutinized every passenger as they filed into the waiting area. I didn't want to miss him. The minutes dragged on, then I
finally spotted him. Quickly I slid behind a pillar to watch him alone
for a few precious seconds. Just as I remembered, he was at least six
feet tall with a compact musculature that favored quickness and endurance more than brute strength. His hair was milk white, and his skin
was the color of parchment from months of little sun. He wore a dark
suit, white shirt, and conservative tie. First impressions were apparently
important to him.

He walked over to a leather lounge chair and set down his carry-
on bag to adjust his suit coat. With a look of controlled confidence, he
scanned the terminal for me. When he picked up his bag, I stepped out
from behind the pillar and held out an uneasy hand.

"Peder, I'm so glad you made it," I said with genuine relief.

Peder shook my hand warmly and said, "Yes, of course."

"Did you have a good trip?"

"The flights were long, but I managed."

His perfect English was delivered in the seductive British accent that
makes most American women drool. I led Peder to the baggage claim
area, where we stood in awkward silence until he retrieved his bag. It was
ten at night, and it occurred to me that he might be hungry.

"Would you like to stop and get something to eat?"

Peder nodded his head politely. "Yes, that would be perfect. I'm rather
starving at the moment."

We walked into the airport garage, where Peder loaded his luggage
into the rear seat of the Ramcharger. I wondered what he was thinking.
After all, I hadn't briefed him very thoroughly. I wouldn't have made such
a long trip on so little information. As Peder adjusted his seat belt, he
looked around at the vehicle and noted his approval.

"This is fine transportation you have."

"Yes, I like it," I said lightly.

Peder's presence was definitely a distraction. I became extra conscious
of my driving as I negotiated the neighborhood near the airport. I drove
past several restaurants that were already closed, but finally spotted a
small cafe still open.

"Do you like Mexican food?" I asked.

"I don't know, actually. I've never given it a try."

"I think you'll find something you like. After all, every country in the world has their version of the burrito."

Peder smiled. "Don't worry, I trust you."

Inside the restaurant we settled on a table near the door. As Peder perused the menu, his blue eyes gleamed like glacier ice, but then they registered a questioning look. "Can you suggest something?"

"Sure, do you want breakfast or dinner?"

"I'm in the mood for breakfast, actually."

A young Hispanic waiter appeared to take our orders, and I suggested huevos rancheros for Peder.

The waiter looked at Peder and asked, "Red or green?"

"Red or green what?" inquired Peder.

The waiter made no effort to conceal his impatience. "Do you want red or green chile on your huevos? You get to pick."

"Make it red," I interjected. "On the side."

"You got it," replied the waiter as he turned to me. "What do you want?"

"Just a Corona."

"I'll have that as well," added Peder.

The beer and food arrived quickly, and I found myself transfixed by the way Peder ate. He consumed each bite with an exactness that suggested high manners. He used his knife with his left hand. Then he laid it down and transferred his fork from his right hand to his left as he was left handed. When his plate was clean, he organized his utensils at the top of his plate with his fork turned downward. A signal that he was done.

"Well," he said as he finished off his beer. "That was fine. Thank you for stopping."

It was pushing midnight and the cafe was closing when we walked out the door. I drove him to his hotel and helped him check in by providing a US government card to cover his lodging for the night. I insisted on escorting him to his room. Although this was a high-end chain hotel, the room was in bad shape. Wallpaper was peeling in places, and there was a decisive hole in the wall that suggested violence.

"Don't move," I said, picking up the room key. "I'll be right back."

I trotted back to the clerk's desk and demanded another room for Peder. The clerk explained that the room was the only one available at the discounted government rate.

"The man who just checked in is a foreign diplomat. He expects better accommodations. Give him a better room or else I'll have to change hotels."

The clerk handed me another key. "Thanks," I muttered.

The better room was two doors down the hall, and the change was quickly made.

"Much better," said Peder as he glanced around the room.

"Can I pick you up around ten tomorrow morning?"

"Shorr, that is fine."

I left Peder in his room. Walking past the front desk on my way out, I waved to the clerk. "Much better, thanks."

— ⁓ —

The next morning I found Peder in the hotel's dining room. He was reading a Norwegian paper while his plate sat with a knife, fork, and spoon arranged perfectly across the top.

"Good morning," he said as he put his paper down. "I hope your night was good?"

"It was fine," I replied, holding back a yawn. "And you?"

"Very good, but of course I always sleep when I'm so exhausted. So, what is the plan for today?"

"We're going to drive up to Santa Fe, the long way around. I want to show you some of New Mexico before we get too busy."

"That sounds fine. I'll get my bag and greet you at the front."

As we drove out of town, I provided Peder with a short history of the city. "Albuquerque is named after a Spanish duke. Sometimes it's even called the Duke City." I told him about Coronado, the early Catholic friars, and the Pueblo revolt of 1640.

Peder's interest in New Mexico history surprised me until he told me that he'd studied world history at the University of Oslo. This led to a short conversation about the Vikings when they brutally invaded England in the year 793. Peder told me that to this day sunken Viking ships are considered graves and are protected by law. I was very impressed to learn that cultural heritage crime was a high priority with Norwegian police organizations.

Thirty minutes later we were deep in the Jemez Mountains, which were resplendent with deep-emerald hues. At the Jemez Pueblo, I pulled off at a rest stop that consisted of a few open adobe structures with thatched roofs that housed picnic tables and grills. While the amenities were sparse, the backdrop was stunning. An ancient volcanic mutation had exposed huge walls red with clay. This was a sight that couldn't be seen anywhere else. Each side of the pull-off was punctuated by boulders of the same red rock that formed huge walls. For centuries Jemez potters have utilized the red rock to make their now-famous trademark pots and vessels.

We both got out of the Ramcharger to take in the view. An elder from the pueblo sat nearby selling fry-bread. For a few bucks, I bought some for Peder to try.

"Hum, this is good," said Peder, encouraging conversation from the elder.

"My wife makes it," said the elder.

Peder commented on the beauty of the surroundings. Meanwhile the elder's eyes were glued to this unusual alabaster man with deep curiosity. Native American custom dictated that probing another person's business was rude. But the elder couldn't stand it anymore and finally popped, "Where about do you come from?"

"I'm from Norway, way up north," replied Peder.

"You mean up by North Dakota?"

Peder laughed politely. "Norway is in Scandinavia—the most northern part of Europe."

"Oh, way over there, I know now."

As if I'd disappeared, Peder and the elder talked on and on about life on the pueblo. I was impressed at how quickly Peder had connected with the Pueblo Indian, who was far removed from his own culture. The conversation told me something about Peder's sensitivity and appreciation of other people. Overall, I sensed a deep kindness in him. On the business side, his ability to quickly develop rapport would be a huge benefit when he started rubbing bellies with the bad guys.

Driving north in the Jemez Mountains, I negotiated the winding road that had been pushed through a dense forest of ponderosa pine. Eventually it opened up to the Valle Grande that stretched for thousands of acres.

"Look, there are some elk feeding," I said, pointing across the valley.

"Where?"

"They're across the valley, near the trees. It's a little unusual for them to be out this time of day. We're lucky to see them."

I stopped the Ramcharger so Peder could take pictures of the elk and the spectacular mountain landscape. It was obvious that he loved nature, and I was certain that he would care about the Indians and the wildlife we were trying to help.

By the time we reached Santa Fe, daylight was folding into a striking purple sunset. We had stopped for dinner at an American restaurant and then checked into a hotel five miles from the Santa Fe square where the Spirit Bear Gallery was located. I selected it because it had a low profile and was not one of the hotels where tourists usually stayed.

Later that evening I met with Peder in his room to explain more about his assignment. "Before you get started," said Peder, "let me show you something."

He went to his camera case and withdrew a jewelry box. "Do you think this will help my image?" It was a new diamond-studded Rolex watch—the $50,000 kind.

"It's fantastic! Is it yours?"

"It is for this assignment. A friend owns a jewelry store. I thought it might be useful. A man notices two things in another man: his watch and his shoes."

I looked down at the athletic shoes he was wearing.

"No, not these," said Peder. He went back to his suitcase and retrieved a pair of fine leather loafers. "These are Italian, the best brand there is."

"You are simply amazing, Peder. You've come prepared." Then I laughed. "With your good looks and fancy stuff, the crooks will be chasing you around the block."

Peder nodded his head with satisfaction. "I know how to fool these guys."

I showed Peder something I'd made for him. It was a higher-end black camera bag meant to be slung over the shoulder. I opened it so Peder could look inside to see the recording equipment I'd installed.

"This is called a Z-Box, which will do a video and audio recording at the same time. Check out the front. Can you see the camera lens?"

Peder studied the front of the case and then pointed to a tiny hole in the leather. "Is this it? I can barely see it."

"That's what I was hoping you'd say. This gadget is great—"

"Sorry to interrupt," said Peder, "but what is a daget?"

"Oh, I'm sorry about that. A gadget is a device."

"Good, go on."

"But the problem is that while you're recording, you won't be able to look through a viewfinder the way you can with a camera. So you won't know exactly what you're recording. You might want to practice a bit."

"I'll practice now."

I showed Peder how to turn on the recorder. He placed the bag's strap on his shoulder and marched around the room.

"This is special investigator Sandbakken trying out his new toy. Can you hear me? Testing, testing."

I rolled back on the bed, laughing as if I'd known Peder forever.

"This is an excellent device. Where did you get it?"

"The recorder is specialized government property. But I made up the concealment. I make all my own concealments—the crooks are keen to anything you can buy in a spy store."

"Like a camera in sunglasses?"

"Exactly, the FBI still uses those."

Peder rolled his eyes. "I don't believe that."

Just then there was a tap-tap-tap on the door. I opened it to find FBI agent Scott Wilson standing in the hallway with a pleasant-looking man in his early fifties. The two agents took over the room like they owned it.

"How in the hell did you find this place?" barked the man yet to be identified.

"Hey," said Scott. "Sorry we're late. I was just showing Wally around the Plaza. Yeah, this is Wally Shumaker. You must be Peder." Peder would use his real name throughout the investigation, while Wally's real name was never used.

While the introductions were being made, I was cringing over the fact that Scott, a known FBI agent, was parading our undercover agent around downtown Santa Fe. Given what I'd been through, I was paranoid over anything that might expose us. Undercover agent Wally Shumaker was a slightly overweight man who obviously carried the traits of more than one culture. I later learned that his mother was Japanese, which explained his slightly hooded eyes. He had the fair skin of the Irish. Unlike Peder, he wasn't a naturally composed man but fidgeted constantly, moving his hands in and out of the pockets of his cargo pants.

Right off the bat I felt rattled. Although I'd agreed to let Wally be Peder's partner, I now felt it was a huge mistake. They weren't at all alike. Peder was very serious about the case, while Wally joked around as if the assignment was all fun and games.

"Hey!" Wally said, pointing to Peder. "Didn't we meet at the FBI's Organized Crime Conference in Budapest?"

Peder looked unsure, but said, "*Ja*, that's possible. I was there."

"I remember. You and your partner gave a talk on human smuggling."

"Well, yes, that's right. . . . Nice to see you again."

"Okay," I said, "let's get to work." I directed their attention to a table in my room. I'd created a small display of Indian beaded paraphernalia, leather pipe cases, and old belts along with pictures of ceremonial items I'd secretly copied from books in the Coronado Room at the university library. I told Peder and Wally I wanted them to be somewhat familiar with what they'd be looking for. I also said that the crooks would not expect them to be experts but they had to have some idea.

"Let the crooks pontificate on what they know," I advised. "Let them be your teachers; they'll love you for it."

While Peder carefully studied each piece, Wally gave the display a scant look but otherwise poked jokes at Scott. At one point I showed the two covert operators a sturdy stick from a cottonwood tree that had a river rock solidly attached to it with straps made from deer sinew. I had purchased the item at the auction in Wisconsin.

"What the fuck is that?" said Wally with a belly laugh.

My mind screamed, *Stop swearing! Peder is a diplomat, not a street thug.*

I skipped a beat and explained: "This is a genuine skull cracker used to finish off seriously wounded enemy soldiers. According to the story, this one may have been used by Indian women at Custer's Last Stand—although I wouldn't put my life on it. But it is true that the women of a tribe were responsible for scouring the battlefield to make sure the white soldiers were DOA."

"That's so cool," said Wally. "Can I hold it?"

He took the piece and, laughing, pretended to knock the rest of us on our heads—just like a kid. Bonk-bonk-bonk. I was horrified at this behavior, especially in front of Peder, who was clearly confused.

Then Wally asked, "Why are you two staying so far from the Plaza? Peder should be with me at La Fonda, which is right where the action is."

I straightened up as if to reinforce the point I was about to make. "Look, Peder is my informant, so I decide where he stays. The fact is, I don't want him downtown. If something goes wrong, I want to make it a little harder for the bad guys to find him."

"Gotcha," said Wally, smirking as if in reality I had a hidden agenda of being alone with Peder.

"You know," said Scott, "I think Wally has a point. They don't have to share a room, but it would make more sense if they were at least at the same hotel."

Hackles on my neck shot up. "I need to know where Peder is every minute he's here. He's totally my responsibility, and I'm not losing control of him. Scott, don't tell anyone where Wally or Peder is staying. That jeopardizes security. In fact, Scott, don't tell anyone about these two."

"Sure," said Scott, his eyes sweeping the floor.

As long as I had everyone's attention, I continued, "Also, I don't want any deals done in a hotel room. All illegal transactions have to be done at the place of business of the target. That way we'll be able to get search warrants to search for other evidence. Otherwise we'll end up searching one of your hotel rooms for underwear. Got it?"

Even Wally laughed at my comment, and I was relieved he took it so well. But then the older FBI agent turned to Peder and quite inappropriately put him in a corner.

"What do think about staying out here, Peder? After all, it's your ass."

Peder's response was certain. "I like the idea of keeping me safe, and I hear she's a good shot. So, I'll stay on here."

Finally I'd won a round, plus a show of confidence from my own informant. But Wally wouldn't let go. He put his hand on Peder's shoulder and said, "Let's get out of here and go have a couple of drinks. We need to be buddies before we start shaking up the bad guys."

"*Ja*, shorr," said Peder, sounding eager to get going.

While Wally had a good point about spending some face time with Peder, I was fuming. My informant was now in the hands of a fast-talking FBI agent who acted like a rodeo clown. One minute ago I was flying high, and now I was frustrated, collapsed on the bed with my fists clenched. Who would Peder listen to—the FBI or me?

CHAPTER TWENTY-FIVE

The next morning Peder, Scott, and I were waiting for Wally Shumaker to arrive appropriately late. Peder was dressed in khaki shorts, a Ralph Lauren polo shirt, his borrowed Rolex watch, and his fine Italian shoes. He certainly didn't look like a standard American tourist. He was decidedly different.

Finally Wally showed up. "Hey, sorry I'm late. I had to call a US attorney back east. We're working a stolen Old Master art case. It's a hot one."

Wally was wearing dark blue cotton-polyester slacks and a light pink shirt. Pink isn't normally worn by men in the West, so for our purposes pink was good. His pink shirt would reinforce his backstory of being from frilly Philly.

"Okay," I said. "Listen up, I want to give you two a briefing of what to expect."

"I'm . . . what you Americans say . . . 'all ears,'" said Peder.

"You're good, Peder," I said, laughing.

Turning to Wally, I said, "Here's a page from the phone book that lists the galleries I'd like you to visit. I put little checks on the ones where I think you should spend some time. Use these places to practice up on your spiel. I don't have any information that these places are dealing in anything illegal, but you can't hit the main target without having been around town a bit. Believe me, by this afternoon most dealers will have caught the scent of the green stuff in your pockets."

"So what exactly is our story?" asked Peder.

"It's a little loose right now, but as you go along, the story will develop on its own. Basically Peder is to claim to have an extensive collection of Laplander artifacts. Wally will explain that Peder now wants to expand into North American Indian material but is especially interested in ceremonial items. He believes in Indian spirits and all that. Remember, Wally, you're Peder's broker, so speak for him. Peder, I'm afraid your English is too good. Can you dummy it down at bit?"

"Ya betcha, en cop koffee pleez?"

I just laughed. Peder knew what to do.

"You think we should ask for ceremonial items right off the bat?" asked Wally.

"You should hint at it," I responded. "Otherwise people will be begging you to buy beaded moccasins all day long. You're not interested in what most collectors have—you want the rare and sacred stuff. Besides, the Indian Arts Festival only lasts three days, and Peder has to get back to Norway on Monday. So if a crook wants to deal, he's gonna have to do it quickly."

Using a deadline to put pressure on a suspect is a tactic I've used many times. It keeps things moving and reduces the exposure of the undercover agents.

"What about headdresses? Everybody wants a headdress, right?" asked Wally.

"Historical headdresses are legal to possess, but they can't be sold. Bald eagles have been protected since 1940, and golden eagles since 1962. As we talked about, *all* eagle feathers are illegal to sell and everyone knows it. Unless someone straight out offers you an eagle feather fan or hair tie or a headdress, don't even bring it up. You don't want to appear too eager. Besides, eagle feathers are not what we're after unless they're attached to a sacred artifact."

Wally laughed. "Hey, I don't even know what an eagle feather looks like."

"There are plenty of them on the table. Take another good look and feel them. Eagle feather shafts are rigid in order for these heavy birds to sustain flight. If you see some feathers and you're still not sure, get a picture with the video and I'll be able to identify it."

"You can identify an eagle feather just from a picture?" asked Wally.

"I can, but there are some good fakes out there, so I'd actually have to see it to make sure. Also, any article with eagle feathers on it is going to cost a lot. Fake feathers are dirt cheap."

"Speaking of money," he asked. "How much do we have to play with?"

I went to my bag, pulled out a flash roll of $15,000, and handed it to Peder. I told him how the roll was organized and suggested that he let a few, but not all, of his contacts get an eyeball full.

"It's all American money." Then I joked, "No pesos."

"I like that," said Peder, grinning.

Wally's eyes widened when he saw the cash. "What if we get robbed?"

"Wally, it's your job to make sure Peder doesn't get robbed. What are you carrying, anyway?"

"Uh . . . it's, it's a Chief's Special, a five-shooter."

"Well, where is it?"

"I've got it in an ankle holster. I'm more comfortable carrying it that way. Besides, art thieves don't carry guns, so I don't go powered up."

I refrained from arguing, but I was astounded that an undercover FBI agent would be so slack in his weaponry. A Smith and Wesson's Chief's Special didn't have the firepower most agents preferred, although it had the advantage of being highly concealable. Also, at that time, agents had no specific practice drills that involved drawing from the ankle. I suspected that Wally had never drawn his Chief's from his ankle holster. He probably qualified on the gun range by drawing from the hip, as all federal agents did. In a tight situation his brain would turn to mush and he'd immediately go to his hip for his gun, just like he'd practiced hundreds of times. But his weapon wouldn't be there.

"Can I see it?" I asked.

"What's the matter, don't you believe me?" he said, patting his ankle. "Don't worry, it's there."

I never saw the gun, and this worried me. As far as protecting Peder was concerned, Wally seemed worse than nothing.

Out of the blue Scott said something surprising. "I'm . . . I'm afraid I can't stay on with you guys. I have a stolen Indian ledger drawing case I'm working on."

Penciled ledger drawings were made mostly by soldiers who used off-white lined school paper to chronicle battles between soldiers and Indians, bison hunts, and everyday Indian life. They weren't artistically exceptional but were revered for their showing of life and important battles in the American West. They were also very fragile, and consequently finding one in good condition was rare. The ledger drawing Scott was speaking of had been stolen from another gallery. There must have been an interstate commerce component to the case, or Scott wouldn't have the authority to work it. But unless he had a good informant, the chances of recovering this piece were slim.

I couldn't believe Scott was backing out, though in a way I could see his point. He was a smart kid, schooled as an accountant, but I never saw a hint of *High Noon* bravado in him. He probably wasn't comfortable with an undercover investigation. I suspected that Scott was recruited by the FBI to work on bank robberies and high-level financial crimes. Most agents joked that FBI accountants carried a .38 caliber pencil for a weapon. I thought these FBI accountants deserved much more credit, as they did an incredible job unraveling worldwide financial fraud. This backroom cadre of agents had put a lot of serious crooks in jail. I hoped that Scott would be given that chance someday. I told him that I appreciated his help and would call him if we ever got lucky enough to secure search warrants and needed extra hands.

Wally jumped up and motioned me to the window. "See that red convertible sports car in the parking lot? I rented it for Peder and me. Cool, huh?"

"It's great looking ... but I thought I mentioned to you that I was driving a red Camaro when my cover got blown. This car looks pretty similar."

Wally dropped the curtain. "No one will notice. Peder and I don't look a bit like you." He winked at Peder and added, "Everybody will love us so much they won't notice our car."

I touched my throat and choked down another hard swallow at the backhanded slap.

With Scott gone, there were only the three of us—which was fine with me. I set up the hidden camera for Peder and refreshed him on how to use it.

"Remember, no floors and no bellies," I said.

Peder excused himself to go back to his room for a minute. In his absence Wally told me that while in Budapest he'd seen Peder very intoxicated with an American woman.

"Yeah, they were both hanging all over each other ... drunker than shit."

Wally was clearly trying to spread dirt on Peder, which I found very distasteful.

"And your point is?" I asked firmly.

"Well, nothing, except that she works for Interpol in the art crime division and was really all over Peder."

"So then what happened?"

"Oh, I don't know. They went off somewhere . . . if you know what I mean."

I remained silent with my arms folded across my chest, listening to Wally as he spread just enough manure to stink up the whole room. I suspected that Wally was trying to knock Peder down a notch to give himself room to come up. After all, in our crowd of three, I had the knowledge and Peder had the looks. Wally needed a spot, but I didn't like the way he was doing it. This was tension that was only beginning to fester.

There was a knock on the door and Wally didn't get a chance to answer. I let Peder in and tried to erase the crappy look I knew was on my face.

I handed Peder his camera bag, patted him on the shoulder, and said, "Go have fun. I'll be here when you're done and will need a complete briefing."

"Wait a minute," said Wally. "What's Peder's undercover name? What's his backstory?"

I responded quickly, "His name is Peder, and he'll show his real passport if he has to. We didn't have time to dummy up a complete backstory; besides, the bad guys will never find him in Norway. As for his work, he runs an Internet service business in Oslo. Here's his business card. Also, he has money from the North Sea oil boom. That's why he's so rich."

"*Netman, Oslo, Norway,*" said Wally, skimming the card. "Okay, Peder the net man, let's go."

A drawing of one of two sacred wooden parrots stolen from an ancient Hopi shrine and offered for sale for $30,000. The parrots were repatriated to the Hopi Tribe.

ILLUSTRATION BY ROBERT L. PRINCE

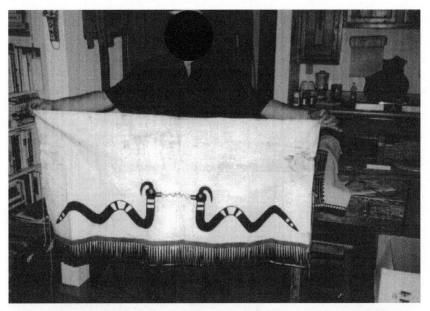

Tony Lorenzo holding a dance kirtle illegally obtained from the San Ildefonso
Pueblo and offered for sale. The kirtle was repatriated to the San Ildefonso Pueblo.
PHOTO FROM AUTHOR'S COLLECTION

An old Kiowa ghost shield with horse hair and migratory bird feathers, offered for
sale for $25,000. The shield was appropriately repatriated.
PHOTO FROM AUTHOR'S COLLECTION

Eagle feather bundles used by Navajo *hataalii* in healing ceremonies, on sale for $20,000. These bundles were repatriated to the Navajo Nation.

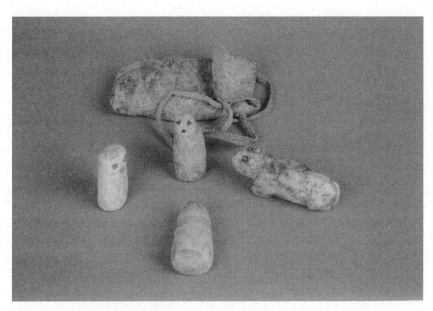

Four fetishes with leather pouch containing corn pollen, confiscated during Operation Monster Slayer and later repatriated to Mother Earth, as none of the tribes would claim them.

PHOTO FROM AUTHOR'S COLLECTION

One fake Native American hair tie, claimed to be worn during ceremonies, made by Tony Lorenzo and purchased during Operation Monster Slayer for $5,000. Artifact was destroyed by the US Fish and Wildlife Service.

PHOTO FROM AUTHOR'S COLLECTION

One parfleche container offered for sale for $16,000 during Operation Monster Slayer. This artifact was seized and later repatriated to the appropriate tribe.
PHOTO FROM AUTHOR'S COLLECTION

1875 Northern Cheyenne eagle feather headdress offered for sale for $160,000 during Operation Monster Slayer. This headdress was seized and later repatriated to the North Cheyenne Tribe.

Informant Peder Sandbakken in the red convertible he drove during Operation
Monster Slayer
PHOTO FROM AUTHOR'S COLLECTION

Informant Peder Sandbakken with Alfonso at the Isleta Pueblo during Operation
Monster Slayer
PHOTO FROM AUTHOR'S COLLECTION

CHAPTER TWENTY-SIX

Being sequestered in a well-worn hotel room that grew smaller with every hour was driving me up a wall. I hated not being part of the action and having to sit on the sidelines like a kid sent to the corner for spitting. The torment reminded me of when I was stuck for two days in a six-by-eight-foot cabin in Alaska waiting for my informant Mark Hanson to come back to base camp after an illegal bear hunt. Dense fog had left Mark and his two guides sitting on the tundra until the weather improved so they could fly again. I had no idea what Mark would do or, worse, what he'd say. I worried that Mark would break under such intense pressure and tell the guides who we were. This had happened with informants before. In the end Mark maintained our cover, but he told me later he was so weary being under scrutiny that he almost folded. While the circumstances were different, the stress felt the same.

Sitting by the window of my hotel in Santa Fe, I envisioned my surrogate spies trudging up and down Canyon Road, the center for high-end galleries that carried exquisite sculptures, incredible original artwork, and the finest of Indian weavings. Peder and Wally would be drooling over superior examples of baskets, rugs, parfleches, beaded shirts, and doeskin dresses costing much more than their annual salaries.

They'd also see early fifteenth-century *retablos*, notebook-sized wooden boards used as canvases. Early Catholic friars painted images of various saints on them and gave them away as part of their Christian mission. Collectors craved them. Intermixed with the fine galleries were shops that filled in the gaps with lower-end Indian paraphernalia and modern Indian-made trinkets for the tourists to buy. For today, my agents were to stay away from the Spirit Bear Gallery and focus on the gallery scene in general. Spirit Bear would be on the radar tomorrow.

Five hours later Wally and Peder stumbled through the door of my hotel room. Both looked bushed to the bone.

"Man," said Wally. "I've never seen so many people crawling around the streets. Man, it's crazy out there."

Peder, whose Nordic face was bathed in sweat, looked at Wally, clearly annoyed. "Why do you Americans always say 'man'? What does it mean?"

"Hey, bud, no worries," said Wally. "It's just slang. But whatever. . . . I've just never seen so much Indian crap for sale. How are we supposed to know what's legal and what's illegal? It all looks the same to me. Frankly, I don't think it can be done. All I saw was enough turquoise jewelry to fill a hundred bathtubs."

Meanwhile Peder collapsed in a chair. He was short of breath and had a slight nosebleed. I gave him ice water and Kleenex.

"What's wrong with me?" he groaned. "I'm usually quite fit."

"You've got a little altitude sickness going on. The stuff just wipes you out. We're at seven thousand feet here—that's about twenty-one hundred meters. Just relax and get some oxygen in your lungs. You'll feel better in a few minutes," I said, playing nurse.

Wally, who was now prone on *my* bed, threw in, "I think I have the same thing. I can't believe how hot it is out there. Can I have some water too?"

I put a glass of water next to the bed. "Well, how did it go?"

"I've never been thrown out of more places in my life," Wally groaned. "Every time we mentioned ceremonial artifacts the shopkeepers got pissed and demanded that we leave. Man, we got turned down more than a bedsheet."

"I don't quite understand what . . . you know about the bedsheet, but I'm shorr no one thought of us as policemen."

"You did fine," I said, trying to boost up the two arts festival fighters. "Tomorrow will be better. You only have one gallery to check out."

I was genuinely surprised at the level of compliance Wally and Peder had found among the galleries. I thought at least one person would take their bait, but no one did. Had the East-West Trading Post case put the fear of God into traders? Or was there something wrong about my plan? I'd already told Wally that catching crooks violating NAGPRA and eagle protection laws would be difficult. He couldn't believe that the bad guys didn't literally line up to be caught by him. In the gold Peruvian funerary figurines case, all he had to do was show up and give some guy money. Operation Monster Slayer was proving to be much more of a challenge.

Wally sat up with his back against the headboard. "You know what I think? I think pretty Miss Dana has got these people trained. Buying a ton of cocaine would be easier than what we're trying to do."

"*Ja*," added Peder. "No one would trade with us." He looked at me and said, "Are you sure we're on the right track?"

"Look," I said, "I know it's frustrating. I've been to all these places and understand what you went through. Just keep going—you'll make a hit. I think the guy I have you set up with for tomorrow will take the fall. I just couldn't send you there first."

"So you've already checked this guy out?" asked Wally.

"It's all in the case reports I gave you. I told you I've talked to the suspect. He has ceremonial items openly displayed in his shop. The contacts you made today only confirmed what I already suspected. There are probably just a few bad boys in town, and I already know who they are."

Wally sounded miffed. "Well, as far as I'm concerned, you scared everyone off when you got burned. That's the real reason we're not getting anywhere."

I shot back, "Maybe the real reason is because you're working within blocks of the jewelry store where you made the Peruvian bust. Maybe every crook in town knows you're back and they're diving for cover."

"Listen," spouted Wally, "I've done covert operations for over twenty years and I can see what's happening. Everyone's paranoid after they found out about you. I don't think we could buy popcorn out there!"

"I bought something," said Peder, holding up a modest turquoise and silver bracelet. "It's for my girlfriend. She will like it?"

"Oh, she will," I said, admiring the jewelry. "It's a very thoughtful gift. Your girlfriend is a lucky woman."

"Uh," said Wally, "I'm collecting these new quarters with the states on them. They're for my kids. Anyone have one with New Mexico on it?"

Later I would thank Peder for bringing out the bracelet, which broke the tension between Wally and me. Things were getting heated and he stopped it. While Peder begged off to go to his room, Wally grumbled about having to drive in heavy traffic back downtown to his hotel. Before he left, he agreed to pick up Peder later to go to dinner.

"Okay," I said. "Please be back here in the morning."

———

At eight the following morning, the phone in my room rang. It was Peder. "Can I come over now?"

"Sure." By the time I got to my door and opened it, Peder was already there.

"Did you sleep well?" I asked, passing him through.

"Not so well, I'm afraid. I'm not so sure what I'm to say to this Dutchman we are to meet today."

"Have a seat," I said, pointing to a chair. "Look, Peder, just being you will make the Dutchman fall for you. After all, he's looking for a man who is wealthy and happens to be on an Indian spending spree in Santa Fe. Isn't that you?"

"Well, yes, I'd rather say so."

"So, be that man. Show interest in everything he shows you. He doesn't sell junk. Don't talk too much; let your face do the talking. Do you know what I'm saying?"

"Very much so," said Peder, who was now grinning.

"Keep him guessing as to what you're thinking. He's a greedy man and will want everything he can get from you. Remember, you don't have to convince him where you're from. After all, you *are* from Norway—"

"—and that's the truth!"

"Exactly, and it's his job to convince you to buy from him. I've been in his gallery. There's contraband in there, and I feel strongly he'll offer to sell it to you. Once you get what he has on tape, I'll be able to send you and Wally back in with a list of what to buy."

"But I thought the FBI was low on funds."

"Yes, but we'll buy small and then create the illusion that there's much more to come. Wally will do this. It's only normal, because the more you want to buy, the more money your 'broker' gets. But there is something else you can do to get him on your side."

"What is that?"

"The Dutchman is very visual."

"What on our earth does that mean?"

"He has an artistic view of things, so he uses visual phrases like 'this is how I *see* things' and 'the way it *looks* to me.' Whenever he talks like that, agree with him and try to use the exact words he uses."

"Ah *ja*, I'm catching on now."

"Am I going too fast?" I asked.

"No, I like this kind of cleverness. Keep going."

"Good. Keep your English down—it's too good. Say as little as possible and eventually this guy will think you don't understand anything and will start talking to Wally like you're not even there."

"You mean like parents who talk in front of their kids, when the kids understand everything."

"Exactly. But make it known that Wally works for you and you have to approve any purchases. Don't buy anything on the spot. After I see the tape, I'll tell you what to go back for."

Then I heard the door handle rattling and Wally yelling, "Hey, open up!"

I opened the door. "Can't we be a little more discreet?"

"Ah, I see Peder's already here. So, who knows what been going on," he said, laughing as if he was walking into a Champagne breakfast party.

My nerves prickled. But I let it go. "You guys ready?"

"Yeah, I got a different wire on today," said Wally, exposing a standard covert audio recorder clipped inside his pants. "I didn't like the one I had on yesterday. There were too many wires crawling up and down my chest. I got itchy."

"Fine," I said, handing Wally a creamed-colored guayabera still in its plastic wrap.

"What's this?"

"It's a typical casual shirt worn by Mexican men as well as white guys in the Southwest. Go, try it on."

Wally retreated to the bathroom and came out wearing it. The cotton shirt had short sleeves, a collar, two wide pockets on the top and bottom, and buttons down the front. Each side of the shirt was embellished with thinly stitched ribbing.

"Wait a minute, it's still got the wrinkles in it."

"That's the point. Say you just bought it yesterday—there are thousands of them around here."

"That's true, I noticed the same thing. It looks fine," said Peder.

"Okay, guys, you know where the place is, so get going. Peder, remember you only have an hour on the Z-Box before you have to change the tape." I looked at my watch—it was just after ten a.m., so the gallery would be open. "Get going before our guy disappears for lunch!"

I eased the door shut after them and listened as their footsteps shuffled down the hallway. From my window I watched them climb into the killer red convertible, top down, with Wally in the driver's seat. The pure confidence and sureness that radiated around them made me feel much better. They exuded the aura of men who had it all—hidden behind chic sunglasses and breezy expressions that would make anyone believe every word they said.

The convertible swung out of the parking lot and north onto Cerrillos Road toward the centuries-old Spanish plaza. The day exuded cool sunshine. I imagined the blue-and-yellow Spanish tiles that bordered the window panes sparkling in the high-altitude sun. I remembered the pots of bloodred geraniums that lined the Palace of the Governors while a handsome young man strummed a guitar and sang in Spanish a tragic ballad of love. I'd always said that only the Spanish could sing while sounding like they were dying. I wished so much I was with them.

Wally and Peder were parking now, probably a few blocks from the corner of Washington Street and the Palace of the Governors where the Day of the Dead shop was. The stakes on this contact were huge. If they didn't make a hit with DeVries, it would be at the end of the road. The case couldn't go on, and the Native Americans would lose the dignity of their spiritual life to greedy men who had the empathy of a common sociopath. This plan had to work.

Meanwhile I was stuck in a hotel room worried and wondering. I hoped I'd given my team everything they needed to know about their target and they'd play him just like I told them to. My gut felt like it was being attacked by fireflies. I swallowed pain pills, hoping that no infection was setting in. I couldn't afford to end up in the emergency room again, and I couldn't take any more sick leave.

Alone, several thoughts festered. First came nagging thoughts of the lowlife individual that blew my cover. Whoever he was had every intention of seeing me hurt. I'd racked my brain but still couldn't come up with anyone. If Tony believed the rat over my vouch, he had to be someone beyond reproach—someone that even I couldn't overcome. Like a fox, I'd sit and wait as long as it took. The rat would turn up eventually. They always do.

My second issue was the unspoken matter between Wally and me. Since Peder was my informant, I knew I hovered over him like an overprotective mother. When Wally saw this, he flatly implied that Peder and I were involved in an inappropriate relationship. He said it that morning after eyeing Peder and me alone in my room. Wally's comment was unprofessional, and it cut deep. I knew he wouldn't keep this dirt to himself and it wouldn't be long before the lie would take on a life of its own.

Wally's despicable imagination could not only ruin my career, it could easily render our case un-prosecutable. Defense attorneys didn't need much to discredit a prosecution's witness, and sexual impropriety was the perfect toxin to get the job done. Wally was trying to destroy his own team just so he'd look like the good guy. While it made no sense to me, Wally was becoming a real problem, and eventually I was going to have to deal with it. But for now, I wanted everyone to get along.

CHAPTER TWENTY-SEVEN

It was just after noon when I heard Wally and Peder babbling in the hotel's hallway. I opened the door and welcomed the warriors back to the castle.

"How did you guys do?"

"Oh," crowed Wally, "you'll have to watch the movie to see. Plug in the monitor, Peder, it's showtime!"

Bursting with anticipation, I sat close to the monitor as it blinked to life. The audio began with Peder's first words, "Okay, we're on," accompanied by clonk, clonk, clonk, as the video showed pictures of feet climbing the never-ending staircase I was so familiar with.

"Geez, these stairs are a bitch," groaned Wally.

"Watch it. We're *on!*" whispered Peder.

Totally focused on the screen, I watched as the camera moved across the wooden floor and showed its worn patina. Meanwhile footsteps echoed back and forth. The lens adjusted upward and picked up the image of a red-haired woman who emerged from behind a Mexican-made Indian-style blanket that covered a doorway.

"May I help you?" asked the woman.

"Wow, I hope so," answered Wally, who couldn't hide his first impression of the glowing Mona.

Then the camera's lens caught the woman's eye as she stared at Peder. His demeanor as a privileged gentleman wasn't lost on her. She ran her hands down her skirt in a modified act of primping.

"What are you looking for?" she asked.

"My name is Peder. And you are Miss . . . ?"

"Milne. Mona Milne. I'm Mr. DeVries's assistant."

"Great," interjected Wally. "Peder—I mean, Mr. Sandbakken is looking for old Indian stuff. I'm his broker, Wally Shumaker. I'm not from around here—the East Coast, you know."

Mona laughed lightly. "We have plenty of Indian things. Please feel free to look around. Hopefully, I can answer your questions."

The camera lens flashed by the rugs, blankets, pots, and odd wooden figurines I'd seen, before stopping at the pair of carved parrots decorated with the feather necklace. I'd already told Peder about them, but this time they'd been moved and were set on an old Spanish chest.

"And these are . . . ?" asked Peder as he struggled to hold the camera bag still.

"They're parrots used in a Jemez Pueblo rain dance," replied Mona. "Mr. DeVries told me the Indian maidens carry them in ceremonies and sing for rain."

"Is this a church thing?" asked Peder.

"Yeah," said Wally. "She's saying the parrots are part of a special religious ceremony the Indians do."

"Then I think I should have them," demanded Peder.

My mind was swirling. *Not so fast! What's going on here?*

"That fast?" asked Mona. "They cost thirty thousand dollars."

Peder's tone didn't change. "Is the shop manager here?"

"Sure, I'll get him." Mona exited the room through the Indian blanket curtain, and within seconds a man walked in with Mona trailing behind.

"Hi, I'm Dirk DeVries."

"I'm Peder. It's excellent to meet you." Peder shook his hand and held it for a few beats, hoping that Dirk would notice the Rolex that gleamed on his wrist.

"You have an interesting accent. Where are you from?" asked Dirk.

"Norway."

"Norway? Some of my relatives were from Sweden."

"Norway is another country, you know."

"Yeah, but they're close, aren't they? Never mind. What can I do for such a special visitor?"

Finally Wally took over. "He wants old, very old things, used by the Indians in their religions. You see, Peder has a huge collection from the Laplanders, but he wants to expand into our Indian stuff."

"Mona tells me that you were looking at these parrots. They're exquisite, don't you think?"

"*Unnskyld?* How you call them?" asked Peder to stress his question.

"Exquisite," Dirk repeated.

"Could you explain it?"

Dirk drummed his fingers on a nearby table while he spoke. "Exquisite, I don't know . . . it means good, great, fantastic—very rare. Does that make sense?"

"Mulch beder," Peder said as if he'd been totally enlightened. "But I should know more and I should see more before deciding. *Ja?*"

Wally's voice echoed in the background: "*Ja*, yeah much *ja*. He'll show you everything."

While I hadn't expected the contact to go this way, I had to admit that I could almost hear Dirk's heartbeat hammering for more.

"Come over here . . . you might find these interesting."

As Mona and the men walked to another part of the gallery, Peder dropped back to scan the camera slowly throughout the gallery to pick up as much as he could. As I watched the film, I felt an instant urge to turn around and give Peder a huge hug. This was great! After a few seconds the camera settled on a white fireplace mantel.

Referring to some flattened sticks smeared with a black substance, Dirk said, "These funny-looking things are part of the Navajo *jish* and are called bullroarers."

"Jeesh! Bull-what?" asked Peder.

"A *jish* is a medicine bundle. Think of it as an Indian doctor's bag. The bullroarers have these leather straps on them. See? The chief medicine man swirls these over his head to making a roaring sound—you know, like a bull. This is supposed to call in the gods for healing."

"This is super!" said Wally, genuinely pleased. "So they're used in actual sacred ceremonies?"

Dirk's voice lowered. "Yes, they are. Supposedly they're illegal, but everyone sells them. Besides, the pot cops think these are just flat sticks with black tar on them. But to the Navajos they work magic—especially the black stuff."

"Who are the pot cops?" asked Wally.

"Oh, every so often someone from the Bureau of Land Management or the Park Service will snoop in my gallery looking for illegal Indian artifacts. I've never been caught with anything, because I know more about Indians than they do. They wouldn't know an illegal artifact if one bit them on their asses. Besides, everything I have isn't being used any-more, so it's okay."

"Do you understand, Peder?" asked Wally.

"*Ja*, most of it."

"See," said Wally, looking directly into Dirk's eyes, "I don't know much about this stuff either. I mostly deal in high-dollar Civil War relics like rare flags, rifles, and medals. I've brokered deals with stuff that had some incredible history with it. It's all big-money stuff. After all, why spend the same amount of time on trivial memorabilia?"

Catching a glimpse of Dirk, I noticed that his body language was open, which was good. Mona's face seemed to be perched on his shoulder like a great horned owl with wide eyes.

"Yeah," continued Wally. "I hooked up with Peder in Budapest last year and we hit it off. I agreed to help him find some genuine Indian stuff, since I was from the US and at least knew where to start looking."

"Yeah . . . great shirt, by the way. I see you're going native on us." Dirk laughed. "Mona said you were also interested in the birds. Let's go take another look at them."

I heard the echo of footsteps and then the two parrots came into focus. Without touching them, Dirk reiterated his fake story of the Jemez Pueblo dancers. He added a bit about the so-called maidens dancing in circles to make ribbons on their outfits flutter like bird feathers.

"This is right?" asked Peder, looking at his broker.

"Oh yeah," said Wally. "Even I've heard of this. I think they're legit . . . I mean, just look at them!"

"Well, what will it be? I can make you a deal—the seven bullroarers and the parrots for fifty thousand dollars."

Suddenly my mind went fuzzy on the math. Dirk was bugling num-bers like a bull elk in rut. There was no way we could keep up with this guy.

"Wait one minute!" spouted Peder. "I want to see how these bull things work."

Good. Peder was working Dirk like a greedy barracuda on the hook. He'd drag Dirk in closer to the bait, increase the tension, and then let the line out to make him wait. Even I wondered if Dirk would live through this.

"No problem," said Dirk, in an upbeat tone. "Follow me upstairs to the terrace."

With the hidden camera bouncing, I couldn't catch much until the three men were standing on the roof of the building. In the background I could see a rickety garden bench and a few potted geraniums, two of them dying and one dead. Peder held the camera bag high on his waist and caught Dirk attempting to swing the bullroarer above his head like a lasso. The seven-inch flat stick wouldn't stay in the air and kept hitting Dirk's head like a falcon dive-bombing its prey. This relentless head-pecking went on until Dirk, clearly annoyed, gave up.

"Are you okay?" asked Peder.

Dirk rubbed his head. "Yeah, I just can't get it to swing like the medicine men do."

He paused for a moment to regain his composure. Watching Dirk get pounded by a Navajo bullroarer made us all collapse in laughter.

"That's Indian ju-ju at work," I said. "He's getting what he deserves."

"Anyway," said Dirk on the monitor, "the beauty of these is that no two are alike. Each one holds its own significance in the spiritual lives of Indians to call in the gods when they're needed. There's nothing else that holds as much power as they do."

Back in the gallery Dirk replaced the bullroarer on the mantel. "So, are you ready to deal?"

"I think Peder and I need to talk about this," said Wally. "I can see the parrots and maybe one of the sticks. How much is one of the sticks?"

"I'd rather sell them as a set. As you see, I have seven of them. With the birds, they make a truly exquisite collection."

"Wait a minute," said Wally. "You said the sticks came from individual medicine bags, so why is having a set so important?"

"They display better that way. Look how the shadow from each one casts against the one next to it. It's a matter of beauty and artistic equilibrium. Their magic is apparent by the way they dissipate light like nothing else does."

"What a bunch of crap," I remarked.

In the background I could hear Peder's baritone voice echo in a reflective hum. Wally paced back and forth in front of the camera, the sound of his shoes bouncing off the high ceiling, his arms folded across his chest. Peder pulled out the cash roll and thumbed the bills like a deck of cards. Mona's eyes popped wide, while Dirk's hand rose to cover his mouth.

"It's unfortunate, but I don't seem to have the proper cash with me," lamented Peder.

Great! I thought. *Dirk will now have come up with something to keep the boys in the gallery. He won't want to lose them.*

"Stay here," said Dirk. "Let me show you something really special."

Dirk disappeared from the camera's view but quickly returned. I could tell that Peder was doing his best to film the object, which seemed to fit perfectly in the palm of Dirk's hand. I found myself leaning closer, as if to see beyond the scope of the lens.

"Looks like a rock to me," said Wally flatly.

"This is not just any rock," said Dirk, whose voice was ratcheting up in intensity. "Notice the shape—it's flat, rounded on the top, and has a bit of handle, so it can be held, like a hatchet. I was going to show it to someone else, but I'm showing it to you now. It's that special."

"Why is the curved part so sharp?" asked Wally.

"Your observation is very astute," said Dirk, obviously trying to pander to the poker-faced bogus art broker. "Check out the handle and the bladed edge."

"It's not one of those skull crackers, is it?"

"Not even close. This is one of the most important parts of a medicine man's bundle. It's used by Monster Slayer."

"Never heard of him," said Wally as he glanced at his watch to show his disinterest.

"Wait, let me explain. Monster Slayer is one of the most powerful of the Indian gods. He appears in ceremonies to slay the evil spirits that are harassing the Indians."

Wally picked up the piece. "Gee, maybe I could use something like this."

Dirk went on. "The Indians can't sleep at night unless Monster Slayer is there to protect them. Symbolically, this is his big stick. It's called a *chamajilla,* and it's the only one I have."

"Wow! How much?" asked Wally.

"Eight thousand," said Dirk.

"For a rock!" blurted Wally.

I groaned. While this was about the worst thing to say, Peder saved the day by turning the *chamajilla* over and over in his hands, obviously intrigued.

"I like the meaning of it," he said.

Wally said, "Are you sure? Eight thousand dollars for a rock is a lot. Let's look around a bit."

Peder raised his tone in irritation, pounded his fist on a table, and said bluntly in improved English, "If I say I want something, then I shall have it! Don't bother me about money. Work with Mr. Dirk!"

Peder played this scenario perfectly. In front of DeVries he showed that he was the boss and wasn't interested in Wally's babbling. Wally was definitely out of role on this one. Peder peeled off the cash and handed it to DeVries. He held the ax in his hand and swung it around like he was using it. I sat stunned. While neither of the undercover agents realized it, Monster Slayer had just slipped me his weapon.

CHAPTER TWENTY-EIGHT

The Z-Box clicked off just before Peder and Wally made it out the door of the Spirit Bear Gallery. Wally had managed to convince Dirk DeVries that Peder was very interested in the parrots and bullroarers but needed time to think about buying them. He told DeVries that Peder had to send his pictures to his wife and call her. Peder would be in town for a few days, so there was time.

DeVries had invited the two agents back to the gallery that evening, when he was hosting an antique postcard show. He was holding it to lure the throngs of Indian arts people into his gallery, and he wanted Peder and Wally to be his special guests. They agreed to return to the gallery at seven.

Meanwhile I took the tape Peder and Wally had cut and labeled it as evidence. I congratulated the two of them on the fantastic job they'd done with our target. Dirk DeVries was now chomping at the bit to deal with an FBI agent and a confidential informant, and the irony of it all made me shiver with pure glee.

From the research I'd done, I knew that bullroarers were used by Navajo healers, but I didn't know exactly how they were used. I felt the "calling the gods" story was probably part truth and part fiction. But the black substance made from ashes of a tree struck by lightning was considered a powerful symbol, and I could see why. *Chamajillas* were also part of a Navajo *jish* and symbolized the magic hatchet used by Monster Slayer. Peder was smart to buy it, as it was within our budget, and the purchase let Dirk know Peder was serious about sacred Indian artifacts.

Peder went to his room while Wally remained with me and relived his act with Dirk over and over again. He was truly in his glory. We talked about how the rest of the case could now go down like a routine investigation. With the probable cause Peder and Wally had developed, we were in a good position to get a search warrant and seize anything that might be considered evidence. That way we'd get the parrots without having to plunk down a bunch of cash.

Then Wally said, "Man, I couldn't believe how good Dirk was at appraising Indian art. He knew the number for everything. He could tell you how much every one of those pots, rugs, and figurines was worth. He's got hundreds of things. I was really impressed."

"Don't be fooled by his so-called expertise. It's easy to be an expert when there are no comparisons. Remember, there's no legal market for ceremonial stuff, so his so-called appraisals are nothing more than what he thinks he can get out of someone."

"Yeah, but did you hear the money he was talking—millions of dollars!"

"I'm sure," I said as I went to the door to let Peder in.

"I'm sorry to have such bad news," said Peder, looking solemn.

"What is it?" I said, fearing something very serious had happened.

"I must report back to Oslo. There is a complete shakedown ongoing at my department."

"When do you have to go back?" I asked, nearly in shock.

"Tomorrow morning or even late tonight. Can you manage these arrangements?"

My mind spun with the difficulties of changing a nonrefundable ticket on short notice, on top of the obvious problems Peder's disappearance would have on the case.

"Peder, this is a disaster. Can't your people give you one more day? After all, we spent a lot of money getting you here."

Peder's official side was in full gear. "No. What is going on is serious. Immediately I have to return. I'll begin packing now."

"Wait," I said. "Can you at least go back to the gallery tonight to Dirk's postcard show? I know I can't get you a flight out before then."

"What on earth good could I do there?" asked Peder.

"I want you and Wally to work on your rapport with Dirk. Tell him you have to return to Norway due to an emergency and assure him that you'll be back. Tell him you'll make it up to him. You've got Dirk on the line, so it's just a matter of keeping him there. Tell him how very sorry you are about your business troubles."

"Will Dirk fall for that?" asked Wally.

"Sure, he's extremely hungry for Peder's money. Wally, convince Dirk that Peder is sincere and will be back. Lay it on as hard as you can. You will be back, won't you, Peder?"

"Surely. I want to keep this investigation going."

"Man, this is a bummer," moaned Wally.

"Why do you say 'man' about everything? It's so annoying," said Peder as he abruptly left the room.

In an instant Wally and I were left alone to figure out how to handle the situation at the antique postcard show. Wally would wear his wire and keep the conversation between him and Dirk. It would be hard to record much in a gallery filled with people sipping wine and dripping pico de gallo all over each other. I instructed Wally to keep his conversation with Dirk short and as close as possible. Any agent who had ever recorded anything knew the perils of excessive background clutter.

"Should I hit him up for a headdress?" asked Wally.

"No. He hasn't offered a headdress, and bugging him about getting you one is on the border of entrapment."

"Well, shit, he's selling everything else. I don't think asking for a headdress would be out of line. Someone like Peder would die for a real Indian headdress."

"Okay," I said just to get off topic. "When Peder comes back from Norway, we can talk about it. It might be worth at least bringing up. But our focus is still on illegal artifacts."

I rushed to the phone to call my supervisor at home at nine Eastern time, to get approval to change Peder's airline tickets. Changing tickets wasn't even allowed under government rules, but since this was an under-cover operation, rules could be bent and I would be able to do it.

Right around seven that evening, Peder and Wally returned to the Spirit Bear Gallery. Just over an hour later they were back. Wally handed me the digital tape he'd cut and said, "It's all set. I told Dirk we'd both be back in October. He's not happy."

"I guess when you chew on greed all day, patience doesn't go down well," I said.

Just before they went back to the gallery, Wally's wife called him and said that Hurricane Hugo was breaking loose in southeastern Pennsylvania. Apparently water had intruded through the sheetrock and she wanted him home. Quickly we decided that the undercover agents would head to the airport in Albuquerque that night and take a flight to the East Coast. Peder would continue on to Oslo. Meanwhile I packed up and went home, only to sit up half the night listening to the antique postcard show that had just been held in Santa Fe.

As expected, even with high-quality earphones, listening to the tape was like trying to understand a scratchy radio signal punctuated by laughing cows. Deepening my concentration, I picked up Dirk's voice as he welcomed Peder and Wally like old friends. According to plan, Peder drifted off to look at the postcard display and mingle.

"Look," said Wally, speaking quickly. "Peder's got an emergency going in Norway. He's leaving tonight, but he wants you to know that he's interested in the parrots and the bullroarer."

DeVries: Shit! What the . . . garble, garble, garble.

"No, no, it's not that. It's just this guy owns his own business and wants to be in control of everything. I know this man, and he's completely trustworthy. In fact, if you work with me, I'll get him back here a lot. I found out he's got North Sea oil money. That's a lot of reindeer, man."

Dirk sounded irritated. "Look, it isn't very often that clients with, you know, the right attitude come along. Don't you lose this guy!"

"No, I won't. That's what I'm sayin'. He's so good, we can notch the price up and split the extra profits. That way we'll be in business together, but he won't know it."

"Yeah, I like that idea," said Dirk, who I imagined was drooling. "Remember, the key is to generate sequential deals—one after the next. Got it?"

"No problem. Look, I'm already an expert in appraising masterpieces and Civil War memorabilia, but I don't know squat about Indian stuff. You've got that. Together we could really do a bang-up business. It'd be an East plus West kind of thing worth millions. How cool is that?"

I turned off the recorder and backed it up to listen again to what I'd just heard. Although I had no idea Wally was going to use the tactic of bringing in Dirk as an ally against Peder, I thought it was clever. In fact, I would never have thought of it. With Dirk and Wally working together, we wouldn't lose Dirk—he would do anything to keep Peder buying. But this tactic also had a downside—it was a bit underhanded.

I'd told Wally not to ask about eagle feather headdresses, since we were mainly after sacred artifacts. But he did it anyway. Dirk said that headdresses were hard to get, but he had a friend, code name Sam, who had one for around $260,000, but only if the seller was assured that the piece would be leaving the United States. Quite appropriately, Wally asked about the provenance. Dirk explained that it was an 1875 Cheyenne historical piece that had been bought and sold many times on the black market. Sam was ready to part with it because he feared legal trouble if he ever got caught with it. Dirk explained that, by law, eagle feathers acquired prior to 1942 could be legally possessed but not sold.

Then he said, "We'll write it up as a gift to cover the sale."

I turned off the recorder to make some notes and get a glass of water. When I began listening again, I jumped when the microphone nearly exploded in my ear.

Dirk was screaming, "Hey you, come over here. I want you to meet some people. This is Wally, my new partner from the East Coast. And over here is Peder; he's from Norway. Come here, Peder, meet one of my guys. I told you about him; he's the one with the Indian friends."

I struggled to hear the stranger's voice and was loath to think that I'd have to figure out who this guy was later—which would be very difficult.

"Yeah, nice to meet you," said Wally. "Say, we've got planes to catch in Albuquerque, so we're in a hurry. Come on, buddy, let's go."

The pocket recorder rustled against Wally's clothes as he moved through the crowd. Then it stopped and the stranger's voice picked up much more clearly. "Hey, I uh, I heard about you and your Swedish friend being in town."

"He's from Norway," said Wally, "but go on."

"Well, if you're ever back, come see me. I get better things than Dirk. You see, I'm allowed on the reservations, and the people, well, they trust me. Maybe we could do some business, but I'd have to keep it separate from the gallery. If you know what I mean."

"Sure," said Wally casually. "I'll think about it. So, what's your name?"

"Tony. My phone number is on this card. Here, keep it."

CHAPTER TWENTY-NINE

Tony was back! I had been trying to figure out a way for Peder and Wally to meet Tony, but he came to us! This was a significant development, as now I could show that Tony and Dirk were definitely connected. I listened to the entire tape several times until I got a headache from all the irritating background noise. Now that Wally had met Tony, he could work him to find out exactly who Tony was buying or stealing from on the reservations. It would be a little tricky working both Tony and Dirk at the same time. The key would be to work quickly before Dirk found out the team was also buying from Tony.

For the next several weeks Dirk badgered Wally on his undercover cell phone to find out when Peder was returning to Santa Fe. Wally was under a lot of pressure, keeping Dirk at bay while he kept up with his other casework and worked on the flood damage done to his house. Wally managed to tape all his conversations with Dirk, reminding him that Peder was coming back and was worth so much money and that it was important to keep him happy for future deals.

One day Dirk called Wally in a panic. He had sent Peder an article about Native American paraphernalia at the post office box noted on Peder's business card. Two weeks later, the envelope was returned as undeliverable. "No such address."

Dirk was seething with suspicion as he screamed into the phone things like "Who is this Norwegian anyway? Is he for real?" Finally, "If I find out you guys are trying to scam me, someone's gonna get hurt! Do you understand?"

At the time Wally had no idea that Peder had rented a post office box in Oslo and had no idea that the box number on his business card was wrong. Apparently Peder hadn't double-checked the print job, and now the mistake had landed squarely in Wally's lap. Once again, Wally's ability a sell a boat in the desert convinced Dirk that this sort of thing always happened with international mail. He made a joke that the

US Postal Service people probably didn't even know where Norway was even located, and said things like "Maybe they sent your letter to Monga Ponga—wherever the hell that is."

Regardless, the incident put Wally in a tough spot. Desperate to keep an important defendant, he promised that he and Peder would be in Santa Fe by Halloween—only three weeks away.

When Wally called me with the news, I shrieked, "Why in the hell do you make promises that I can't keep! I can't get Peder here that soon."

"Just call him," said Wally. "He'll come back if you ask him. Besides, he's the one who made the mistake on the address, so he needs to correct that. I'm getting jammed up and it's not my fault."

The mistaken address was about to make the whole case implode. I hung up the phone and waited until the next day when I could catch Peder in his office. To my surprise, Peder answered on the first ring. I explained the situation involving the wrong address and that we were about to lose Dirk. Peder said he was too busy to travel on short notice. He was sorry for the mistake but said that traveling to the States was impossible. Once again he wouldn't tell me why, for high-level national security reasons. I felt completely helpless.

Meanwhile Dirk DeVries was starting to smell a rat and was slipping away. We had to do something to keep him on board with Wally and Peder. I was concerned that Dirk would start moving evidence that he had in his gallery. I especially didn't want to lose the sacred parrots. Although it would be a hard swallow financially, I told Wally to call Dirk and tell him that Peder couldn't travel now but would buy the parrots as a gesture of goodwill.

"Negotiate with him the best you can," I said. "Get him to send them to you in Philly—you're Peder's broker and will make sure he gets them. Dirk is getting too nervous with all the inconsistencies he's been handed."

"We got the money to do this?" asked Wally.

"In fact, we do. I've been selling some of Dana Delaney's inventory she bought at an auction. She's made a nice profit on everything she bought. We can make it work. But no bullroarers."

"Shit," said Wally, "I hate paying Dirk for this stuff he probably paid little or nothing for. Hopefully this will be the last buy we'll have to make."

Wally called Dirk and tried to make a deal on the sacred parrots, but Dirk insisted that the seven bullroarers be included in the deal. He argued that Peder obviously liked them and that they were becoming extremely rare, as the Navajo spiritual leaders were hanging onto their bundles more than ever. Wally and Dirk haggled back and forth until they finally agreed on $35,000. This was a lot of money, but the chances were good that we'd get it back after Dirk was busted and found guilty. This buy would provide solid evidence against Dirk, but I still wanted everything he had in his studio and his house. To get this we needed to update our probable cause for a search warrant. Peder had to come back.

Wally paid Dirk with a certified check drawn on his undercover business bank account. He called me and said that Dirk was more ecstatic than he'd ever been before. He talked of future deals to capture Peder's money and then building a partnership with Wally in the near future. He saw millions of dollars coming his way and relished the idea of exploiting Peder to get it.

Wally was doing a terrific job, and my dismal opinion of him was changing. The situation with Dirk had been difficult and intense, but Wally was handling him like a pro and was putting up with a lot from the annoying art dealer in Santa Fe. For the first time in this investigation I found respect for Wally, in spite of his sometimes childish nature.

CHAPTER THIRTY

It was a rare misty morning in Albuquerque when Wally called and told me that he had just received an e-mail from a woman curator at the University of Pennsylvania. She had come across someone on the Internet offering to sell a war bonnet once worn by the Apache warrior Geronimo. The ad was rather cryptic and went like this:

> SUBJECT: *Authentic Geronimo headdress one million dollars, serious inquiries only. The headdress is for out of country sales only—serious international inquiries only.*
>
> *Contact:*
> *Richard.**

In a long-winded phone call, Wally told me he had called "Richard" and ended up talking to a Marco Romero* who was a car salesman from Marietta, Georgia. Wally asked about the headdress's availability and its provenance. Marco explained that Geronimo had worn the headdress in October 1907, at the Last Powwow commemorating Oklahoma's acceptance into the Union as a state. At that time Geronimo was a seventy-eight-year-old prisoner of war but was allowed to appear at public events—like a circus act. According to Marco, the great warrior had worn this eagle feather headdress at the powwow and later presented it to a half-Cherokee named Jack Moore. Moore in turn gave the headdress to his good friend Lee Walton,* whose grandson C. W. Walton* had inherited the headdress and had kept it mothballed in a trunk for decades. Apparently C. W. Walton was ready to cash in on the headdress and had asked Marco to find a buyer.

Wally asked Marco to send pictures and background information, as he might have an interested buyer in Europe. Wally received the supporting documents at his undercover post office box. Unbelievably, Marco also sent a copy of 16 United States Code 668, the Bald and Golden Eagle Protection Act of 1940, which clearly explained the prohibitions of selling eagle feathers in interstate commerce. This meant the two men from Georgia were operating with full knowledge that they were breaking the law. When the federal prosecutor in Philadelphia learned about this, he nearly leaped for joy.

Wally already had devised a plan in which he and I would do a short buy/bust on these guys in Philadelphia. In fact, he was very excited about doing it and was surprised that I wasn't.

"Why don't you hand the case over to the local US Fish and Wildlife Service in Georgia?" I argued. "They make headdress cases all the time. The point is to get the headdress off the market and then repatriate it to the rightful tribe. We don't need that kind of exposure, especially after all the money we just spent to keep Dirk in the boat. It's too much of a risk."

Wally argued that making the play in Pennsylvania wouldn't hurt our case in Santa Fe. "I'm not gonna pay them a million bucks, of course! But I'll need you out here to play the role of an expert who can authenticate the headdress as being old and make sure that the eagle feathers are real. I don't want to arrest these guys for selling dyed turkey feathers."

"Come on, Wally, a US Fish and Wildlife agent can do a buy/bust in Georgia. Let the local agents handle it. These bozos have openly advertised their desire to sell the headdress and even admitted that it was illegal. This is a slam-dunk case that can be wrapped up in the next few days. Besides, I don't feel right doing something like this while we're working a case on DeVries in Santa Fe. The world of wildlife and Indian crime is small. We could get tripped up in a bad way."

"God, you're paranoid. It'll work out great! Besides, I really want my buddy prosecutor in Philly to handle the prosecution. He'd get a kick out of it. After all, it's Geronimo's headdress! What a wild story!"

I further argued that the two Georgians had initially wanted to sell the headdress within their home state. Normally, violators were charged in the state in which they violated the law. Wally was luring them into another state, which was called "manufacturing jurisdiction." While doing this wasn't illegal, it didn't look good, especially when the only reason for the change was to put on a good political show for the US Attorney's Office and the FBI. As much as I resisted, Wally worked me like one of his targets and convinced me to help him.

———

A few weeks later I found myself in a hotel room at an Embassy Suites near the Philadelphia airport. The FBI had rented two rooms on the third floor that had a door between them. FBI technicians drilled a hole at the baseboard near the door, threaded a wire through the wall, and hooked it up to a lamp that had a camera concealed inside.

"Does the hotel let you drill holes in their walls?" I asked one of the technicians.

He looked up at me from the floor and said, "They don't like it, but we do it anyway."

The efficient technicians quickly set up a video recorder and a monitor in the so-called command-center room where my boss Matt Miller and an FBI supervisor had arrived to watch the action. A dead-serious four-agent arrest squad stood by. This would definitely be Geronimo's last stand.

I was dressed in a pair of tan business slacks and a turtleneck sweater covered with a maroon overshirt. My SIG Sauer 9mm was concealed firmly on my body in a pancake holster. My husband's botany loupe and a pair of latex gloves were my only props. I felt inadequately prepared for this but hoped that my so-called "expertise" would get the job done.

Finally the door was closed, but not locked. Wally and I positioned ourselves in front of the camera and waited. Wally paced the room while he whistled. His arms were planted across his chest. I'd seen this dozens of times on tapes he and Peder had cut.

"You nervous?" I asked.

"I always get buggy before a deal goes down." He shot me a dubious glance and added, "You never know what might happen."

Wally's attitude started to make me jumpy, but I quickly calmed down. This was a simple buy/bust. In my line of work this was standard.

Just before the time when Marco and his buddy were to arrive, Wally's cell phone rang. I could tell from the conversation that it was Marco, who wanted Wally to meet him and his partner in the parking lot. My guess was that they were nervous about going into a hotel room.

"C'mon, I'm waiting for you in room 311," said Wally. "I ain't got all day. My expert is here and she's got some equipment she has to use."

I squeezed my "equipment" in the palm of my hand and fired a fuming look at my partner.

"So, hurry up!" Wally closed the phone, giving Marco no chance to argue. Less than two minutes later there was a knock. Wally opened the door. "Hey, guys! Come on in!"

Two men walked in and took seats next to the table where the hidden camera had been positioned. The larger of the two men, C. W. Walton, was carrying a turn-of-the-century wicker basket, which he set on the floor in front of his feet.

At first glance these two guys looked like polar opposites. C. W. Walton had pasty white skin with a pinkish bulbous nose. Dated, tinted bifocal glasses didn't do much to hide his tired blue eyes, which were pushing sixty-five years. From his background check I already knew he was a lawyer who worked in a small Georgia town where he'd been forever. He had no criminal history.

By comparison, Marco Romero looked like a bookie of some kind. He wore a brown leather jacket, jeans, and leather shoes. At forty-two he was beefy, with thick brown hair that receded, leaving a small point on top of his head. At one time he was probably a smooth and confident guy who chased women with great success, but that was a long time ago. Now he looked slovenly, and as he collapsed in a chair, his knees bounced as if they had rubber in them.

Wally pointed to me. "This is Dr. Susan McIntyre from the University of Pennsylvania; she's an expert on Indian stuff."

Neither man stood up to shake my hand. They acted like they didn't care who I was, even though I stood between them and a million dollars. I just hoped they didn't ask me any questions about a university I'd never stepped foot on.

C.W. started his well-rehearsed spiel. "My grandfather was friends with a half-breed named Jack Moore. Here's his picture." C.W. handed Wally a four-by-seven-inch daguerreotype photograph that was secured inside a plastic sheet protector. Jack Moore was a good-looking man in his twenties who could very well have been half Indian and half white. I took notice of the swirly cursive signature and thought that Jack probably had someone else sign it.

Marco squirmed in his chair while C.W. droned on: "My grandfather was in the oil business out there, and Jack Moore used to come to his home, break down the door in the middle of the night, and sleep off the whiskey. Then two weeks later Jack would be all sobered up and come back and bring him a cow or something. One day he showed up with this headdress and said that Geronimo had given it to him. He wanted my grandfather to have it."

Marco finally broke in. "Geronimo was a prisoner of war but was eventually let out. Toward the end of his life he made his living by selling trinkets, hats, and whatever he claimed he owned. People went nuts over having anything that had to do with Geronimo. Back then he was one famous Indian."

Finally C.W. opened the basket and gently pulled out a bonnet covered with eagle feathers. He had to stand up to get the back trailer loaded with thirty-seven foot-long eagle feathers out. Carefully he moved the piece onto the coffee table we'd cleared off, and I immediately got to work.

"These are definitely feathers from an immature bald eagle," I said confidently.

"Of course they are," said C.W. flippantly, not realizing that he'd just admitted knowledge of the fact that he was selling eagle feathers and not turkey feathers.

I took the loupe and carefully examined the beads on the headband. "These are Venetian glass beads that are consistent with those used around the turn of the century. I see the right colors . . . rose-lined white, mustard yellow, ruby red."

In the middle of my analyses, Wally broke in and asked the sellers what they were going to do with the million dollars headed their way. C.W. said he was going to set up a college fund for his grandkids, while

Marco said he had already made a substantial down payment on a new Lamborghini. Marco's story had all the elements of a midlife crisis, which was just about to take a hard hit. Still scrutinizing the headdress, I could tell that the sellers didn't want me spending too much time with it. It was as if they didn't want me to find something that might blow the deal.

Fingering the headband, I was surprised at the poor workmanship on the piece. While the beadwork resembled a Cheyenne pattern, the wool cloth showed even stitches, as if it had been sewn on a sewing machine. I had read that when headdresses were hot tourist items, Cheyenne women had acquired sewing machines from white women to make headdresses in half the time it took to sew them by hand.

I ran my hand over the trailer and estimated that the feathers from at least three different bald eagles had been used to complete the headdress. It was very possible that the birds had been killed specifically for their feathers, which is why the federal government had stepped in to prohibit the killing of these birds. Killing eagles to make Indian items had been a problem for a very long time. Meanwhile Wally led a brief discussion with C.W. and his broker on how stupid the federal laws were about selling eagle feathers, while I had a conversation with myself about how stupid I felt.

Before flying to Philadelphia I'd done some research on the famous Apache and learned that traditionally Apaches didn't wear eagle-feathered headdress. I uncovered pictures of Geronimo wearing headbands, stovepipe hats, and other headgear just for a picture that he was paid for. I did stumble across one picture of Geronimo wearing a short feathered bonnet, but the eagle feathers were from a mature golden eagle, not a bald eagle. The headdress I was holding was not the same one I'd seen in the old photograph. The sellers did not have any direct evidence that Geronimo ever wore or owned the headdress I was examining. Its contrived legend reminded me of the stories told about the treasures held in Al Capone's vault, which turned out to be empty.

Meanwhile Wally was explaining that his client wanted a bill of sale from C.W. to prevent his descendants from making a claim on the headdress years later. Speaking almost cryptically, C.W. said he'd sell the letter and photograph for one million dollars and would loan the headdress to the buyer for an indefinite period of time.

Out of the blue, C.W. looked at me and said, "I'm sure you're a nice lady, but I don't know you." He didn't trust me, and I didn't blame him.

"Dr. McIntyre, would you mind stepping into the hallway for a minute?" asked Wally.

Quietly I eased out the door and went to the adjacent room where the supervisors and raid team were waiting. I got there just in time to watch as C.W. presented two sales receipts to Wally.

"All bullshit aside," Wally said. "I'll sign this one for the headdress and when she comes back in I'll sign another one for the letter and picture."

My boss Matt Miller leaned toward my ear and said, "They don't trust you. Ha, ha."

"I don't care. The way things are turning out is better for the case. The bad guy is admitting that selling the headdress is illegal and he wants to cover it with a second sales receipt. The fact that he wants to hide this from me shows his extreme culpability."

"I just thought it was funny that they kicked you out," said Matt with a smirk on his face.

I ignored Matt and listened as Wally said, "Before she comes back, between us, how many other people are involved in this? I don't want to get into trouble."

C.W. responded, "No one else knows. Once you get this thing overseas, it ain't never coming back. We understand that, right?"

"That's right," said Wally. "You did the right thing bringing it to me. Okay, I'll let her back in."

"It's time for act two," I said as I left the command center.

Wally met me in the hallway and we went back into room 311. C.W. showed me a sales slip for the picture of Jack Moore and accompanying letter. The amount noted "paid" was exactly one million dollars. As if he was going to issue a check, Wally went to his briefcase and pulled out a manila envelope. Then he turned to the two bunglers and said, "Hey, you guys hungry?"

Instantly the adjoining door flew open and four FBI agents wearing raid jackets burst in screaming, "Hands in the air, you're under arrest. Hands up! DO IT NOW!" C.W. shot his hands in the air as blood drained from his face and his jowls trembled. While C.W. was being patted down, his knees collapsed and he crumpled awkwardly into the chair he'd been sitting in. I worried he was going into shock and told one of the arresting agents to make sure C.W. was okay before moving him. Meanwhile Marco had been patted down and was already in handcuffs. Tears filled his eyes, and abject fear seemed to consume him as he babbled that he didn't mean to do anything wrong. I wondered if he was more worried about losing his freedom or his car.

For me, the whole arrest scene was overkill. This was not a dangerous drug bust, but the FBI treated it like one. The sellers deserved to be caught, but I didn't agree with all the drama. I'd arrested dozens of people for wildlife crimes and always treated them with professional respect as long as they behaved. The Georgians needed to be stopped, but they didn't deserve this kind of trauma.

The FBI agents collected the evidence, and we all headed downtown to the federal courthouse. C.W. and Marco appeared before a federal magistrate and were arraigned. They both pled not guilty and were released on their own recognizance. Meanwhile Wally was busy working the phones to line up a press conference the FBI had announced for that afternoon. I kept telling Wally that we had no proof that the headdress had ever belonged to Geronimo and I thought that making this claim at a press conference would come back to bite us.

"Listen to me," I insisted. "I've seized Sitting Bull's bustle three times. Crazy Horse's peace pipe is all over the place. For God's sake, Apaches didn't even wear feathered headdresses. We can't make an official claim that this was Geronimo's headdress. We can't come close to proving it."

"Well, you never know, and it's what these two dummies think."

"So, you're taking the word of a couple of money-hungry losers over the truth?"

Wally wouldn't listen. The show had to go on, and I felt like I'd just eaten a rotten meal.

The FBI's local public relations officer was now on board and was riding high on being able to showcase the FBI's remarkable recovery of "Geronimo's headdress." In a conference room at the US Attorney's Office, the PR man hung the headdress on a coat rack and laid the feather-laden trailer out on a table to demonstrate how long it was. Podiums and microphones were set up, and the press flooded in. But to my greatest relief, Wally and I were not paraded in front of the mass of cameras.

That night I left all the craziness behind in Philadelphia and flew back to Albuquerque. The next day I was frantically working on Peder's travel arrangements when Wally called. He told me that Dirk had called him and read a part of an article in a Santa Fe newspaper that reported an undercover agent in Philadelphia had purchased an illegal eagle feather headdress. Two men from Georgia were arrested by the FBI after the sale. Dirk went on to accuse Wally of being the FBI agent mentioned in the article.

"Damn it, anyway," I screamed. "This is bad! I thought something like this might happen. How bad is it? Is your cover blown?"

"Hey, calm down, would ya," said Wally. "I think I got it straightened out—so things are cool now."

"Are you sure? This is a major bungle just when we're so close to hammering Dirk."

"Yeah, everything's cool. Don't worry. It's all on tape."

"Please send it to me overnight. I don't even want to talk about it until I hear the tape."

⌒

It seemed that the only thing working well in my life was FedEx. The delivery man was right on time as he handed me the package at my front door. Inside, I ripped the package open, put the tape inside a recorder, sat at my desk, and braced myself.

The call began with DeVries screaming, "Tell me you're not a fucking FBI agent!"

Wally: "No, man, what are you talking about? I just got back into town."

DeVries: "I'm really wondering about you. It's been in the papers; the FBI busted a couple of turkeys for trying to sell a bonnet they said belonged to Geronimo—which is a bunch of crap because as an Apache Geronimo would have never worn a headdress like that. The Plains Indians wore headdresses. Are you sure you weren't involved in this? You're scaring the shit out of me."

Wally bounced back, explaining all the traveling he'd been doing. He'd been in Peru, Bulgaria, and Paris, working on deals he was brokering. I had to admit, Wally was a great liar. Eventually Dirk sounded calmer. Wally spent several minutes convincing Dirk that someone was using the Internet to sell a headdress that supposedly belonged to Geronimo. Over and over again he said it was a scam. "Remember I told you about this guy and how wacko he was."

"I don't really remember us talking about it, but you may have said something," Dirk admitted.

Finally Wally said, "I did tell you. Look, I could have been caught up in this bullshit, but thank goodness I was out of town."

As I shut off the recorder, my emotions shuttered with the realization that we'd barely survived yet another glitch that could easily have killed the case. I never said a word to Wally over his insistence on buying the headdress in Pennsylvania and what a bad idea I thought it was. Instead I banked on what I'd learned: Wally could still be reckless but had enough Teflon on him that everything bad just slid off. One day I thought his work was terrific and the next day I could strangle him. I wondered what was going to happen next.

CHAPTER THIRTY-ONE

November 29, 1999. I was standing with Peder at the Albuquerque Sunport inside the baggage claim area when his bag came off onto the conveyer belt in two pieces. His clothes flew off the belt and landed everywhere on the floor. I felt horrified—even the man's silky white boxers were in full view. Quickly a hefty baggage handler and I collected Peder's belongings and stuffed them into a large garbage bag provided by the baggage office. Peder stood by obviously disgruntled.

I literally flung the plastic bags into my Ramcharger and drove Peder to a comfortable suite hotel located off South Guadalupe Street in Santa Fe. He had made it clear that he was accustomed to five-star lodgings when he traveled and needed an upgrade from his previous US hotel arrangements. I hoped this hotel would keep him happy—especially after the fiasco at the airport. Peder had also insisted on flying in business class, which gave him a sleeping compartment so he could sleep a full eight hours. He argued that this allowed him to land feeling refreshed and ready to go to work. While this made perfect sense, "keeping Peder" was getting expensive, and I wondered how much time I'd have to spend on my knees begging for forgiveness for breaking government travel rules by overspending on airline tickets and accommodations.

At the hotel Peder and I made several chaotic trips carrying his personal belongings into his suite. As for the room, he said it was better. Not great, just better. Peder picked up one of his shirts and tried to shake out the wrinkles, but it was hopeless. I popped up the ironing board and began ironing shirts. I was on my third shirt when Wally showed up.

After giving Peder a manly bear hug he turned to me at the ironing board. "Are we playing house here?"

"Shut up," I hissed. "The airline demolished Peder's suitcase, and his clothes are a mess. I'm just trying to make things right."

Peder kindly told me I'd done enough ironing. He wanted to start planning our workday. I did too. With iced Cokes to soothe our throats, we sat in the living room area of the suite. I spread my copious case file on the coffee table. Wally had no file or notes. He had been furnishing his bosses with case reports I'd spent days writing, never writing any of his own, which was fine with me. While preparing case reports took days, under these circumstances I didn't want Wally writing reports that contradicted mine. That could kill us in court. Besides, I didn't think he'd keep anything straight.

I began the discussion by pointing out that since Tony Lorenzo had done us the favor of approaching Wally at the Spirit Bear Gallery's postcard show, the only polite thing was for Wally and Peder to pay him a visit. Wally had called Tony the night before and had arranged to drop by Tony's house at three p.m. Since I'd been in Tony's house, I was able to give the undercover agents a full description of what to expect. With the show going back on the road, my spirits were high.

"I think that his really hot stuff is stashed in boxes throughout his place. Keep asking questions so he'll bring out what he has. If he offers anything with feathers on it, buy it. I suspect there's a lot of contraband in that house, which we'll get to eventually with a search warrant."

"How much can we spend?" asked Wally.

"Keep it around eight thousand if you can. Also, be sure and tell Tony to keep his mouth shut about Peder or else you won't do business with him."

"He told me not to tell Dirk if we hooked up," said Wally.

"Well, then, we must be honest about that," added Peder, grinning.

I was beginning to feel giddy. "I love it when crooks devoted to each other turn fickle. This couldn't get any better! Please send Tony my best regards." Just joking, of course.

Wired for sound and video, the duo were now dressed in long pants, business shirts, and light jackets. I readjusted Peder's jacket to cover a wrinkle I spotted in his shirt. Wally smirked at my motherliness.

"Details are important," I retorted.

"Come on, buddy, let's get out of here before she starts combing your hair."

"Just one more thing . . . try and keep Tony in front of the camera. Some of the other tapes show too much of Wally. You're not a movie star.

Also, Wally, your constant whistling is making it harder to transcribe the tapes. Peder, if Tony hands you something, see if you can get it on tape. All we want to see is Tony and evidence. And don't forget to ask him to take Peder to a reservation—like we talked about."

Wally and Peder marched out to the parking lot and got into the flashy red car. As they drove off, I thanked Monster Slayer for giving me another shot at bad-boy Tony. With this new development I hoped that it wouldn't be long before we'd have enough evidence to bury him in it.

—

With the team gone, I slipped out to a trendy luggage store and bought a quality suitcase for Peder. I liked it so much, I wished I had one. Back at the hotel I wrote up the justification I'd need to cover the official purchase. I hoped my paperwork would land on the desk of a lazy bean counter who didn't want to fuss with law enforcement. I was in enough trouble.

Around four-thirty that afternoon, the team came through the door of Peder's room screaming victory. Peder's camera bag even had something wrapped in tissue paper in it.

"I'll set up the monitor. I want to see this before the tape even cools down," I said.

"Man," said Wally. "What an idiot that guy is. He can't be Indian; he's got a New York accent, for God's sake. And what an ego! He thinks he's the god of hot shots."

"I know this guy, and you've got him pegged spot on," I said. "He's definitely not an Indian. I checked with the BIA and he's not registered with any tribe."

"Here," said Peder. "We bought this. Tony said it is for warriors. Is that right?"

The item they had purchased was a seven-inch arrowstick. The shaft above the point was wrapped with string to hold five feathers. The first was an eagle feather. The two largest were tail feathers from a red-tailed hawk. The middle feather was wild turkey, and the last one was a blue Amazon parrot feather.

Wally said he was impressed with my feather identification skills. "Do they teach you that in fishy-wildlife school?"

I ignored him and turned on the tape. The first image was of Wally's round stomach filmed about ten feet from where Peder had set the camera bag. Wally's arms were folded in a closed position across his chest—once again something savvy undercover agents never do. There was little to no background noise except for a faint whistling sound.

After the introductions were made, Tony faced Peder and said, "I can't exactly place your accent. Where are you from?"

"Norway. Would you like a mint?" Peder thumbed a mint from a wrapper that had Norwegian writing on it and offered it to Tony.

"Sure. What should I say, *danke?*"

Peder laughed. "That's German."

"Well, I'm close, aren't I?"

"Not bad," said Peder, putting the package of mints in his pants pocket.

"Hey, these are really tasty," said Tony, smacking his lips.

"And what about you?"

"I'm Italian."

"Ah, Italy. I've spent some time in your country."

"Oh, I'm not from Italy. I mean I wasn't born there. I'm actually part Apache."

"Interesting," replied Peder.

Tony, who was eating up the attention he was getting, launched into his often repeated spiel about his credentials as a person who could be trusted to find authentic Indian material that no one else could. Unfortunately I couldn't catch all of what Tony was saying.

I looked at Wally. "Why do you whistle all the time?"

"It calms me down. That a problem?"

"Yes, it is. I can't hear Tony. What's he yakking about?"

Peder turned off the recorder and explained to me that Tony was bragging about being the only person who was allowed on the reservations, which was why he had the most authentic Indian paraphernalia used in secret ceremonies. Tony claimed that all the tribes trusted him—especially the Navajos because he had a Navajo girlfriend. I'd heard all this before, of course, and figured that the reason Tony could talk so much was because he repeated everything over and over again.

Peder turned the tape back on and the viewing became a little better. Wally was still in the picture, this time pacing back and forth, but Peder was examining artifacts right in front of the camera. I got a good look at several cylinder kachina dolls with painted faces, a four-hundred-year-old ceramic bowl that Tony claimed was used to hold sacred corn pollen inside a kiva, and several wooden hair ties decorated with eagle, parrot, and turkey feathers. According to Tony, the hair ties were worn during religious ceremonies and the feathers connected with the warrior energy in the sky to make the dancer stronger.

I thought Tony's Indian "expertise" was as pathetic as it was tragic. His interest in Native American spirituality could only be measured in cash. He sold sacredness without the slightest compunction about helping to disintegrate a culture formed by some of the earliest people in the region, whose lives revolved around the organic rubrics of the universe. Tony was running a terrible scam. But I took comfort in the fact that we were onto Tony and he wouldn't be in business for long.

As the tape rolled, Tony brought out a plain cardboard box filled to the brim with stone fetishes. I stopped the tape and explained to Peder that these fetishes weren't carved by electric drills but were made by hand by Indians. They began as found rocks that, to the eye of the finder, resembled an animal or even a person. The finder would refine the rough form with a knife until it took on the shape of a bear, coyote, fox, badger, or human. The eyes always consisted of tiny turquoise stones, and some had zigzag arrows carved into them. In the final creation, a spiritual leader would blow life into the fetish and declare it to possess living energy consistent with the animal it represented. The art form and tradition of fetishes came from prehistoric times.

Finally Peder asked me, "Why does Mr. Tony have so much of these? That doesn't seem right."

"I don't know where he's getting them. But it's obvious he'll sell them to anyone who will open his wallet. I wouldn't mess with a fetish from another person. The Indians believe that they come with spiritual baggage that could be harmful. It's okay to take one as a gift, but it's not okay to take one under bad circumstances."

"Mr. Tony is facing bad spirits, I'm sure. Don't you think? But wait, take a listen."

Tony was now in front of the lens holding a fetish that had been carved into a humanoid figurine. Indeed, it had a large head with big owl eyes that were dotted with turquoise pupils. Tony explained that he had several of these and believed they had been carved to resemble space aliens that still appear in New Mexico and Arizona from time to time.

"You see these carved on canyon walls where nobody goes," he said. "They're spooky little guys, but I'm the only one who has them."

Peder and I looked at one another and poured out belly laughs. Peder spoke first. "How far do you carry this theory?"

While Peder and I were absorbed in analyzing the tape, Wally sat wedged into the corner of the couch, his arms planted on his belly, watching the television set with a blank stare. He was in an avoidance mode, but I didn't know why. On the tape, I could now hear Peder talking directly to Tony. Only Tony's Hawaiian shirt and right arm were visible on the screen.

"You can't show these marvelous things to just everyone, can you?" asked Peder.

"No, I have to be careful. Those of us in the business watch out for one another. In fact, we just ran off a federal agent who was snooping around."

Peder reeled backward. "How could you know such a thing?"

Tony's chest swelled. "All of us dealers know Garry Sullivan. He's a retired FBI agent and he told us. Her name was Dana Delaney—you know, like the movie star."

Peder raised his voice and said, "This is astonishing! I don't believe it!"

"It's true," said Tony. "Garry doesn't like women who carry badges. After I ran her off, she just disappeared. Good thing or she might have ended up dead by now. She was a looker, though, and I thought about hitting on her." Tony laughed. "Now I'm glad I didn't even try."

Wally's response sounded something like "Looks like we just slipped by—" but I slammed the off button before his sentence could be finished.

Shooting up out of the chair, I walked over to Wally and screamed, "Why didn't you tell me about this!"

"We thought you should hear from the tape . . . you know, not from us. We figured Tony was bullshitting, you know, like he always does," muttered Wally.

Meanwhile a short breath stalled in my lungs, and I thumped my chest just enough to get air moving again. Wooziness invaded my brain like a virus, and my body simply froze in place. The treachery of the FBI hit me that hard.

Peder shook me gently. "What is wrong? Are you okay?"

I plopped into a sofa chair. "Shit, no, I'm not okay."

"Why are you so upset?" asked Wally as he squirmed on the couch. "So some idiot said you were a cop. It's not like he really knew. Maybe you were competition and he wanted to blow you out. I mean, you didn't get hurt or anything."

I paused to measure my words carefully. "Listen to me. Tony said a guy named Garry Sullivan was the leak. Well, I know who Garry is. He's an FBI agent who retired the same week I started hitting the galleries as Dana Delaney."

"So how does this Garry know what you look like?" asked Peder, who sounded genuinely concerned.

My eyes were still drilling through Wally, and my words felt like exploding spit. "I met the son-of-a-bitch at his retirement party." I lowered my voice and added, "Excuse my language, Peder."

"That's quite all right. I'm on top of what you're saying."

Then I continued. "I could tell from the get-go that this bottom feeder had no use for me."

"This is astonishing!" said Peder, his booming voice thundering inside the room.

I was both surprised and suspicious over how calm Wally remained. "Listen," he said. "Shit happens. So I say, let's just keep moving and get this over with. We have to finish Tony and Dirk off."

"Yeah, we'll keep going," I said. "But this fart by the FBI means we need to finish up in hurry. Eventually Sullivan will find out about you two, and then he'll rat you out. Sullivan changes everything."

Wally walked over to me and put his arm around my shoulder. "Everything will be fine. Peder and I will catch these two thugs, and you'll be happy."

"Right now, I'm just pissed. Is there anything else that's important on the tape?" I asked. "I need to get going. It's my anniversary and I should at least be home for that."

"Yes," said Peder. "Here is a camera picture Tony let me take. I told him I wanted to show it to my wife."

The still photograph showed Tony holding up the ceremonial kirtle worn by a dancer of the Snake Clan of the San Ildefonso Pueblo.

"How were you able to get Tony to pose for this?"

"I just asked him. Politely, of course, but as you might notice, he's not happy about it."

"To get a crook to pose with contraband is unbelievable. You're very good, Peder," I said.

Wally piped up and said, "You'll be pleased to know that Tony is taking Peder and me to a pueblo tomorrow morning. Peder insisted that he wanted to meet a real medicine man, and Tony fell for it."

I perked up. "Hey, that's great! Which pueblo?"

"Uh, I think it's the Eslet . . . does that make sense?"

"The Isleta," I said. "It's about fifteen miles south of Albuquerque."

"Is it safe?" asked Peder.

"I think so; just don't go anywhere in Tony's truck. Have your own wheels—take the red car, but stay with Tony. Be sure and get this so-called medicine man's name, and get a picture of him if you can. He may be one of Tony's suppliers. There's no doubt that Tony is getting help from the inside. I'm sorry, but it's too risky to get you any backup. It's wide-open country out there, and the tribal members are liable to run down whites they don't know. As much as I hate it, you'll be on your own."

"We'll manage," said Peder.

"Just do your business and leave," I said to reassure them, even though I wasn't so sure myself. "Let's meet up back here tomorrow afternoon. I'll want to debrief you on what happened at the Isleta and plan our next move. We need to step things up."

I put on my coat, grabbed my bags, and headed toward the door. "Good luck at the pueblo," I said as I let the door slam behind me.

I jumped into my Ramcharger, cranked the engine, and headed south on I-25 to Albuquerque. I don't remember much of the fifty-mile drive, as my mind was screaming mad over the unbelievable treachery of a former FBI agent. The puzzle was quickly solved. Sullivan was an avid antique collector. Several antique shops intermingled with antique Indian art galleries on Canyon Road. The shop people and their customers were like a coffee klatsch. They talked and gossiped all the time. Sullivan only had to tell *one* person about me and the word would have traveled faster than a barn fire. But I was sure that my undercover role was a titillating topic in Santa Fe that everyone enjoyed at my expense. And I didn't even know it.

I squeezed the steering wheel. Damn that miserable jerk! He was supposed be on my side. Instead he took the dark side—the evil side that was out to destroy a mission to save Native American spirituality. I was almost home when I felt Monster Slayer slipping a plan into my mind.

CHAPTER THIRTY-TWO

December 2, 1999. I dressed in my courtroom clothes, which consisted of tan dress pants, a white shirt, and a navy blue jacket. I always wore an American flag pin on my lapel. My gun and my badge rode comfortably on my belt.

The night before, I'd called FBI special agent Scott Wilson and told him that I wanted to meet with him and Garry Sullivan. I made it sound like I needed to talk to Sullivan about an old case in which his name had popped up. No big deal. As an aside I mentioned that I also wanted to update Scott on the Indian artifacts case. I figured Sullivan wouldn't be able to stay away from a meeting like this one. I also thought about Scott, and why he had backed out of the investigation early on. He and Garry were good friends. Maybe Scott felt like he'd told Sullivan more than he should have and was worried that things would eventually blow up. I didn't let on that they almost had.

As furious as I was about my cover deliberately being blown by a fellow law-enforcement officer, I didn't tell a soul. I didn't want or need any advice. Monster Slayer had said that evil originates in the minds of evil people. He said it was critical that it be eliminated to maintain balance in the world. I couldn't let this evil go unchecked. I had to confront it in order to squash its power.

The oversized tires on my four-wheel-drive spit gravel from the orange barrel sites in all directions as I zoomed north on I-25. For the full hour's drive my ferocity seemed to have no limits. I charged La Bajada Hill faster than Geronimo's raiders. I felt like an eagle that had just landed on fire. Over and over I mentally rehearsed the verbal thrashing I was about to give the FBI. This might not help my career, but I didn't care. I had decided that something very evil had to be made right, even if it involved taking on the biggest and most powerful law enforcement agency in the world. After all, I had the tape, and it was my big stick.

I parked in the public parking lot across the street from the US Post Office building, where the FBI hid out in plain sight. At the office I was buzzed in right away, which meant I'd been there too often. Even the clerks knew I was an undercover agent. I marched directly into the conference room, where I saw three FBI agents sitting at the conference table next to each other. Arrayed in a phalanx like Roman soldiers were special agent Scott Wilson, retired agent Garry Sullivan, and senior resident agent Rick Ferris,* the local supervisor.

Introductory preliminaries took almost no time before I plunged into the malevolence I was there to confront. "Listen to this tape. It's less than thirty seconds."

The tape played, and when it was over everyone except agent Wilson was silent.

"When did this happen?" he asked.

"Yesterday."

"Who's talking?" asked Sullivan.

"Can't tell you," I answered. "This is part of an ongoing investigation that you have no part in."

"Who's listening?" asked Sullivan again.

I shot up from the chair and jabbed a finger in Sullivan's face. "Look, you don't get it. What matters is that you blew my cover while I was actively working in a covert capacity. That's obstruction of justice, which is a felony."

Sullivan puffed out a nervous laugh. "Oh, good grief, everyone knew you were an undercover cop. In fact, I think you're lucky to be alive."

I blurted words soaked in sarcasm: "As if you give a shit about me!"

Sullivan mopped his forehead and turned his face from me. Like a common criminal, he didn't specifically deny what he'd done. He diffused the blame by claiming that hundreds of people already knew I was a federal undercover agent.

He shrugged his shoulders and said, "C'mon, everyone knew," as he tried to make his culpability slide off him like an egg off a rock.

Scott and his boss remained still and silent as the ruins at Chaco Canyon. Nothing moved except nervous thoughts. If Wilson and Ferris tried too hard to cover for Sullivan, their own words might implicate them. If Sullivan's betrayal became a legal issue, they surely didn't want to go down with him.

I leaned across the table and put my face well within Sullivan's personal space. I'd done this before with some pretty sleazy criminals.

"So, how do you suppose *everyone knew*?" My words were mixed with spit.

Sullivan reeled back and tied his arms across his chest like shoelaces. I braced myself—the hard lie was coming.

"You blew it," he said. "One of the Indian art dealers called your office and a woman answered 'New Mexico Game and Fish.' It was you. You see, you screwed up."

With blood pounding in my ears, I felt like the she-wolf about to eat her lunch.

"Your story is bullshit, Garry! I don't work for New Mexico Game and Fish. I don't even go near their office. I work for the US Fish and Wildlife Service. I have the same federal authority as you used to have. No one touches my undercover phone except me. I answer it the same way with my undercover name, each and every time. I work alone, in a secret location. I didn't slip up. You're lying, Garry! You blew my cover and put me in a very dangerous position!"

I plopped back down in my chair and slammed my pen on the table.

Wilson and Ferris watched their own fingers dance on the table, apparently unable to utter a word. It was pathetically obvious that they didn't believe their buddy, yet couldn't abandon him. FBI agents protected each other, but in this case they too were exposed to criminal liability. I sensed that Wilson felt bad about the injustice I'd suffered. His face looked grim and painful. As for supervisory agent Ferris, he drew in his shoulders as if to make himself look like a smaller target. He understood that he could be held accountable for Sullivan's misconduct. He also understood the possible consequences of losing his Crown Victoria, his career, and his pension. No wonder he wasn't fighting me.

Wilson finally pitched in with a stuttering string of feeble words that made him sound like a little kid who had just broken a window.

"I, I can't see Garry doing, doing something like that. Be-besides, he didn't know that much about, about the case. He, he retired right about the time we were getting started."

"I know, Scott. You told him who I was at his retirement party. Remember, I talked to you about it later. I didn't like it then and I really don't like it now."

As if his memory tightened, so did his lips. Meanwhile I was angry at my own inability to fight off my emotions. I had to stay calm and focus on every word the FBI agents uttered. Monster Slayer had my back, and I was ahead in the war of words. None of the agents outright denied my harsh accusations. Instead Sullivan came up with a pathetic theory of how my own carelessness had caused me to go under. As if to bolster Garry's fine character, Wilson mumbled that Sullivan wasn't capable of ratting me out. But there was something wrong here—it was my long experience that innocent people fought like hell when they were being wrongfully accused. Instead of standing up for themselves, these guys took my rage as if they deserved it. I'd seen many guilty people react this same way.

Suddenly Garry Sullivan stood up and raced out of the room toward the door of the FBI fortress. "I've got another appointment," he bellowed as he ran.

This behavior was typical of guilty people who were not under arrest and were free to leave. In Garry's case it was as if he'd been hit with a sudden realization that the more he said, the more trouble he could get into. The atmosphere was getting too hot for him, and his only recourse was to extricate himself from the scene. He couldn't take it anymore.

Garry Sullivan's betrayal put me in a unique position. If I reported Sullivan to the federal prosecutors in Albuquerque, they would go after him for at least obstruction of justice. The tape was that damning. The downside to this was that Sullivan's misconduct had tainted the role of the FBI in the entire investigation. Any half-brained defense attorney would use Garry's actions to impeach the credibility of the FBI in Santa Fe and could even argue that not even Wally could be trusted.

With such serious credibility problems, the US Attorney's Office could drop my case—especially a case in which no one died and the alleged crimes were committed against Indian cultures and dead wildlife, both of which have little political clout. Even though I still had the *chamajilla* that could make FBI careers drop like flies, I had to be cautious. Monster Slayer warned that when fighting monsters, you have to be careful not to turn into one. With the spiritual lives of Native Americans at stake, I refused to let the investigation collapse because of the wretched betrayal by one FBI agent. I would let Sullivan, Wilson, and Ferris worry themselves to death over what I might do. Meanwhile, Monster Slayer and I would carry on in secrecy—but first I had to know one thing.

"Scott," I asked. "Does Garry know about Peder and Wally?"

Scott's pale face flushed the color of a peach. "No! I swear he doesn't. Only agent Ferris here, me, and a guy at headquarters know. With an international informant involved, we've kept this case very quiet."

I wasn't about to let Scott off the hook right away. "You better be telling me the truth, because if there's another leak out of this office, I'll be your worst nightmare. I've got another team out there, and I want you to assure me that they aren't going to be ambushed by one of Garry's friends or anyone else you've talked to."

"I swear," said Scott. "We wouldn't do anything that would jeopardize our own people."

The irony of this statement stung like a scorpion bite, but I let it go. "Good," I said. "I'm leaving now. Let me know if you hear anything that could cause trouble for our guys. Their butts are on the line, and I'm trying like hell to protect them from assholes like Garry."

"No problem," muttered Scott. "Sorry about Garry."

I left the FBI office drowning in trepidation. I hadn't told the FBI agents that at that very moment Peder and Wally were in the most vulnerable situation they'd been in so far. They were alone on a remote Indian reservation with a known crook who knew all about undercover agents. The harsh reality was that this trip could very well turn out to be a trap organized by Tony. With no backup, Peder and Wally could disappear without the slightest trace. Remote Indian lands were like the Alaskan wilderness. What could happen was both unpredictable and unforgiving.

CHAPTER THIRTY-THREE

I headed toward a hotel located near the old Santa Fe train station on Cerrillos Road. (I kept changing hotels so as not to establish a routine that could be traced.) To my greatest relief, I saw the red convertible in the hotel's parking lot. I hadn't even considered that Peder and Wally would be back by now and wondered if for some reason their trip had been cancelled. Or did they have to leave in a hurry?

I didn't bother to check in but went straight to Peder's room, where I found Wally reviewing the photos Peder had taken on his digital camera. The moods of both men were upbeat and I was anxious to hear what they had to say.

"Tell me what happened. I want to hear the whole thing."

Wally spoke first. "We got everything that was on your laundry list. You'll be happy. But man, I gotta tell you that Tony is totally wacko. He couldn't keep his mouth shut long enough for me to even talk to this Indian—all he talked about was how great he is at fooling people."

"We'll see about that," chuckled Peder. "He's the real fool."

"Forget Tony," I said. "I want to know what happened on the reservation with the Indian."

I learned that Tony had met them just outside the Isleta Pueblo and then led the way past a sign that read ISLETA PUEBLO—DO NOT ENTER. Wally and Peder followed Tony's Toyota pickup to a remote part of the reservation, where they stopped at an adobe house with a flat roof and a wooden door painted turquoise. Just from the picture, I estimated that the house had been sitting in the hot New Mexico sun for many decades. But the place had a surreal look lent by the backdrop of stunning red cliffs topped with a mixture of piñon pines and Utah junipers.

According to Peder, a Puebloan man came out of the house and waved to Tony. Tony hopped out of his truck and introduced Peder and Wally to Alfonso—supposedly an important medicine man on the Isleta. Alfonso was alone at the house and didn't invite his guests inside. I took a minute to study the photograph Tony had taken of Alfonso and Peder together. Standing next to Peder, who was just over six feet tall, I estimated Alfonso's height to be about five and a half feet. He had long black hair braided down his back and wore a red headband, a red T-shirt, a blue jacket, and camouflage pants. He also had a fanny pack tied around his waist and tucked beneath his bulging belly. Fanny packs weren't typically worn by Indians, which made me wonder what he was keeping so close to his body.

I took my magnifying glass and examined the picture more closely. "What's wrong with his nose?" I asked. "It's all crooked."

Peder replied, "He broke it in a fight and never got it properly repaired."

Looking at me, Wally asked, "Do you think this guy is really a medicine man?"

"I don't think so. Tony told me about a guy named Alfonso who was one of his main suppliers. I think he's a thief. The day Tony blew me off, he said he couldn't get any good material because Alfonso had died."

Wally laughed. "He don't look dead to me."

"So, Tony lied to you," said Peder, pretending to look put off.

"Amazing, isn't it?" I laughed. "Anyway, Tony claimed that since he had lost his main supplier, he was getting out of the business. But here he is, back in and obviously happy about it. He can't resist messing with Indian stuff. We've got to stop him."

I complimented Wally and Peder on the great job they did getting such good pictures. Prosecutors loved pictures, while crooks hated them. Sometimes it was hard to coax suspects into posing for a few seconds. But in this case their openness was an obvious sign that they would do almost anything to keep Peder and his pesky broker in their company. Meanwhile Tony and his buddy acted like they were on the verge of winning the New Mexico lottery. At one point Alfonso zipped open his fanny pack to reveal a stone bear fetish and offered it to Peder.

"Is fifty dollars enough?" Peder asked.

Alfonso snapped the fifty-dollar bill out of Peder's hand faster than a desert lizard. Over the next few minutes Alfonso bragged that he had special access to sacred items that he would be willing to sell to

Peder—only if Peder kept everything strictly between them. It seemed that stealing from his own tribe was fine as long as he didn't get caught doing it. He also justified his thievery by saying that if the money brought by selling ceremonial objects was used for good things, then the spirits would allow it. Wally and Peder left Tony and the so-called medicine man with the sincere promise that they'd be back in contact to buy more ceremonial artifacts.

I explained to my partners that the contact they had made at the Isleta Pueblo was critical. Tony's suppliers were the missing link in the circle of illegal artifact trade. The circle was now complete at one pueblo, and now we could break it.

Unbeknownst to any of us, while Wally and Peder were at the Isleta Pueblo, Dirk was leaving frantic messages on Wally's undercover cell phone. Apparently Sam, the owner of the 1875 Cheyenne headdress, was now very anxious to sell. Sam had read the article in the Santa Fe newspaper about the FBI's Geronimo headdress bust and was nervous about being caught up in a similar sting operation. The idea of selling the piece to an overseas buyer appealed to him, and he wanted to move forward with a sale to the Norwegian.

All of the messages left by Dirk carried the same ring of panic: "Where the hell are you! Call me, this is important! Call me now!"

Listening to Dirk's messages, the three of us laughed, saying that by now Dirk was probably bouncing off the walls. Wally had to call him back right away. As Wally dialed Dirk's number, I could feel tension gathering in the room.

"Hey, bud, this is Wally. What's your problem? You sound totally wacko." Wally listened for a while and said, "Yeah, I told you we might be interested. But there's no way my client is going to agree to spend that kind of money on something he's never seen. He has to look at it first. Yeah, yeah. I don't blame you for not keeping it at the gallery, so get it somewhere so Peder can see it. Can't we go to Sam's house? No? Oh, I get it, he doesn't want us to know who he is. Okay, gotcha. . . . We'll be there. Calm down, man, we'll be at the restaurant at seven o'clock. . . . Just calm down. You're starting to freak me out! What's the name of the restaurant again? You're kidding, aren't you? The place is called Geronimo's?"

Wally looked straight at me, but I held my reaction to the irony so as not to interrupt the course of his deception. While the intense conversation lasted only a few minutes, Wally looked sapped as he closed his phone.

"Shit, man, dealing in this Indian stuff is worse than rescuing a stolen Picasso." He sipped his Coke and continued. "Dirk wants us to have dinner with him and his wife at this place called Geronimo. He says it's a fancy place and the food is great."

"Wow, Geronimo must be high-dollar," I said, rolling my eyes. "So, what's this dinner all about? There has to be a reason for it."

Wally shook his head. "I can't figure it out, but he wants to introduce us to another couple. I guess they're big-deal collectors in Santa Fe that want to meet Peder. After dinner he'll take Peder and me to his house to look at the headdress."

Peder had been deadly silent until he said, "The other man who will be at the dinner is Sam, and he's checking us out."

"What?" wailed Wally. "Checking us out for what?"

"Peder's right," I said. "These guys aren't stupid. They want to make sure they're not being set up by the two of you. Wally, your credibility with Dirk is sky high, but this mystery Sam is not so sure." I looked at Peder. "Remember, you're a rich guy, so don't react to the big bucks they want for the headdress. Dirk is desperate to get this headdress deal through, so you can hardly make a mistake. Right now, he's blind to everything except for the money he thinks he's getting. I think Sam is one of Dirk's very best friends and clients. Dirk really wants to make this deal go through to keep his friend happy."

Wally and Peder turned even more serious as we talked about the verbal strategy they should use with their dinner companions. I suggested to Peder that he act reluctant at first about buying the headdress, to check Sam's reaction. I told him to ask questions about the authenticity of the headdress. Sam's reaction would tell us something about the level of his involvement in the deal. Overall, I wanted to give Sam the opportunity to convince Peder of the value and legitimacy of the headdress. Later, this would show prosecutors that Sam had a major interest in selling the piece for the money and that he was legally liable.

My comrades retreated to their rooms to rest and get ready for the dinner. Later when the three of us met, Peder made an announcement that I simply couldn't believe.

"Sorry to say this, but there is more trouble going on in Norway. I have to go back. Tomorrow."

"What!" I screamed. "What on earth is going on over there?"

"I can't tell you. National security concerns."

"Peder," I screamed, "don't do this to us! We're getting so close. Make the deal tonight for the headdress and we'll serve the warrants early next week. Can't you stay for that?"

"Noooo," said Peder. "I might can [*sic*] return, let's say . . . let's say . . . in two weeks."

"Whew!" said Wally. "I don't even know if I can wait that long. This is getting old."

"Two weeks is an eternity!" I said in a near-panic voice.

Peder seemed to know what I was going to say next and interrupted me. "Calm down. We'll manage. Besides, Wally can handle this quite alone. I think."

"Oh no!" barked Wally. "You're the big money guy. Dirk won't sell just to me."

I thought Peder was right. Wally could set up the last deal. He'd purchased the parrots from Dirk without Peder. He could set up final buys with Tony and Dirk and then we could serve warrants without Peder. But Wally would have nothing to do with the idea. He argued that the bulk of their credibility was built on Peder's false pretense. Peder couldn't disappear at this point. Wally was totally dependent on Peder and even argued that without Peder his safety would be compromised.

"If Dirk gets suspicious," Wally said adamantly, "it'll be my butt on the line."

I always yielded to Officer Safety. If an agent didn't feel that a particular move was safe, then it couldn't be done. I'd had too many nonparticipants tell me that what I was doing was safe when I felt otherwise. I wasn't going to do that to someone else. Reluctantly I agreed that we'd wait for Peder to return before we'd do the takedown. But this meant that Wally and Peder would have to make additional contacts with both Dirk and Tony to update the probable cause for a search warrant. This had to be done no more than ten days before the warrants were served. This was another stall that could jeopardize the traction of the case. Things were getting worse.

I looked at my watch and noted that it was getting late for the dinner date.

"Look, you guys need to get going. You've got Dirk in your hands, so keep him there. I'll be here when you get back. If things really go to hell . . . well, figure your way out."

"Yeah, that's why we get the big bucks for doing this job," Wally said with his eyes rolling to the ceiling.

There would be no audio recording of the dinner at Geronimo's restaurant. The sensitive recorders would pick up clanging glasses and general background noise that would obscure the dinner conversation to the point where it would be impossible to accurately transcribe it. I said it would be better to have no recording than to have a bad one for lawyers to endlessly pick apart and use against the prosecution. When I wrote my official report documenting the dinner, it would be based entirely on what Peder and Wally reported to me. I hoped this would be enough.

Alone again in a hotel room, the pain in my stomach began to flare up. As usual I took painkillers and lay down on the bed. Worry and dealing with problems all the time was taking its toll. This was serious stuff. If Peder and Wally didn't pass the heavy scrutiny they were about to undergo, the case was once again in danger of going under. I wished Wally hadn't been so insistent on buying a headdress. We could have easily left this alone and been done by now.

CHAPTER THIRTY-FOUR

Just after midnight Peder and Wally were back. Tired, to be sure, but still willing to be debriefed while I took notes. As I had figured, Sam was really William (Bill) Silverjack.* He and his wife, Janice*, wanted to meet Peder, the exotic and wealthy collector of high-end Indian artifacts. Courteous and gracious, they were obviously longtime friends of Dirk DeVries and his wife, Bonnie.* In fact, Dirk described Silverjack as someone who had been with him during the "Indian wars with the government."

Wally and Peder didn't know that Dirk was referring to a decade earlier when Silverjack was indicted for buying and selling Navajo *jish* items, eagle feathers, and kachina dolls decorated with protected bird feathers. His collection was confiscated by the FBI and the National Park Service, after which he'd pled guilty and paid a fine. Silverjack's name and illegal activities peppered numerous government intelligence reports, all of which I'd read.

To defend against the barrage of burning personal questions by his dinner companions, Peder said he filled the time with stories of the ancient culture of Sami reindeer herders on the Finnmark mountain plateau. He told his guests that it gets so cold that in an instant snow particles turn to ice on one's face. These traditional herders endured centuries of hardship as they cared for their herds and raised their families. The handmade awls and other implements made by these people were prized by collectors. Peder talked about this migratory culture's shelters, which closely resembled the tepees used by Indians in North America. According to Wally, Dirk's wife, Bonnie, was totally enthralled with her husband's client and asked if Peder could bring her a reindeer hide the next time he visited. He promised he would.

Peder filled more time by explaining in detail his collection of artifacts looted from Viking graves. He described a noblewoman who was interred in the year 834 inside an ornately carved seventy-foot Viking ship. Carts, slaughtered horses, and dispatched servants were buried with her, so she could maintain her position of prestige in her next life. Peder claimed to have centuries-old silver and bronze inlaid swords, a copper-plated box, and a gold-and-silver circular brooch his ancestors used to fasten their cloaks—all legally protected Viking grave items.

Later Wally reported that everyone at the dinner was mesmerized by Peder's extensive knowledge of Norse history and of his country's indigenous peoples. They genuinely found Peder fascinating even as he admitted that much of his collection consisted of grave items that are protected by the government. In the end, he echoed the attitude of his dinner mates: "If collectors don't protect historical items, who will?"

In a side conversation DeVries told Wally that in Silverjack's opinion there was no way the FBI would go to the trouble of sending a Norwegian informant to set Dirk up. Silverjack gave DeVries his approval to do business with Wally and his intriguing client, but he never said outright that he was the owner of the 1875 Cheyenne headdress. Unfortunately, the headdress was never discussed at the dinner. Silverjack maintained his stalwart wariness.

Dirk, his wife, and the two undercovers left the restaurant and went to Dirk's home on a quiet street in old Santa Fe. As expected, the home was decorated nicely with Spanish colonial furniture, fine Navajo rugs, and exquisitely carved kachina dolls. Dirk led his clients into his home office and opened the lid of an old Spanish-style wooden trunk. The magnificent Cheyenne eagle feather headdress lay inside.

In his resonant baritone voice, Peder issued an *aaah* to express his profound feelings at finally seeing something so extraordinary. The magical moment was lost in an instant when Dirk's cell phone rang. Irritated, Dirk glanced at the number and for some reason felt compelled to leave the office to answer it. Wally surmised that the call was from Silverjack checking on how things were going. While Dirk was out of the room, Peder quickly positioned his camera to take a picture of Wally lifting the headdress out of the trunk. Later this photograph would serve as critical evidence of the illegal $160,000 offer for sale taking place in the home of Dirk DeVries.

When Dirk returned, Peder expressed sheer delight at buying such a historically important Indian artifact. While Dirk salivated over the prospect of being paid an enormous sum, Peder explained that he couldn't buy the headdress that night and that he wanted something legal to cover the illegal sale. Dirk said he had a legal bow-and-arrow set in his gallery. He said he'd increase the cost of that item to cover the illegal headdress.

"I have to talk to my wife more about such money. You understand, I hope." Peder added that he was leaving the following morning for Norway but would return to Santa Fe in January of 2000 to finish the deal. Dirk's reaction was a roller coaster of emotions. While he seemed thrilled that Peder was willing to part with so much money, he was agonized that Peder was making him wait.

Wally now had his body wire on and recorded Dirk saying to him in private, "Look, I feel like I'm being jerked around and I don't like it. You said Peder was good for his promises. I'm pissed, and I want you to make this deal happen tonight. All this bullshit is fucking ridiculous! If there's something wrong, tell me right now!"

Wally could feel the whole deal was on the verge of collapsing. Dirk had been built up and now was being shot down. He wasn't taking it well and seemed near to backing out.

Wally pressed Dirk to remain patient. "Look, keep your eye on the prize. Peder is worth the sequential deals that you want in a client. He's just feeling some pressure right now. Let him go home and talk to his wife. All hell has broken loose at his business, and he's got to get that straightened out. He'll come back, I can promise you that. I've got a lot in this too, and I'm on your side. I'll make it all work—just be patient. Think about it. Two weeks isn't that long."

Dirk's face flushed as he used his finger to poke at Wally's chest. "I don't want him leaving the country before paying us."

Wally tried to lighten the mood with a laugh. "Oh, he'll be back. I'll make sure of it. He owes me money too." A second later he added a stern precaution. "Keep your mouth shut and don't piss him off. Don't let him know you're mad."

Wally had masterfully turned the tables. A few minutes later at the front door Dirk put his hand on Peder's shoulder. "Don't worry about it, I understand. We can talk some more. I have more material I can show you when you come back. You'll be very pleased."

"You're very kind," responded Peder. "I'll be back soon. So, we can take our time?"

Back in the hotel with me Wally said, "Dirk agreed, and that's basically how it all went. It was nerve-wracking as hell because the ball kept moving."

I looked at Peder and Wally with misty eyes. "You guys went through a lot tonight. Silverjack is a very suspicious man, and yet you were able to convince him that you were real and then stall Dirk. You did a fantastic job. I really mean that. I'll starting working on the affidavits for the search warrants in the morning. I've already told the US Attorney's Office that we're getting close, so they'll be ready."

The next morning I drove Peder to the airport for his flight to Norway. Later that day Wally Shumaker boarded a plane to Philadelphia. I was alone now and would soon find myself acting as a dizzy ringmaster trying to coordinate three federal agencies and a dozen agents in the takedown of our targets, Dirk DeVries and Tony Lorenzo.

CHAPTER THIRTY-FIVE

We now had legal probable cause to search the Spirit Bear Gallery and the residence of Tony Lorenzo. We couldn't go to Dirk's house, since he'd told Wally that he'd moved the headdress to his gallery. I didn't truly expect that Dirk would keep contraband at home. A smart man wouldn't put so much at risk.

Throughout the investigation I had additional suspects I had wanted Wally and Peder to check out, but we simply didn't have time. Besides, the longer the investigation continued, the more vulnerable we'd be to leaks and mistakes. The case couldn't survive many more hits. Dirk and Tony rose to the top from the very beginning, so it was natural to focus on them. Meanwhile, Assistant US Attorney Rainey Swanson* took on the case with vigor and wrote the affidavits required to support the warrants.

To my despair, problems arose at every turn. Peder's availability changed twice, as did the availability of several members of the search team. It was impossible to make the two-week deadline we'd promised Dirk. Wally carried the burden of keeping Dirk waiting, as patiently as possible, but it was becoming more difficult by the day. Wally, however, was doing what he did best—convincing the bad guys to see things his way. I'd never seen anyone do it better.

As good as Wally was, both Dirk and Tony continued to pester him with phone calls demanding to know when Peder would be back. At one point Tony said he had just acquired a 150-year-old parfleche, a tanned buffalo hide container, which was used by Puebloan spiritual leaders to hold their sacred objects. Lorenzo insisted that it was clearly a ceremonial piece and that he'd hold it for $16,000, but not for long.

Meanwhile Dirk had somehow heard that Tony had taken the undercover agents to the Isleta Pueblo. In one phone call to Wally he screamed, "Don't buy anything from Tony! He sells fakes! Don't screw around with him or it'll mess up our business relationship." In another phone call Dirk told Wally that he had something extra special for Peder when he returned. "Your client won't be able to resist this. I'll show it to him when he gets here. You won't believe your eyes when you see this—it's totally priceless."

When I heard this, my gut simply gnawed. We had to stop these guys before they did more damage. Our constant delays only gave Tony and Dirk more time to steal or buy more rare artifacts to sell to Peder. This could come back to haunt us in court. A defense attorney could claim that the defendants were able to continue their pillage because of my failure to shut them down. Popping pills to ease the relentless pain I was having, I set a drop-dead date for a takedown. Fortunately, Peder was able to make yet another trip across the ocean.

———

January 18, 2000. I rented a large suite at one of the better hotels in Santa Fe. The suite would serve as the command center for the takedown operations. The two bedrooms would be occupied by my supervisor, Special Agent in Charge Matt Miller, and Wally Shumaker. The rest of the team, including me, would stay at a smaller hotel nearby.

Miller wanted to be present at the takedown as an observer, but I diplomatically explained that I needed working agents and put him on the team assigned to search the Spirit Bear Gallery. He had been nitpicking me over my case management to the point that I wanted him to see for himself how difficult covert investigations really are. He agreed to participate and just asked that he be given light duty.

Throughout the day, two teams of five federal agents assembled at the command center. They were from the US Fish and Wildlife Service, the FBI, and the National Park Service. Team #1 would search Tony Lorenzo's house. I'd carefully solicited Jemez Pueblo chanter F. Shando* to assist this team with identifying sacred Indian material that would be seized. Thirty-five-year-old Shando's quiet demeanor reflected the many years he'd spent guiding his people in deeply spiritual matters. He was broad shouldered, dressed in a green shirt and blue jeans. A red headband wrapped his forehead, and a leather prayer bag hung around his neck, as it did every day.

His Buddha-like face twisted nervously as his brown eyes darted around the room at the eager law enforcement agents reining in their adrenaline. I understood that Shando was uncomfortable watching the bravado of white men, but I also knew he'd pull through for the sake of his people.

Team #2 would go to the Spirit Bear Gallery. Special agent Susan Morton, a skilled anthropologist with the National Park Service, was a natural pick to go with this team for the same purpose of identifying sacred artifacts. Susan was a perky blond woman in her forties, with a short haircut that suited her life as a busy agent. At five feet five inches she was solidly built from years of exercise, and her demeanor was equally solid with a no-nonsense attitude that everyone respected. Dressed practically in a tan raid jacket, black pants, and a white blouse, she was ready to dig through drawers, closets, or wherever she thought contraband might be concealed. Meanwhile special agents Phil Young and Scott Wilson were mobile and were to travel between the two search sites offering assistance when needed.

As part of the normal protocol, I gave each team a detailed briefing on what to expect at the search locations. I showed them sketches of the physical premises and explained the personalities of both suspects. I had no reason to expect that Dirk or Tony would be violent, or else I would have solicited extra backup help from local law enforcement agencies. Even so, I instructed the team members to watch the two suspects constantly, just in case.

I introduced Peder and Wally, who added their suggestions on how the teams should handle their respective assignments. I was pleasantly surprised by how insightful they were. For example, Wally encouraged the team members to treat the suspects with respect and allow them to remain on the premises as long as they stayed in one location. They would not be allowed to follow the agents around as they conducted the searches. Dirk and Tony could "lawyer up" at any time; this would not affect the searches but would prevent the agents from interviewing them. Overall the agents were highly impressed with the covert work done by Peder and Wally and were enthusiastic about the objectives of the investigation.

Finally at approximately one-thirty p.m. Peder and Wally left the command center and drove to Tony Lorenzo's house on Piedra Lane. As I later learned, Tony was overjoyed to see his friends. He lost no time in showing them the parfleche container he'd promised to hold for Peder. Tony bragged that the piece was very rare and unique, and in this instance he wasn't lying. Peder put on a show of how excited he was to own the parfleche. He *ooh*ed and *aah*ed as he turned the piece over and over in his hands like fine china.

Wally cut things short by saying he had to rush Peder to a bank in Santa Fe where Peder would authorize the wiring of $16,000 from his bank in Oslo, which would soon be closing. Tony didn't realize that it was evening in Norway when the banks were actually closed. Wally promised they would return within two hours with the money and would pay Tony and pick up the parfleche. After his clients left, I imagined a totally euphoric Tony nervously pacing the floor of his small abode, rubbing his hands over the windfall that was soon to come.

After nearly three decades of undercover work I was familiar with what Peder and Wally were going through. Even though I'd done my job well, I didn't like hurting people. I actually became fond of some of my targets, except for their penchant to manipulate others and destroy wildlife just to feed their egos. I learned that most people were not *all* bad, but some needed extra lessons in leading a life that was not based on destroying wildlife and cultural beliefs.

Wally called me and said they were done at Tony's and were on their way to the Spirit Bear Gallery, where Dirk was undoubtedly anxiously waiting for them. Little did Dirk know that his life was about to change drastically. During this time my thoughts turned to how Peder and Wally were dealing with their final ruses. They had deeply befriended Dirk and Tony to get to this point, and their deception would be an emotional blow to the two suspects. It would be brutal. It would be cruel.

For many undercover agents this causes internal dissonance. While undercover agents know all along about the eventual fall, a part of them wants the relationship with their targets to remain the same. No one wants to be despised, but in a successful undercover play it has to happen. Wally had once told me that he actually admired Dirk for his business acumen. I didn't quite understand this, since most of Dirk's business was illegal. It's easy to be successful when you cheat and use exploitive tactics. Although

I never said a word about this, I felt uneasy as I listened to Wally telling Dirk about a future business relationship between them. In one of the tapes he made a very convincing pitch that he and Dirk should become partners and set up an appraisal business that would generate millions of dollars. Wally would appraise, buy, and sell Eastern memorabilia such as Civil War relics. Dirk would do the same with Navajo rugs and Indian artifacts. Wally described a booming business in which the two antique aficionados would rake in a fortune. He boasted that the two of them were natural partners and that bilking money out of Peder was just the beginning. I thought this play on Wally's part was overdone. His promises were too tempting for the part he was playing. No jury would like this tactic.

Peder, on the other hand, had played his part perfectly with little emotional investment. He understood the harsh reality of undercover work, which usually amounted to "bait and bust." The crooks operated with impunity and with no expectation of ever being caught. Their greed and unabashed selfishness justified hurting people, cultures, and anything else that got in their way. They had to be stopped. Not crucified, but stopped in a meaningful way. Peder understood this.

The agents were now on their way to their final meeting with Dirk. While they wanted it to be flawless, they were also eager to get it over with. Maintaining their deception was grinding on both of them. As the undercover video later revealed, the weary men met a jubilant Dirk who looked as if he could jump out of his skin. He led the undercovers to the back room of his gallery and closed the Navajo curtain behind him. He opened a large moving box to reveal the 1875 Cheyenne eagle feather headdress with a $160,000 price tag on it. As hard as it must have been, Peder and Wally made an excellent show of salivating over it.

"I never dreamed of such a thing," said Peder as he exhaled with deep satisfaction.

"Great!" said Dirk, deeply gratified. "But I have something that will knock your socks off!"

"Socks?" asked Peder, who again was stumped by a strange American idiomatic expression.

Dirk's spontaneous laughter sounded like a kid at Christmas. "I mean that this is something you'll absolutely love."

He retrieved a box the size of a shoebox from a wooden chest and set it on a table. As he raised the lid, he seemed to be holding his breath in anticipation of something magical. The camera lens captured a cylindrical object that rested on a bed of soft white tissue paper. This presentation seemed to imply that the artifact represented something of purity. Dirk explained that the relic was hundreds of years old and had probably never been seen by whites before. It was so exceptional and so difficult to obtain that he needed $90,000 for it.

Dirk's voice had a ring to it. "It's called a corn mother and comes from an underground kiva in one of the pueblos. It's like the center-piece of an Indian altar. You simply can't get anything more sacred than this."

Holding it up for inspection, Dirk revealed that the piece was shaped like an ear of corn padded with cotton from a cottonwood tree and wrapped in muslin. Eagle feathers protruded from the top and were kept in place by a deerskin robe. The wraparound was held together with leather ties to which a few turquoise beads and white shells had been attached.

"This is a once-in-a-lifetime find. I hope you're pleased."

Dirk went on to pontificate that a corn mother is the most sacred object to Native American ritualism and that this one, in his opinion, had been worshiped inside a kiva for hundreds if not a thousand years. I would later learn he was being more truthful than he'd ever been.

Peder's enthusiasm went into overdrive over acquiring such a rare gem. In reality he knew nothing about corn mothers, but with contrived jubilance he exclaimed, "This sacred mother will take the highest position in my collection!"

Once again Wally cut the celebratory mood short and insisted that he had to take Peder to a bank in order to approve the wiring of some $250,000 from Oslo to Santa Fe. Wally promised they would return within the hour with a certified check to finalize the long-awaited trans-action and make Dirk's and Mr. Silverjack's wallets bulge.

"I'll be here," said Dirk, grinning. "Wally, maybe you and I can talk more about what future deals we can set up."

"That would be great," said Wally, shaking Dirk's hand. "See ya later."

Peder extended his hand and said what would be his last words to Dirk, "What a pleasure; see you shortly."

—◂ ▸—

When the two undercovers arrived back at the command center with the recordings they had made, I updated the search warrant affidavits, stating the government had fresh information that contraband existed at Tony Lorenzo's residence and at the Spirit Bear Gallery. I rushed the affidavits to the local federal magistrate and swore under oath that the information in the affidavits was true. The magistrate signed the actual search warrants and wished me luck. She did not, however, authorize the arrest of the two suspects, as we had no indication that they were flight risks. But with the search warrants in hand, the wheels of justice began to creak forward.

CHAPTER THIRTY-SIX

The command center at the suite was packed with agents hyped on adrenaline. I couldn't believe that they were all gathered because of my case. This was the endgame, the time when we'd find out how much damage Tony and Dirk, with crimes fueled by their supposed love for Native American culture, had been doing to the Indians.

Just before leaving the hotel, chanter Shando stopped the buzz of agents by raising his voice and announcing he wanted to give a blessing for protection. Though his chant was in Towa, a language spoken only by the Jemez people, it resonated in the command center with an unseen force. When he was done, he told us in English that he'd sent a prayer to the Great One asking that the good they were doing would overpower the inevitable evil they were headed for. The evil he was speaking of was the artifacts that had been desecrated and could cause harm to the agents seizing them. This set the tone in the minds of agents mustering up strength to do the job ahead of them.

At approximately four p.m. the raid teams, armed and wearing bulletproof vests and visible badges, set out to the Spirit Bear Gallery and to the residence of Tony Lorenzo. The teams waited near the search targets until they could make their approaches at exactly the same time. At the two locations the teams' leaders advised DeVries and Lorenzo that a federal magistrate had authorized the premises described on the warrants to be searched for contraband. While the search warrants didn't reveal the undercover agents' true identities, they revealed mine: "Lucinda Schroeder, also known as, Dana Delaney." The soon-to-be-defendants would learn the truth about Peder and Wally when their lawyers retrieved the affidavits written to support the search warrants from the federal clerk of court. This was standard procedure.

I later learned that Dirk reacted to the search of his business as if he'd been slugged by a gorilla. Unable to stand, he collapsed in his office chair and sank his face into his hands, muttering repeatedly, "Oh my God, I can't believe it. This can't be true. Oh my God! I'm ruined . . ." As a bit of composure returned, he asked, "Are you guys arresting any of my clients?"

"Which ones?" asked the agent.

"Their . . . their names are Wally Shumaker and . . . and Peder Sandbakken."

The agent's response was, "No."

Dirk looked to the ceiling as if he was thanking the heavens. "Those guys didn't do anything wrong . . . leave them out of this if you can . . . please."

Wally and Peder had done their jobs so well, Dirk was actually looking after them. This is the kind of human connection that good undercover agents make.

An FBI agent was assigned to sit with Dirk to keep him calm and under control. There was no way of predicting how a suspect might react to such a shocking turn of events. As with the senseless death of a loved one, his life had been turned upside down in every way imaginable. An agent got Dirk a glass of water and watched him carefully for signs of physical distress. The team already knew how to get to the closest hospital.

Dirk was allowed to call an attorney in Albuquerque, who advised him not to give any statements to authorities. This was expected and was not considered a major setback, given the mounds of evidence the team was about to seize. Agents asked Dirk to open a couple of locked cabinets, and he cooperated. Contraband found in these cabinets alone accumulated so quickly that one of the team members had to run out to a local hardware store to purchases more boxes.

The corn mother was found in the back room where Wally and Peder had last seen her. The agents searched the shelves of the back room and found boxes full of *jish* items including two Navajo eagle feather bundles and ten pairs of talking prayer sticks. The Cheyenne headdress was in plain view when the agents entered the premises. The search warrant also gave the agents authority to seize records, which were located in Dirk's desk and in an antique four-drawer wooden file cabinet. These records had the potential of revealing who Dirk's other clients were, who had bought protected artifacts from him, and who overall had any place in the web of an illegal enterprise that Dirk had every intention of expanding into an international scheme.

Meanwhile anthropologist Susan Morton of the National Park Service did an excellent job of differentiating Indian art pieces from religious artifacts found at the gallery. Later she commented that although she'd studied religious accoutrements of the Southwest Indians, she'd never actually seen very many. The search of the gallery produced more than she could have imagined. All of the search team members wore latex gloves and treated each artifact as if it were alive and needed special handling.

Over a period of seven hours the agents seized more than two hundred pieces and photographed each piece in the exact location where it was found. They completed the tedious task of filling out and affixing to each piece a US Fish and Wildlife Service evidence tag, as I would be the eventual evidence custodian. (Initially the FBI wanted possession of the evidence, but I secured another parcel of control by convincing them that, as the lead agent, I needed instant access to the evidence until I repatriated everything to the respective tribes.)

At Tony's house, the team leader reported that after the agents knocked on his door, Tony reacted with full compliance. His brother was a deputy sheriff, and he probably knew that putting up a fight would cause even more problems. One agent said that as his body sank onto his bed, he slumped over like a deflated balloon. Another agent described Tony as a defeated warrior who knew his best chance was to surrender. This didn't surprise me, as I'd always thought that subconsciously Tony had been preparing for this day. Compared to Dirk's, Tony's business looked like a garage sale. His modest lifestyle gave the impression that he didn't have much to lose. Even if he lost everything he had in his house, his real assets were hidden.

The agent assigned to watch Tony found him genuinely interested in how the agents went about their official business. Tony watched every move and as usual couldn't stop blabbing about what an expert he was in Indian artifacts. He didn't ask to contact an attorney, as he said he was going to ask for a public defender at his preliminary hearing. Meanwhile he maintained an almost itchy demeanor, as if he wanted to help the agents do their jobs.

At one point the agents showed chanter Shando a paint kit and some old wooden carved arrow sticks found beneath Tony's kitchen sink. In an explosion of emotion the chanter sharply accused Tony of making fake warrior hair ties to sell. Tony shot back that he was only freshening up some hair ties that weren't being used anymore. But when the agents found hair ties that had been freshly painted and had macaw, wild turkey, and eagle feathers attached, Shando's resentment grew even further.

"The feathers are in the wrong order!" he shouted. "This is the ultimate desecration of our tradition and could bring bad things to happen!"

The chanter dropped the toxic artifact and stomped outside to air out his tainted soul. He had touched something very offensive and would now need to undergo cleansing rituals to make things right. Shando would not go back into Tony's house after that and sat in an agent's car for hours until the search was completed.

One of the surprising things found among Tony's stash was a box that contained centuries-old stone fetishes along with leather pouches filled with corn pollen. An agent asked Tony where he got them.

He merely shrugged his shoulders and said, "Oh, different people gave them to me. I don't even remember."

The team leader called me about this at the command center. I told him that we knew of one Native American from the Isleta Pueblo who might be a supplier of fetishes, but not for a hundred of them. I told the agent to seize them all—we'd get to the bottom of it later. Tony also had dozens of cylinder and flat kachina dolls that chanter Shando said were used by individual Puebloans to attract the favorable characteristics of certain spirits. One, for example, was a flat doll lying in a bed of cotton that represented an appeal for a child. A woman had used it to pray for fertility, and now it was in Tony's house being tossed about like a trinket.

Since Lorenzo's house was relatively small, it took the agents only about four hours to properly photograph, tag, and seize evidence of crimes. One of the agents found a receipt for a storage shed Tony was renting in Santa Fe. When an agent called me about this, I suggested that Tony was probably hiding illegal material there. Unfortunately, we didn't have a single shred of information to prove this and consequently couldn't get a search warrant for the shed. We'd never know what was in there. In this respect Tony had beaten us, and I'm sure he knew it.

———

Around midnight the exhausted search teams arrived at my hotel room. We loaded dozens of boxes full of evidence into my room, where it would remain secure with me, placing the evidence seized from Lorenzo's residence on one side of the room and the evidence from the Spirit Bear Gallery on the other. The agents were excited about the success of the searches and eagerly filled me in on every detail. Finally a hotel guest called the front desk because we were making so much noise. Embarrassed, we stopped what must have sounded like a college party, and the agents quietly retreated to their rooms. Peder was in a room next to mine and had apparently slept through the whole thing.

Alone in my room that night, I couldn't shake the creepy feeling that I was being watched by dozens of spiritual entities. I tried to sleep, but anxiety and fear seeped into my consciousness, tormenting me until dawn. I was glad to finally get up and leave the room for breakfast.

CHAPTER THIRTY-SEVEN

January 19, 2000. As prearranged, the exhausted agents that had been on the raid teams reported to my room at ten a.m. I conducted a short debriefing, and two hours later the room cleared, with only me, Susan Morton, Matt Miller, Peder, and Wally remaining. Out of curiosity Wally wanted to see the corn mother. He found her wrapped inside a box of evidence and put her on the round table in the room.

A shiver spun down my spine as Susan explained that the corn mother was an extremely rare piece used in the raw beckoning of spiritual blessings by indigenous peoples. If a corn mother became too time-worn, holy men would make another one, using the exact materials and procedures used to make the previous one. The actual corn cob was carefully selected by the spiritual leaders to represent the perfect ear of corn that formed the foundation of ancient agriculture. Susan explained that the corn mother was kept in an honored place inside a kiva and was revered for her life-giving powers. From the beginning of time, the corn mother served to represent the gift of life to plants and to people. Her kernels, which actually produced a milky substance, made her the perfect representative of universal nourishment for the born and unborn, for the yield of crops and the fertilization of seeds that produced them. She nourished souls and was so sacrosanct I felt myself apologizing to her for having her inside a hotel room instead of her precious kiva home. I even felt partly responsible for this dire situation.

Out of the blue, Wally asked Peder to take a picture of him with the artifact.

"No!" I shouted. "No trophy shots! The Indians insist on humility, and a picture of you holding the corn mother as bragging rights is disrespectful."

"Go ahead, Peder, take the picture," urged Wally. "This thing can't bite."

Peder put the camera down, but things got worse. Wally carried the corn mother to the bed and began untying the leather strings around her.

"Don't do that!" I shouted, my nerves nearly exploding.

"I want to see what's inside," he protested.

Raging with frustration, I rushed to her side and slapped Wally's hands. "Stop it! The medicine men will know someone has been messing with her. Stop it!"

I took a mental snapshot of how the leather strings had been tied and quickly tried to replicate the exact pattern. When I was done, my boss Matt Miller stepped in, took the artifact from me, and put her away. While I was relieved, I still had the urge to choke a certain FBI agent.

We were all emotionally and physically wiped out from the previous day's grind and struggled to load the evidence boxes into my Ramcharger. In the parking lot we shook hands, but that seemed unceremonious given what we'd been through. I wanted to tell Peder how much I appreciated all his work and concern about the case. He was not just a government informant; he was my personal hero and always would be. I never got the chance to genuinely thank him. Peder got into Matt's rental car and within seconds they wheeled out of the parking lot on their way to the Albuquerque Sunport. Peder's leaving felt like a great and sudden loss. I put my hands over my face to hide my sadness. It was hard for me to accept that it was time for Peder to go home to his real life in Norway.

Wally hopped into the red convertible that had served him and Peder so well and drove off, giving Susan and me a light wave. I knew I might see him again—in court. I wish Susan could have known how much comfort she was as I watched my comrades go their separate ways. I felt like a new widow who'd been surrounded by family but was now alone with nothing to do but clean up the last casserole dishes. Because of Susan I didn't feel abandoned, and because of her the real work continued.

In Albuquerque, Susan and I secured the boxes in the evidence room of the bunker where I was once a supervisor. The agents I used to supervise had been on the raid teams and were aware of the magnitude of the case, but they wouldn't be available to help me finish it up. They were field agents with their own caseloads.

Right from the start, Susan explained to me that the artifacts we'd seized weren't just part of a religion; they were like marrow in the bones of the believers. Bird by bird, Susan and I spent five solid days meticulously listing every item seized pursuant to the search warrants served on January 18, 2000. I had to present this list, called a return, to the federal magistrate and swear under oath that it was true and accurate. Any evidence that "turned up" later due to sloppy paperwork would infuriate our prosecutor no end. The return document had to be perfect.

Inside the clammy cinderblock walls of the evidence room, Susan Morton began her evaluation of each artifact to determine which tribal entity it most likely belonged to. Susan was born in 1952, the same year I was, and had a BA degree in anthropology from the University of California at Berkeley and an MA from the University of Arizona. She had worked for the National Park Service as an archeologist before becoming a special agent in 1991. Her background in Native American cultures was so extensive that she could separate the Puebloan material from those of the Navajo and the Hopi tribes. She was amazing, and if I'd known her during the covert portion of my investigation, I would have trusted her with my secrets.

I didn't know this at the time, but I would be with her in 2009 when she was named Outstanding Federal Law Enforcement Agent by the Women in Federal Law Enforcement organization in Washington, DC. We would have lunch together and would reminisce over the artifact case we worked together. We'd laugh about Tony and how ridiculous he was and how indescribably greedy Dirk was. My heart would break when she died in 2010.

In part Susan relied on a stack of a dozen-odd resource books with pictures of very old ceremonial artifacts that were in use in the early part of the twentieth century. The photographs, mostly poor in quality, were taken by some of the first anthropologists to explore Indian Country but remain the last photographic evidence depicting the use of sacred artifacts. These anthropologists traded food, beads, cloth, and alcohol to gain access to everything from underground ceremonial chambers to outdoor shrines secreted high in the mountains.

When these researchers became overly zealous in their collecting, eventually the holy men barred them from entering tribal lands. They did this to protect what was vital to them, as rampant collecting in the name of research was literally destroying their everyday spiritual life.

History tells us that early anthropologists were not the first threat to Native American spiritual practices. In the 1500s Native Americans endured the crushing treatment imposed upon them by Spanish conquistadores, who made a fervent effort to convert the tribes in the Southwest to Christianity. Finally, to stop the constant fighting and bloodshed, the friars allowed native practices to continue alongside the Catholic Church. Even today you'll find life-sized kachinas painted on the white adobe walls inside old churches, or an active kiva yards away from church grounds.

As part of our work, Susan and I photographed the hundred-plus fetishes seized at the Piedra Lane residence. We were both stymied as to how Tony was able to get his hands on so many of these soul-enhancing artifacts. All of them showed the patina of being very old. Each one had once belonged to a person who used it for personal growth and expansion of knowledge. In fact, Indians from several tribes throughout the Southwest used them, making the repatriation of them a challenge.

Among the animal fetishes, such as raven, bear, mountain lion, and owl, were some figurines that looked like humans with oversized eyes. Tony had said these represented the aliens that had visited the earth—and still do. Susan, however, thought the figurines represented earth surface walkers. Their vital inner beings are blown into them with chants, prayers, and messages from the holy winds. Susan thought these figurines might have been placed in outdoor shrines to attract the forces of protection. If this was true, it meant that Tony had been combing the hills surrounding tribal lands and looting the shrines whole. This made sense, as I could see Tony climbing boulders and cliffs in a hunt for shrines. I could picture his gleaming face when he found one, screaming, "Finders keepers!"

Susan explained to me that the key to using a fetish is careful self-examination to determine where a person needs help in his or her journey through life. A hunter, for example, may sit before a mountain lion fetish to help in the task ahead. Mountain lions, with their natural stalking and cunning skills, are considered the masters of the hunt. The user visualizes how the mountain lion hunts his prey and asks to be given these characteristics. With intense visualization the hunter takes on the master hunter skills of the mountain lion.

Fetishes themselves don't hold magical powers, but if used properly they can help the desired characteristics to manifest in the persons seeking help. The power comes from the users as they visualize the reality they want to create in their lives. This self-improvement method is described in many modern books that promote the philosophy that a person becomes what he or she thinks. Fetishes help to sharpen the thinking, which can have positive effects.

Spiritual fetishes most often are in the form of an animal, as the ancient Indians recognized how dependent humans are on the natural order of things. By assimilating the mysterious forces of nature, they were able to achieve superior self-improvement and guidance in matters that were problematic. With greater spiritual vision the ancients were able to achieve balance and oneness with the universe.

Over time one might collect a number of animal fetishes to consult for guidance to resolve personal problems. For example, eagle reminds us to see the bigger picture of a situation and live with dignity and grace. Coyote, the trickster who is fond of clowning around and making light of serious issues, can make us laugh at our own mistakes and remind us that our perceived self-importance is standing in our own way. Fetishes tap into ancient intuitive thinking that has served humans so well for eons. Today this method of spiritual growth is left unacknowledged in our fast-paced technology-led lives. But the basic concept is still practiced by people who meditate or find quiet moments with their own soul, with the goal of living harmoniously with timeless forces of the universe.

Next we examined the parfleche Tony tried to sell for $16,000. Susan told me that the parfleche container was originally made to store a rolled headdress of a Plains Indian. At some point a Plains Indian had traded it to a Pueblo Indian. She pointed out the faded geometric designs in the background that had been covered by the cloud and lightning symbols important to Southwest Indians. The Southwest Indians had found a sacred use for the parfleche, so it all made perfect sense. It irked me that Tony told one of the raid team agents that he paid a Pueblo Indian $200 for the parfleche. We already knew he tried to sell it for $16,000.

Among the seized items were ten sets of what DeVries had referred to as Dreaming Twins. He had shown them to Peder and Wally during one of their contacts, but the agents had passed on them at the time.

Susan laughed and said, "Dirk is a dreamer, all right. Why does he keep making up stuff?"

The artifacts were actually called talking prayer sticks. Also called Hero Twins, they represented Monster Slayer and his brother Born for Water. Dirk had hand-scribbled "To be repatriated to the Navajos" on top of the box. This was his feeble attempt to cover himself in case he got caught with the illegal artifacts. Of course, he never had any intentions of returning the talking prayer sticks to the Navajos; he was going to sell them to the highest bidder. But to protect himself and to erase the timeless rhythm of Indian spirituality, Dirk began calling the Hero Twins "dreaming twins." His pitiful greed was that deep, and his selfishness was beyond words. The Hero Twins were wrapped together with leather ties along with a few eagle fluffies, turquoise beads, and white shell. Typically, a Navajo *hataalii* would have one set in his *jish*. He would meditate and let his hands tremble over them while seeking an answer on how to heal his ailing patient. The *hataalii* used the Hero Twins for many purposes, but these were things I was not meant to know. The profound significance of the twins boggled my mind. The fact that Dirk had ten sets of talking prayer sticks meant that ten different medicine bundles had been stolen and taken apart. This was the ultimate desecration.

In the Navajo creation story, Monster Slayer slayed evil forces while Born for Water watched his brother and made sure he didn't overuse his power. I thought back to the time when I had the opportunity to destroy FBI careers, but didn't because of what Monster Slayer said about turning into a monster while fighting them. I held a talking prayer stick in my hands and silently promised that their drama was over. They were going home.

A few days later Wally called me and complained that he'd been getting repeated calls from Dirk, who sounded desperate to talk to him. I expected this might happen, but so far Wally had been letting the calls go unanswered. I told Wally that he should ditch his old phone number and get a new one, but he didn't want to do that.

"Should I talk to him?" he asked. "This is driving me wacko!"

"Absolutely not! First of all, you can't continue to play your covert role with Dirk. He's represented by an attorney, and from what I hear his lawyer can be a real jerk. So don't make any mistakes. From now on, all communications with Dirk have to be done through our prosecutor, Rainey Swanson, and Dirk's lawyer."

After every undercover project went down, I'd cancel my covert phone number. But Wally had too many other crooks calling the same number. He felt that changing it would jeopardize his other cases. Wally must have felt cornered by Dirk, his long-lost best buddy. But the rules were clear. Wally couldn't communicate with Dirk and yet had to keep track of the messages he left. What a pain.

Then I asked about Tony. "Have you heard from him?"

"Naw, I suppose both he and Dirk are blaming each other for the shit they're in. What a couple of losers!"

"I agree, but you have to stay away from him, too. No communication unless it's through Rainey. She's in charge now."

—◆—

As Susan and I were finally wrapping up inside the evidence room, we found a glaring error. For some reason we'd failed to list the corn mother as part of the evidence seized. I wasn't concerned, as I knew we had her. So, for what seemed like the hundredth time, we waded our way through the physical evidence.

After a couple of hours of searching, my hands began to sweat. If I had to tell Pueblo leaders that I'd lost their precious corn mother, they'd hit me with an insidious curse worse than cholera. While I tried not to believe in Indian ju-ju, I'd definitely seen it, and it terrified me. Then the fireflies in my gut started to rage, and within minutes I was bent over in pain. Painkillers came to the rescue—again. I was taking too many of them, but was beyond caring.

Susan knew that losing the corn mother was catastrophic. She was more afraid of curses than I was. Maybe the corn mother disappeared because we didn't handle her properly. After several more hours of fruitless searching Susan and I finally had to confront our worst fears—the corn mother was gone! Did someone take her? Who and why?

CHAPTER THIRTY-EIGHT

January 22, 2000. My head hung slightly as I tried to focus on the matter being heard by Magistrate Judge Madison.* With nerves cracking under my skin I explained that the list of seized items I was submitting was true and accurate except for one artifact that was inexplicably missing.

"What's it called again?" asked the magistrate. At that moment his black robe reminded me of one that an executioner would wear. I fully expected to be condemned to death for the crime of losing evidence.

"It's called a corn mother," said Assistant US Attorney Rainey Swanson, who stood at my side barely maintaining her professional composure.

Magistrate Judge Madison hit me with questions about when I'd last seen the artifact and how long I thought it would take me to find her. Even though I'm hardly clairvoyant, I said I'd find her within a week. In reality my mind swirled with uncertainties. Susan and I had already turned everything upside down and in my opinion had exhausted every option.

To my surprise the judge was reasonably lenient. While the corn mother meant mountains to me, to the judge she was just a cob of corn with feathers. He acted as if the incident was simply an oversight by an incompetent agent.

Before going to court, Rainey Swanson peppered me with countless questions about the corn mother. Could she have been stolen? Did I let any Indians inside the evidence room? Who else had access to it? While Rainey demanded answers, I had none that would explain the missing evidence. We both knew that losing key evidence could be used by a defense attorney to discredit the entire case.

Rainey snapped up the phone, called special agent Scott Wilson, and ordered him to travel to Albuquerque and tear the evidence room apart. He wasn't to search for the corn mother, he was to find her! Then she called special agent Randy Smith and told him to do the same thing. There was no putting this off—it had to be done immediately!

Special agents Wilson and Smith spent the entire day combing the evidence room, the garage area, and the main parts of the office space and still couldn't find the missing evidence. Part of me wondered if they saw her but kept overlooking her. The artifact had to be somewhere in the office. But she wasn't. Agent Wilson called our prosecutor and gave her the bad news. Rainey didn't like the FBI for a number of reasons and took this debacle as an opportunity to really wring Wilson out.

When he got off the phone, he turned his inflamed face toward me. "I don't understand why she's so ticked off at me. She wants me to go through the evidence again! Somebody screwed up and I'm taking the heat."

"Go home, Scott," I said. "It's getting late and we've beaten this dead horse a dozen times. I'll look for her in the morning. Maybe she slipped out of one of the boxes and is under something we didn't notice. Another fresh look can't hurt."

Drained to the bone, we all left the bunker and went to our respective homes. When I got to mine, I couldn't even talk about the missing evidence. My gut was inflamed after another firefly attack. Wrenching in pain, I cooked a quick dinner, took painkillers, and went to bed. Between the missing corn mother and my illness, the world looked so bad I hoped I'd wake up on a Tahitian beach with zero problems.

—❧—

Back at the bunker the following morning, I walked into the evidence room and spoke to the unseen spirits. "Okay, where is she? I know you know. So give it up, this isn't funny anymore."

I opened a box that contained evidence seized from Tony Lorenzo to take another look at one of the *tablitas* we'd seized. I removed the *tablita* from the box and there she was—the corn mother, snuggled among strangers from other tribes. Unbelievably relieved, I gently lifted her up and carried her into the office where agent Smith was.

"See what I found? Randy, I thought you went through every box. How could you have missed her?"

Smith had an incredulous look on his face. "Oh my God, where was she?"

"She was mixed in with the evidence seized from Tony's house. I thought you went through every box. At least you said you did."

"We went through everything that was seized from the gallery, but we didn't search Tony's boxes. . . . I mean, the corn mother was seized at Dirk's gallery."

My relief was so immense that I didn't bother to tell agent Smith what I thought of his ineptness. He stuttered something I didn't even care to listen to. I had things to do. The first phone call was to our prosecutor. While she was glad that the missing evidence was found, she accused the FBI of lying to her.

"Scott Wilson told me that he searched every box. It's obvious that he didn't. I don't like being lied to," she said, nearly screaming.

The next person I called was my boss in Washington, DC.

"Matt, I found the corn mother, and I think I know how she went missing. Remember when we were in the hotel room and Wally started messing with her? You took her and put her away. But I think you put her in a box that contained evidence seized at Lorenzo's."

"I put her in the wrong box? Well," he said, laughing, "that's what you get for putting a desk agent in charge of anything."

So this was my fault? I was too numb to argue. I couldn't really blame Matt, though, as Susan and I couldn't find her either, and we looked everywhere. I returned the corn mother to the evidence room and placed her in a spot where she'd never be overlooked again.

"You stay put!" I warned.

I left the bunker and went straight to the US magistrate's office and reported that the missing item had been found. When I told the magistrate that an agent had misplaced the evidence, he grunted something about incompetent agents. He scribbled his name on the revised list of evidence and told me the matter was closed. While I'd thankfully cleared this hurdle, I could see more trouble ahead. Due to the bungling of evidence, this magistrate clearly didn't like me. This might hurt us, as he would be the judge to sentence both Lorenzo and DeVries when the time came. Human judges were not immune to human grudges.

—◆—

Special agent Susan Morton had been at her Santa Fe home for about a week when she called me in a near panic.

"I'm in total misalignment," she cried. "I've lost the keys to my own evidence room, and yesterday I rear-ended a Mercedes in that damn post office parking lot. The accident wasn't serious, but it's going to take me weeks to get this straightened out. Then I had a pisser of a fight with my boss. That's three things in a row."

"Susan, you're not going nuts, you're just not focusing on things. Calm down and everything will be fine."

"No," she insisted, "I'm cursed. I can definitely feel it."

Desperate for relief, Susan called chanter Shando from the Jemez Pueblo for help. He told her to close her eyes as he gave her a verbal cleansing over the telephone. After this she told me she'd not suffered a single mishap. She felt certain that Shando's healing words had eradicated evil spirits from her. I hoped she was right.

At this point I was working very closely with our prosecutor building cases against Tony and Dirk and was practically living at the US Attorney's Office. AUSA Rainey Swanson was nearing her sixties but had the energy and vibrancy of someone much younger. She kept her hair, blonde mixed with gray, piled on top of her head in a nest that actually looked groomed. As opposed to conservative suits, she chose flowing skirts and loose tops. She didn't look like a lawyer, but she had the sharp mind of one and could spit dragon fire if she wanted to.

One day she instructed me to get affidavits from a spiritual leader of every affected tribe affirming that the artifacts we'd seized were sacred to them. These statements would be used to block a defense argument that the artifacts were just Indian-made trinkets. Getting these statements meant contacting numerous chanters, priests, and *hataalii* and asking them to reveal what was unspeakable on paper and later in open-court testimony.

I begged Rainey to understand that her instructions were diametrically opposed to Indian ways. No healer would reveal his sacred secrets, as such revelations would be in violation of their most sacrosanct beliefs. I suggested that we use Anglo anthropologists as expert witness. They could explain Native American beliefs as well as anyone, even if they were slightly wrong. After a heated argument Rainey finally said she'd think about it.

Driving home from her office, I was preoccupied by the abysmal idea of getting formal affidavits from Indian practitioners. My mind was dripping in dread as I took an access ramp to get onto I-25. I was behind a white commercial-grade truck when the driver slammed on his brakes due to stalling traffic on the highway. I assumed the driver would keep going, but he didn't. I smashed into a steel bumper of the truck, forcing the hood of my Camaro to fold up like a pup tent. I could barely see over it to drive.

After the accident I banged on the steering wheel and yelled, "Damn these Indian spirits. Leave me alone!"

No one was hurt, and the truck didn't suffer any damage. Officer Duke arrived at the scene on his motorcycle. After hearing both sides, he said I was at fault—which was true. He gave me a ticket for "inattentive driving" and I drove the wrecked Camaro to my house, where I was expecting company. My guests were four Navajo religious leaders who wanted to view the Navajo evidence seized from Tony and Dirk. They didn't want to be seen in an office where there were a bunch of white people around. My house was the best place I could offer them for privacy. As long as the evidence remained with me, it was legal to do this.

In my living room I spread out the talking prayers sticks, the eagle feather bundles made to eradicate evil, small bags of soil taken from sacred sites, bullroarers, and much more. Before we began any meaningful discussion, a *hataalii* named Ronnie Largo* pulled out a bundle of eagle wing feathers from a leather pouch he was carrying and started brushing the walls and corners of my living room. As he danced about, he claimed he could feel negative energy in the room.

"It must go," he blurted.

When he was done, I thanked him and admitted that the previous owners had been unkind and were now in trouble with the IRS for failure to pay taxes. They had left Albuquerque in an attempt to hide, but the IRS found them. I also told him about the corn mother and how she disappeared.

"Ah!" bellowed Largo. "That was the trickster playing a trick on you! I hope you learned something from it."

The other Navajos agreed that trickster (also known as coyote) had messed with me. They laughed as they explained that they had seen the trickster at work many times. Trickster liked to make the best laid plans go wrong and sometimes made things go missing. Largo said there was something about my attitude or someone else's that caused the disruption. I thought back to Wally and how he treated the corn mother at the hotel room in Santa Fe. That's where the trouble began. I couldn't believe it.

CHAPTER THIRTY-NINE

The next day, I drove the Camaro to a body shop and got a ride back to the bunker. After the incident with the trickster, I really wanted to get the artifacts out of my life. I dreaded going into my evidence room, where I could feel restless forces moving about. Painted eyes seemed to monitor my every move, and I felt myself apologizing for everything that had happened to them. It all felt very creepy, as if somewhere people were praying mightily for their return.

The *hataalii* Largo had told me to make sure, when I was with the artifacts, to treat them like living beings. He said if I worked from the deepest part of my heart, my life would flow better. I knew he was right and I had to start doing things differently.

Once again I went inside the evidence room and looked at the artifacts. This time, as if it was the most natural thing I'd ever done, I began talking to them. I said I was sorry for everything they had gone through, but I was going to make things right. I was going to return them home. I reorganized the entire room by grouping the artifacts by tribe or pueblo and then facing them in the direction of their respective homes. I wrapped individual pieces in white tissue paper or set them on a tissue paper pillow. The color white was a sign of purity, and I used it profusely. In a soft voice I told the corn mother that she was safe and would be returned to her sacred homeland soon. When I was done, the dissonance I had been feeling inside the evidence room actually eased.

I was still digging through the files we had seized. It was lonely, dogged work, and after several hours nothing significant had popped up. Discouraged, I grabbed another stack of DeVries's files and began flipping through them. Interestingly, I discovered that Steve Jobs and Ralph Lauren were two of his clients, but there was no indication that either man had violated any laws. Finally I came across a file labeled "M" that was full of handwritten letters. After reading a few pages, I grinned like a mischievous cat. The letters were sent by a woman who affectionately called her lover "heart bear." The lines flowed like heart-wrought poetry: *You embrace me with loves' forever touch; your eyes light up my sky and your soul radiates through me; my heart can't bear to live without you . . . heart bear. . . . I need you always.*

Other letters conveyed the wails of a young woman who fantasized being with her lover in California where at twilight they'd bathe in the mist of golden sunsets. While I could hardly stand to read this mush, the investigator in me loved it. The woman was Mona, and her lover was none other than Dirk DeVries. I thought back to the first time I'd visited the Spirit Bear Gallery and noticed that there were no family pictures there. I'd considered this to be a hint that Dirk had a distant relationship with his wife. Now I knew that he'd been cheating on her with his lovely office assistant. These letters were like striking federal gold. They revealed that Mona had been complicit in Dirk's underworld. She knew that he was running an illegal enterprise and at times assisted him. This exposed her to indictment for at least aiding and abetting. Now Dirk's freedom, his life's work, and his marriage were on the line. He would surely capitulate and plead guilty in exchange for keeping Mona out of legal trouble and keeping his love affair secret. Prosecutors often arranged deals like this. These letters were the best weapon I had. Monster Slayer had been quiet for a while, but I sensed he was back now.

CHAPTER FORTY

October 23, 2001. A federal grand jury heard the cases against Lorenzo and DeVries and found that there was sufficient evidence to charge them with numerous counts of violating the Native American Graves Protection and Repatriation Act, the Bald and Golden Eagle Protection Act, and the Migratory Bird Treaty Act. Given the amount of evidence against the defendants, Assistant US Attorney Rainey Swanson contacted the defense attorneys to suggest that they negotiate a plea bargain. This would mean there wouldn't be a trial, and sentencing would be done by a federal magistrate. Tony's public defender, Rachael Hammer,* agreed to this, as Tony said he didn't have enough money to pay her to defend him in a full-blown trial. Dirk's attorney, Michael Yocum,* who was aware of the Mona letters, indicated that his client would do anything to avoid a trial.

—~——

March 15, 2002. The sentencing hearing for Tony Lorenzo was held at the federal courthouse in Albuquerque in Magistrate Judge Madison's courtroom. Tony's brother, a deputy sheriff, sat in the front row dressed in uniform, as if the shine of his badge would reflect law and order onto Tony, who was sitting at the defense table with his attorney. He was wearing neat blue jeans, a black shirt, and a blue vest with some beadwork on it. It seemed odd that he was still playing part-Indian. The courtroom was filled with reporters, interested law enforcement agents, and spiritual leaders and tribal members from the Hopi and Navajo tribes and several pueblos. The Native Americans were there to see Tony get thrown to the lions.

AUSA Swanson went to the podium and explained to Judge Madison how Tony had raided multiple Indian reservations and lured pathetically poor people into stealing sacred artifacts for a fraction of the money he sold them for. She pointed to the parfleche piece, which he confessed to paying a tribal member $200 for and then offered to sell for $16,000.

Another example was the fake Jemez hair tie with protected hawk and eagle feathers on it, which he made and then sold for $5,000. Rainey presented a strong case that Tony was making a lucrative living exploiting Native American sacred artifacts and should be punished for the damage he'd done to an entire culture. After her short discourse, the prosecutor sat down next to me.

"Mr. Lorenzo," asked Judge Madison, "how do you plead—guilty or not guilty?"

Slowly Tony stood up before the judge. He was unsteady and a little pale. "G-guilty," said Tony in a squeaky voice.

"Speak up!" barked the judge. "I can hardly hear you."

Ms. Hammer shot him a grinding look, as if to say she had no time for his nonsense.

Tony cleared his throat. "Guilty, uh, sir."

"Fine—let the record show that the defendant has entered a plea of guilty. Do you wish to address the court before sentencing?"

"Yes, sir. I'd like to say that I have a lot of respect for the Indian people and didn't mean to hurt anyone. The money I gave them was to help them buy food for their families. I had no idea that the artifacts were so special."

I nudged AUSA Swanson and whispered, "Are you going to let him get away with saying that?"

She whispered back, "It doesn't matter what I say. This judge has already made up his mind."

She was right. Magistrate Judge Madison quickly ordered that Tony Lorenzo pay back the money paid to him by the government agents, and placed him on probation for three years. This meant that if Tony violated any laws, he'd go to jail for two years. The judge also ordered that the government return the seized property to the rightful tribes and that Tony cooperate with the FBI by identifying the Indians he bought or stole from. This would never happen, because by then the focus of the FBI had turned to terrorism after the tragedy of 9/11.

Stunned, I looked at the prosecutor. "No jail time?"

She shrugged and said, "That was a sentence handed down by a judge who doesn't like Native Americans, the government, or you, at least not in this case."

I swallowed hard. I knew the judge wasn't crazy over me, but I didn't think he'd give Tony a light penalty because of personal feelings. Regardless of the sentence, I thought Tony had been hit hard enough to quit what he'd been doing. Besides, my job was to catch the bad guys and not worry about sentences. As long as the crooks were stopped, I could live with a light sentence. In the short term, however, I was incensed.

The courtroom emptied into a grand rotunda where a swirling marble staircase reached three stories to the first floor, even though everyone took the elevators. This was the new federal courthouse in Albuquerque, and being in it made you feel you were in a place of hallowed authority. As I entered the hallway, I was suddenly surrounded by a dozen Indians who looked spitting mad. All I heard was angry voices.

"What went wrong?"

"Where's our justice?"

My mind spun as to what to say to them. I didn't like the sentence either, but I thought the Native American community should be happy that their artifacts were recovered. Somehow I had to make them see things differently.

"Calm down," I said. "You're viewing this from the white man's way. From your way of thinking, you won. You're getting back all the sacred things that have been stolen from you. The heart and soul of your spiritual lives can now be restored. I promise you, I have handled your spiritual objects with deep respect, and my only wish is that they go home to you. I will personally see to this."

The men began talking among themselves. Soon I saw heads nodding in agreement. I heard one say that it was true that no punishment could give them what they really wanted. Then I handed out pictures of Tony and advised that they watch out for this guy and chase him off if he appeared on tribal lands. Overall they seemed to relish being a part of solving the problem. Yes, they would be on the lookout for Tony. In fact, some said they recognized Tony and had seen him in their pueblos during feast days.

As a final word, I told them what they didn't want to hear. Unidentified tribal members had been complicit with Tony in stealing and selling the artifacts recovered in the investigation. It was up to them to find these people and deal with them in accordance with their ways. While heads nodded that this would be done, I wasn't too sure. It would be difficult for tribal leaders to confront the members who had conspired with Tony to line their own pockets. There was a lot of nepotism within the tribes, as everyone was related in one way or another.

━◦━

That night I flew to Tampa, Florida, to tend to my father, who was suffering from congestive heart failure. My diverticulitis was getting worse and I was taking too many drugs. I was also taking too much sick leave, which couldn't continue for long. The overall stress was getting to me, but even though I was eligible to retire, I'd decided to stay on until my work with the Native American people was done.

━◦━

It was early April 2002 when Dirk DeVries was formally sentenced. Once again, medicine men and tribal members from various tribes filled the courtroom in anticipation of finally seeing this white man pay for his crimes against Native Americans. Still not happy over Tony's sentence, they came in force to make a visible impression upon the magistrate that they were outraged about the impingement on what was sacred to them. I felt hugely satisfied. Dirk DeVries had been charged with a total of seventeen felony and misdemeanor counts. There was no way the judge could overlook this. As promised, the Mona letters would be kept secret and DeVries's wife would not learn about his affair with her—at least not in open court.

Inside the courtroom Assistant US Attorney Rainey Swanson took the podium first, briefly explaining what Dirk had done and how his actions had deeply injured the Indian people. With all the evidence we had, she had an easy job of laying out his willful indiscretions and making him look like an insensitive, greedy jerk. When she returned to the prosecution's table, I was there to whisper "good job" in her ear. Magistrate Judge Madison seemed to understand the seriousness of the crimes, and now it was just a matter of hearing what defense attorney Michael Yocum had to say.

"How do you plea, guilty or not guilty?" asked the judge while looking directly at DeVries.

Dirk stood up sharply and said, "Guilty." He sat back down and folded his arms calmly in front of him. He didn't seem a bit rattled, which made me wonder. Just being in federal court makes most people shake. I didn't take my eyes off of him.

The defense attorney asked to address the court, and his request was granted. To me Yocum had a weak personality that contrasted with his tall and robust physique. His whiny, pleading voice irritated me to no end. As he took the podium, I wondered what on earth he could say to justify the crimes committed by Dirk DeVries. I didn't expect that he'd outright lie to the judge, but that's exactly what he did.

Yocum described the government's investigation as overbearing and out of bounds. He painted his client as a victim of persistent agents who were desperate to make a case against DeVries in order to further their careers. He threw the word "entrapped" around like confetti, even though he didn't have a shred of legal proof that this had occurred. He whined that the case dragged on because the agents were having trouble coming up with evidence, and after so much harassment by government agents, his client finally gave in to what they wanted.

Seated next to Assistant US Attorney Swanson, I began to squirm. I scribbled a note to her pleading that she put a stop to this diatribe of lies. She whispered to me to be quiet and let the other side have their say. I couldn't believe what was happening, but without the authority to intervene I was forced to listen to how my hard work for justice was really an outrageous government scheme against one man. Then, to my utter amazement, defense counsel said he wanted to present a letter to the court. The magistrate told Yocum to read the letter and then he'd decided if it was relevant to the case.

Defense attorney Yocum, who had sat down, stood up and spread a smirk on his face. "Your honor, this is a letter sent by an FBI special agent known to my client as Wally Shumaker. Mr. Shumaker sent this letter to my client a few weeks after the government had ransacked his gallery scratching for whatever evidence they could come up with."

When Yocum began reading the letter, I slid down in my chair hoping I was hearing things wrong. But I wasn't. Wally had written Dirk an apology for upsetting his life. He wrote that he was only doing his job and that in reality he liked and respected Dirk. He thanked Dirk for his friendship and expressed admiration to Dirk for being a fine businessman. The letter said that Dirk wasn't really a criminal but had made a mistake selling eagle feathers. If he stayed away from them, he should be fine. Finally, Wally wished Dirk and his family well and even suggested that Peder might send them a reindeer hide as he'd once promised.

Yocum handed the letter to the judge and sat down. A deadly silence overtook the courtroom. A pen in Rainey Swanson's hand shook as if it had been afflicted with palsy. I felt nauseous, hot, and sweaty. I couldn't bear to turn around and look at the Native Americans seated behind me. The magistrate was quiet and obviously in deep thought.

The true nature of Wally had revealed itself. He was a shape-shifter who had once appeared to be my ally but then changed and ended up stabbing me in the back. As suspicious as I had been about his feelings toward Dirk, I never saw something like this coming. Meanwhile Yocum carried on in front of the judge about how even the FBI sided with Dirk DeVries. Every word the lawyer spoke felt like a new punch, a slap and a sting. Feeling mortally wounded, I crossed my arms across my core as if to protect it. My mind swirled as I tried to think back. Where did I miss the signs? No, I didn't miss anything. I trusted Wally, and for that I was left vulnerable and exposed. It was minutes before I could even settle on the reality that Wally had gone to the dark side and was fine with it.

The judge put the letter down and looked over the courtroom with a cool detachment. Then he shrugged his shoulders and said, "If the FBI doesn't care about this case, then neither can I."

"Do something!" I whispered frantically to the prosecutor. "We have to fight this!"

She stared straight ahead as if she was trying to contain her internal rage. She seemed to brace herself for what was to come. She knew what I didn't.

Magistrate Judge Madison ordered that DeVries pay back the money paid to him by the government agents for illegal items. He ordered that the seized items be returned to the rightful tribes. And then he handed down a sentence amounting to three years of probation and one hundred hours picking up trash on Indian reservations. With a single gavel tap, it was over.

My heart sank to the ocean floor. This pathetically low penalty hardly served as punishment, given the commercial scale DeVries was working. The sentence was such an insult to the Native Americans that it hurt to the bone. The judge had no idea what he'd done.

My mind flipped to an image of Dirk picking up trash on a reservation, and then I saw him in a ditch. Dead—with a bullet in his back. I whispered to the prosecutor.

Immediately she stood up and addressed the court. "Your honor, while the government appreciates the community service being imposed upon the defendant, we don't feel the defendant would be safe on a reservation. His transgressions against the Indian people might motivate someone to harm him."

Magistrate Judge Madison grunted, "Oh, I hadn't thought about that. Then I'll order one hundred hours of community service educating people about protected artifacts. Mr. Yocum, you work this out with the probation office."

"Yes sir," said Yocum as he rose slightly from his seat. "Maybe he can work at the Indian Museum in Santa Fe."

This made me groan even deeper. But while I wanted Dirk seriously punished, I couldn't see sending him into a shooting gallery. Someone would take him out and his death would never be solved. I knew that much about Indian ways. If he was smart, he'd never set foot on tribal lands. I wasn't sure that he'd be completely safe walking the streets of Santa Fe.

The chatter inside the courtroom picked up, and the prosecutor turned to me red-faced and furious.

"The FBI screwed us royally," she muttered.

"Isn't there anything we can do?" I asked. "We can't let this sentence sit the way it is."

"It's over," said Rainey. "But you were right about Dirk getting hit while picking up trash. He's a slimeball, but he doesn't deserve to be killed."

I left the courtroom and entered the vast rotunda with pillars and marbled floors. With total dread I faced the twenty or more medicine men and tribal members who had attended the proceeding. While I had worked hard to develop a positive relationship with them, they were now blaming me for the terrible outcome in court.

"Another broken promise by the white man," said one.

"We shoulda known we'd get screwed," said another.

I took a deep breath and repeated what I'd said after Tony's sentencing. "Don't look at the white man's justice as your justice. You have won the real battle. Your sacred beings have been cared for. They have been treated with dignity and respect."

I watched as faces softened, and continued, "The spiritual objects that have been ripped from you will be returned to you. That is what this case has been all about from the beginning—that's Indian justice, not white man's justice. I keep telling you this, but you're not listening. Also, remember . . . some of your own people were helping to supply this white man with sacred artifacts. You must find these people and punish them."

Heads nodded, and some actually thanked me for my work on the case. It spite of what anyone said, I still couldn't get over the anticlimactic feelings running through me. As I walked down the outdoor stairs of the courthouse, I struggled with why Wally had betrayed me and Peder and everyone who worked on the case. I thought back to the promises he'd made to Dirk about developing a lucrative partnership. Wally had less than four years left before he could retire from the FBI. After that he could do whatever he wanted. While developing a case against Dirk, maybe he was also planning his retirement. Maybe he wrote the letter to make sure Dirk got off with a light sentence, so they could be partners. The whole bizarre scenario made me sick. I wondered how Wally lived with the stink of ambiguity and how he rationalized being both the good guy and the bad guy depending on how the wind blew. I guess only a shape-shifter would really know.

CHAPTER FORTY-ONE

It was early 2003 before I was allowed to release the artifacts to the tribes. My first stop was at the Hopi tribe located in the middle of the Navajo reservation in northeastern Arizona. In geological terms the tribe sat on the Colorado Plateau, which consisted of large blocks of horizontal or nearly horizontal sedimentary rock. Each distinct line in the rocks represented thousands if not millions of years of geologic activity. If they could talk, they would reveal a world of information about life on earth. Along the way there were dozens of sites where petroglyphs had been left as remnants of the ancient ones believed to have lived in the area 10,000 years ago.

In modern times, the Hopi tribe was reached by driving west from Albuquerque to Gallup, New Mexico, then north to Window Rock on the Navajo Reservation and then west to the Kykotsmovi Village where the Hopi Cultural Preservation Office was located. The exhausting drive took about six hours. At the HCPO I met with Darrel Selestewa,* a prominent Hopi healer, and Stanley Tomosie,* the director of the Cultural Preservation Office. I carried two large boxes filled with Hopi artifacts seized from both Lorenzo and DeVries and delivered them to a conference room where the two Hopi men closed the door. At first they were concerned because *bilagáana* were forbidden to see sacred items. But since my viewing of the items couldn't be helped and I was there to help them, they reluctantly let it pass. I was thankful that they trusted me enough to handle what was sacrosanct to them.

Overall I returned about thirty-five artifacts to the Hopis. When I opened one of the boxes, the two Hopis gasped when they saw the pair of wooden parrots. While they weren't about to reveal the significance of the parrots, they appeared to be grateful to have them returned. After seeing them, they quickly closed the box. That was my last glimpse of the parrots that had been in my life for so long. They were home now.

Another very rare artifact was a *mongko*, which is a four-by-two-foot board painted with light blue stripes and sacred symbols etched into it.

A sacred wild turkey feather and a corn cob hung from it by common string. This artifact was carried by elaborately dressed priests of the now extinct Two-Horned Society. The priests wore hats with two large animal horns attached. Most people considered the horns to be from a desert bighorn sheep, but to my eye they were too long and narrow to be from a bighorn. They looked more like the horns of an ibex, which is found in Spain. Perhaps the early Spaniards used these horns as trading material. The Hopi men said this relic would be destroyed in a soulful way, as it was no longer used by the Hopis and might carry bad spirits from being in the wrong hands.

During my visit with the Hopis I learned that the tribe believes it sits at the center of the earth and holds a special responsibility for prayer for peace for all peoples of the earth. Like many of the tribes in the Southwest, the Hopis believe they originated from another world, which was underground. They were born of Mother Earth, which makes her the object of greatest respect and worship. The strong interrelationship between nature and the people is inextricable. Mountains, rocks, streams, and plantings are holy, as the ancients dictated that their very survival depended on the whims of nature. The Hopis conduct numerous ceremonies throughout the year at exactly the same time. Each ceremony tells the story of how the Hopis came to be and how they were intended to live.

I attended a ceremony by the Long Hair Dancers, who acted out the lesson of how important it is to give back after something is given. During the ceremony the Long Hairs brought boxes of food into their circle. As they had been given to, they had to give back. They did this by throwing the food to the people in attendance. One dancer looked straight at me and tossed me a banana. I caught it and ate it, thinking how now it was my turn to give something back, to anyone. The idea of always giving back translates to footraces where the winner has to keep running past the finish line to the fields and deposit saliva as a means of passing his strength to the crops. To the Hopis, the concept of giving back is critical to maintaining the cycle of life.

After I finished handing over their sacred items, Darrell cleansed me with corn pollen, blessed me with a prayer spoken in Keresan, and gave me a brief hug of thanks. There was no huge fanfare or celebration.

They did, however, treat me to a tour of old Oraibi, a village built on a high mesa that had been continually inhabited for more than five hundred years.

As I drove away from the Hopi tribe, I saw a handmade sign that read BE HAPPY BE HOPI. Yes, I would work harder at being happy, and I would add to my own life's tapestry the Hopi values of humility, respect, selflessness, and the idea of always giving back. A part of Hopi would always be with me.

CHAPTER FORTY-TWO

On February 23, 2003, I got up early to drive to Window Rock, Arizona, headquarters of the Navajo Nation. The drive from Albuquerque to Gallup, New Mexico, includes a mesa capped with sandstone deposited along the shore of a Cretaceous sea. Just north of Gallup is Window Rock, home to one of the finest examples of a stone arch outside of Arches National Park in Utah. Window Rock is a tourist attraction, and even I never tired of seeing the bright blue sky as it seemed to penetrate the giant boulder.

At the Navajo Nation Historic Preservation Department, I met Ben Begay,* who greeted me with an enthusiastic *ya'at'eeh*! Begay was a twenty-six-year-old apprentice studying to become a *hataalii*. This would take years of intense study, and I admired him for his interest in keeping traditional Navajo medicinal and spiritual beliefs alive. After some introductory banter, I revealed the artifacts that I believed were of Navajo origin. Begay didn't say a word, but his face froze. Finally he asked me how so many sacred items could have left the nation. I had no answer other than to suggest that there were Navajos who were complicit in stealing and/or selling these sacred objects to non-Indians for the lucrative black market in Indian ceremonial artifacts. I had information on Tony's girlfriend, and I gave it to him.

Ben, who was devoted to the Navajo way of living in perfect balance, regarded every action as sacred and believed the goal of every step was to live in joy and balance. How could a Navajo disrupt this basic tenor of the Navajo way? I felt awful having to tell him the brutal truth about the dark side of some of his own people.

Suddenly Ben began scratching his arms wildly. He said, "White people have desecrated what is sacred to us. I don't see how we can take them back—they might carry evil."

Calmly I explained that I'd treated their precious artifacts with humility and respect. I'd kept them safe and secure and had covered them with white muslin cloths.

"I believe the prayers by Navajos have brought these artifacts home to you. They want to be home," I urged.

Ben Begay declared a cultural crisis and called in Alfred Yazzie and two other *hataalii* for their opinion on the matter. From a corner of the room I watched as they placed their trembling hands over the ten sets of talking prayers sticks and chanted in Athabaskan until the room almost shook. Then they meditated in silence, listening for whispers in the holy wind that brought sacred messages of guidance. Then they chanted some more.

When the chanting ceased, Ben said that the talking prayer sticks wanted to return home, but the *hataalii* were concerned that had they been desecrated. After all, several *bilagáana* had handled them in ways that were not respectful. The *hataalii* had to pray on it more, but for now they would take them. As for the bullroarers, the sacred bags of soil taken from the four sacred mountains, the small bag of ashes from a tree that had been struck by lightning, and many other *jish* items, the verdict was the same. The Navajos would take them for now and would decide whether or not the artifacts would be destroyed due to being desecrated at the hands of *bilagáana*.

The *hataalii* also told me that their spiritual doctrine prohibited them from talking about their ceremonial accoutrements. I responded that I understood and found myself apologizing for the white men who had been so disrespectful toward the Navajo culture. They nodded as if they accepted my apology but never thanked me for my efforts in returning what had been taken from them. After all, I'd only done what was right.

Ben Begay explained that the wound of the desecration was so deep that it would take time and healing. In the end, the *hataalii* and Ben dusted corn pollen over the artifacts to cleanse them. Then Ben dusted some on me and chanted as he asked that I be cleansed of any evil I'd been exposed to. I was grateful for any sprinkling of goodness or healing.

During my day with Ben Begay and the *hataalii*, I learned that the sacred sun gives the gift of warmth, and the summer lightning gives the gift of fear. Everything in nature has something to teach us and something to be revered. Everything that is done, said, or thought is considered to be a sacred part of life's journey. I learned that there is no separation between daily life, such as eating, sleeping, and walking, and what is sacred. The supreme goal in life is to walk in beauty by being kind, respectful, and helpful to others. Every wrongful act has to be rectified with a good deed; this is what living in balance is all about.

My drive home went well into the night as I thought about the federal law I was charged to enforce. While NAGPRA was designed to protect Native American religion, there really was no such thing as a specific religion in Indian culture. The law tried to capsulize Indian religion into ceremonies and rites conducted for specific purposes. In reality the Native American way of daily life and "religion" were the same thing. The goal of the Indians was to embrace every moment in a spiritual way. Every object they used was a gift from their deities and was treated with respect. That explained why baskets made by the Navajos always contained a spirit break—a broken line that disrupted the perfection of the basket. A person's spirit was used to create the basket. The person's spirit had to be released, so it would be available for creating other things. This same concept applied to Navajo rugs. The weaver always made a mistake, often indiscernible, as a spirit break.

Every interaction with another person was considered a sacred connection with the spirit of all people. While there wasn't a specific name for this all-consuming spirit, it existed and sent its messages through masked deities and kachinas. Then I thought of the Judeo-Christian concept of God, saints, priests, preachers, angels, and the spirits of loved ones we sometimes feel are with us during times of trouble. To me, the similarities between white man's religion and the Indian way of life were striking. Except that I was raised to fill my soul during one hour on Sunday. To the Native Americans I met, the goal was to do this every day, all day.

CHAPTER FORTY-THREE

In the summer of 2003, FBI special agent Wilson, AUSA Swanson, and I drove to the pueblo where the corn mother had come from. The religious leaders were horrified over the theft of their most precious artifact and asked us never to reveal their pueblo's name. The corn mother's removal was a supreme cultural crisis, and they wanted to keep it a secret.

This pueblo is the most secluded pueblo in New Mexico and is strictly closed to outsiders. It amazed me that Tony was able to pilfer so much material from this highly inaccessible place. I speculated that Tony's coconspirator might have been a shaman, since he was getting material from inside a highly guarded kiva. I felt if this person was ever identified, he'd surely be dealt with harshly by the tribe.

I'd placed the corn mother inside the cylinder parfleche and then inside a large Tupperware container along with a dozen other ceremonial artifacts that had been spirited out of their great kivas. We went inside a modern building and then into a round room where the councilmen met to discuss tribal matters. Four shamans sat on the floor around the box. Their long hair was held back by cloth headbands. They wore off-white muslin tunics that tied at the waist and sacklike muslin pants. I'll never forget the rabid glare of hatred one of the shamans shot at me—as if I were the most evil one alive. Quite the opposite of what I expected.

The shamans ordered us out of the room while they viewed the artifacts. The presumed leader asked if a woman had seen the artifacts. Agent Wilson quickly told him no, only white men. I cringed at the lie but knew that without it the holy men would not welcome their artifacts home. Scott also explained to them that the FBI was certain that one of their own people had worked with a white man to steal these artifacts. It was someone who had access to the kivas. The shamans reeled in disbelief. Wilson added that the FBI was going to let the tribe deal with this as they wished. The shamans eyed each other suspiciously, as if one of them might be the offender. I'm sure this was something unimaginable to them.

After two hours the shamans came out of the council meeting room and declared that they would take the artifacts back but that much damage had been done. Clearly resentful toward us, they complained it would take extensive cleansing before the artifacts could be used again. They would make their final decision after much meditation and ceremony. We agreed and moved on. Silently I bid the corn mother good-bye. Because of the lessons the corn mother taught me, I would give countless thanks to Mother Earth for her bountiful gifts and would never pollute her or desecrate her.

—◦—

The Acoma Pueblo is located about sixty miles west of Albuquerque and a few miles south of I-40. The pueblo sits on top of a 365-foot mesa in order to enjoy protection from raids by other tribes and the Spanish conquistadores. The most famous story about Acoma took place in 1598 when a small army of Acoma Indians ambushed a group of Juan de Oñate's men, killing eleven of them. The Spaniard took revenge on the Acomas, burning most of the village, killing more than six hundred Acomas, and imprisoning nearly five hundred of them. Men over the age of twenty-five years who survived had their right foot amputated. Then they were forced into servitude for twenty-five years. I wondered if the water pot I bought from Tony was used to carry water to wash the wounds of Acoma men afflicted in this atrocity.

On a cool evening that yielded a striking purple sunset, AUSA Rainey Swanson and I drove to the Acoma Pueblo. We had been invited to attend a council meeting in which the members would decide if they'd take the water pot and the so-called desecrated artifacts back. At issue was how badly the items had been affected. Could they be cleansed and used again?

Since we had some extra time, we drove up the mesa and took a short tour of the centuries-old adobe homes where the doors were painted turquoise, the color of protection. Only women owned the homes in this matriarchal society and passed their property down through their daughters. We walked past the great kiva, which had a ladder protruding from it as if it were punching holes in the sky to produce rain. Not far from the kiva sat a church, built by enslaved Acoma men back in the seventeenth century. It was still used in conjunction with native practices. People roamed about selling pottery to tourists and tending to the daily business of life. A few families still lived in a few of the more-than-five-century-old dwellings, but most had second homes in the valley.

At seven p.m. Rainey and I walked into the conference at the Acoma Cultural Center located at the base of the mesa. The conference room was filled with two dozen men, mostly elders but a few younger ones too. As at a Rotary Club meeting, we were expected to shake hands with each man, greeting him with a smile and a "nice to meet you." The meeting began with an elder named Mr. Charlie explaining why Rainey and I were there. Mr. Charlie was a stocky man, somewhat bowlegged, with a round face that grew even rounder when he smiled—and he smiled a lot. He wore blue jeans and a western shirt, which was pretty much what other council members wore in one form or another.

On the table I set a box that contained dozens of artifacts including a centuries-old ceremonial bowl believed to have been used in an underground kiva to hold corn pollen. I suspected it was used in highly spiritual matters. Also in the box was the water pot I'd purchased from Tony at the beginning of the investigation. Minutes later Rainey and I were escorted out of the room into a hallway and told to sit in two plastic chairs and wait. Mr. Charlie would let us know when they had made a decision.

Sitting in the dark hallway for the next few hours felt like Chinese water torture. All we could hear was a jumble of Keresan, some Spanish, and our own names, Rainey and Lucinda. We shifted in our chairs dozens of times and by midnight were in a fitful sleep, using our heads to prop up one another. The situation was miserable and showed no signs of ending. Finally around three a.m. Mr. Charlie came out of the room and invited us inside. Bleary-eyed we followed him. The council members all looked awake and alert. I later learned that their meetings were always held through the night to test their endurance. This had been done since time beyond memory.

Mr. Charlie set the water pot on the table and ran his fingers over the hallowed symbols. "This pot is sacred to our people. An Anglo is not supposed to have it," he said slowly.

"I think it may have been stolen, or that a white man paid an awful lot of money for it," I said, keeping back a yawn.

"No woman would sell her water pot. This one is very old and probably has been passed down through many generations."

"Maybe a woman died and one of her sons sold it," suggested Rainey.

"That would be despicable," replied Mr. Charlie. "I'll find the family and give it back. I'll make it right."

I felt like I had returned a lost child to its home and breathed a deep sigh of relief.

Mr. Charlie held the small painted pot seized from Tony in his hands like a crystal bowl. His eyes began to mist when he said, "I can't imagine how this got out of the kiva. Now it's been desecrated by Anglos."

Rainey agreed that the pot should never have ended up in a white man's hands but said that there had to be an insider complicit in the transgression. After all, only a few Acomas were even allowed inside a kiva. The pilferer had to be someone they knew.

"If I can find out who did this," said Mr. Charlie, "I'll make sure that he is punished."

Finally Rainey and I said our good-byes, left the cultural center, and headed back to Albuquerque. Even though we had accomplished what had never been done before, we were just relieved that the tribe accepted what was uniquely theirs. We also talked about how, by staying up half the night, we'd passed an endurance test the Indians had imposed upon us. If we had not been sincere in our repatriation efforts, we would have left. But we stayed, and our endurance showed that we were working from our hearts. That is what they were testing us for, and we passed.

CHAPTER FORTY-FOUR

In September 2003 a surgeon told me that I needed surgery to remove a large part of my colon. I was in pain most of the time and knew I'd never pass my next government-mandated physical. The surgeon also told me that my recovery could take months. The badger in me wanted to keep working, but after thirty years I knew it was time to go.

Within a couple of months I made quick trips to the Jemez, Zia, San Ildefonso, Zuni, Tesuque, Laguna, and Isleta pueblos, all located within a short driving distance of Albuquerque. At each pueblo I met with the spiritual leaders and handed over sacred artifacts that belonged to their tribe. With my heart in my hand, I apologized for the spiritual damage done and begged them to reconcile their troubled feelings. In each case my sincerity was the barometer used to determine whether the artifacts would be accepted back into the tribe's society. To my greatest relief, every pueblo I visited took their artifacts and the holy men cleansed me in the event I'd been exposed to evil forces. After all, it was taboo for white women to see or handle Indian sacramental objects.

In December of 2003 I stayed busy cleaning up my remaining cases and getting my property ready to turn in. I still had the nearly one hundred stone fetishes seized from Tony Lorenzo in my evidence room. None of the tribes would take them, because their origin was unknown. No tribe would take something that might carry evil spirits. I didn't feel right leaving them in a dusty government evidence room until they ended up in a landfill where they'd really stir up negative energy. They needed to be disposed of properly. Unfortunately, there was no government procedure for this.

I had become friends with a shaman named Kutake* from the Zuni tribe located in western New Mexico. He was a deeply spiritual man whose gentle ambiance radiated around him. When I was with him, I felt I was in the presence of a great healer. His voice had an ethereal quality, as if he was talking directly to my spirit.

I had returned a number of religious items to the Zunis, and he was especially grateful. He reminded me that his tribe was still missing a pair of Zuni war gods. (These gods have been on the Interpol list of stolen ethnographic objects for several years.) There was reason to believe that a collector had them. I didn't tell Kutake that I knew the man who had probably stolen his war gods from their outdoor shrine and sold them. Instead I told him that I'd keep an eye out for them, but for now I needed advice on what to do with the fetishes. He told me to bring them and meet him halfway between Albuquerque and the Zuni tribe at a run-down restaurant that served as a lonely oasis for travelers on I-40, which was once part of the nostalgic Route 66.

New Year's Day 2004 was the last official day of my career. I started up the Ramcharger for its last trip with me and met Kutake at the restaurant as planned. Inside, I recognized him right away. He was in his early forties and was tall and lean, with a narrow face, dark eyes that shimmered, and hair that fell naturally across his brow. His eyes looked strangely Asian, which might support the theory that Zuni ancestors were actually an ancient migrant group from Japan. He had a graceful smile that showed his self-confidence and comfort in his own skin.

We were the only customers in the restaurant and, given the greasy menu, decided to order soup. Kutake told me he was going to take the fetishes and return them to Mother Earth. He would not take them back to his village because of the bad energy they might carry. Buried in the desert, they couldn't hurt anyone. Only he would know where they were, and he wouldn't speak a word of it.

After eating we went outside to where my Ramcharger was parked. I opened the passenger door and pulled out the box full of fetishes. As my last official act, I handed the box to Kutake and had him sign some paperwork, which had no meaning to him but told the government that the Zunis had taken the fetishes.

"I'll take care of these," he promised, "in the proper way."

Jokingly I said that hundreds of years from now archeologists would find this cache of stone fetishes and would spend their careers trying to figure out how they ended up in the desert. Kutake laughed, saying that the trickster would have a good time with that one. He set the box on the pavement and began rummaging through the fetishes until he selected one. It was a mottled white stone in the shape of a bear. The rustic bear had turquoise eyes and lightning symbols etched into both sides of his body. The fetish was an old one and came with an old leather pouch half-filled with corn pollen. Kutake folded the fetish into his hands and held it there for a few seconds while he blessed it, cleansed it, and cupped his hands to blow his breath onto it. Then he handed it to me.

"This is a spirit bear and is the most powerful of the fetishes we Zunis use. The main qualities of the spirit bear are strength, courage, and ability to adjust to new things. It's also used for healing and the ability to connect with the master spirit. If you need help in any of these areas, meditate on the spirit bear for help. He will be especially useful to you in your retirement. Be sure and feed him."

A rush ran through my body. While my agency had given me paper awards on the occasion of my retirement, Kutake had given me something incredibly meaningful. He told me to keep the spirit bear facing the direction of the rising sun that symbolizes new beginnings. Then he said a prayer of blessing for me in Shiwi'ma, his native tongue. I hugged Kutake and was so choked up I couldn't speak. I didn't want to leave him or his world, but I had to. My job was done. I climbed into my Ramcharger, set the spirit bear fetish on the passenger seat, and waited a few seconds to let my emotions settle. Finally I cranked the engine and started straight east to Albuquerque.

While driving, I let my mind drift back to what I'd learned from the Native Americans during Operation Monster Slayer. I'd found great freedom in walking a path enriched by faith in the power and principles of truth, honesty, generosity, peace, and an absorbing love for nature. Whenever I took something for myself, I would make a conscious effort to give back. Nothing would stay with me for selfish reasons. I would learn to find the middle way in all matters. The holy men had taught me that taking the extreme position in a situation would only make the pendulum swing to the other side, causing imbalance and unhappiness. Finding balance was the key to a joyful life. Every tribe I connected with felt that they were the center of the earth and had the responsibility of praying for all surface-walking people. I could do that. I would now pray for the peace and the wellbeing of the people I know and for all people of the earth.

A strong and lasting connection to nature was essential to nurturing the soul. Taking care of the land was a solemn responsibility. Mountains, streams, and valleys appeared in new and awe-inspiring light. I relished the Native American idea of the wind being a sanctified life force and would listen to the soft swish of the wind in the cottonwoods and pay attention to what came to mind.

The Indians had taught me that it was good to call attention to beauty, to express humility and gratitude, and to work for the greater good. Settling your mind on good things brought blessings and left no room for evil. Evil thoughts and acts carried consequences that could be dire. These ideas became my own. I would keep negative people away from me, and would keep friends in my heart and truth on my tongue.

With the sun setting behind me, I looked forward to tomorrow's rising sun, which would be the first day of my life of new beginnings. Monster Slayer had gone to his home on Navajo Mountain. While I was grateful to him, I would never need him again. In the meantime I would go on remembering the lessons of the ancients—one precious dawn at a time.

EPILOGUE

Lucinda Schroeder, special agent, US Fish and Wildlife Service, retired on January 1, 2004. She had successful surgery in April of 2004. In 2006 her first book, *A Hunt for Justice: The True Story of a Woman Wildlife Undercover Agent* (Lyons Press), about her undercover investigation inside a big-game hunting camp in Alaska, was published. See www .ahuntforjustice.com.

Bo Jenkins of the East-West Trading Post investigation moved to Panama and in 1994 was murdered in a crime that was never solved.

Reuben Harris's aviary was shut down by the city of Albuquerque because of bird squawking that violated the city's noise ordinance. He was also convicted in state court for running an illegal chop shop, placing gambling bets, and committing IRS violations. He lost his home for the second time and served three years in the New Mexico state prison.

Paco and Raul, the two Mexican employees in Harris's aviary, were determined to be in the United States illegally and were later deported to Mexico.

Senior special agent Phil Young, National Park Service, retired in December 2000 to take a job with the State of New Mexico's Historic Preservation Division as an archaeologist. He continues to develop heritage protection in the United States and the Middle East, and also works as a safety officer on wildland fires.

FBI special agent Scott Wilson transferred to Washington, DC, but later resigned to work in the private sector as an accountant.

Dirk DeVries completed his federal sentence and later was successfully prosecuted by the State of New Mexico for embezzlement. His crime was selling for $160,000 a rare Navajo rug that he held on consignment for a client and then keeping the money. He was ordered to repay the owner of the rug and to pay a fine of $80,000. He also spent three months in the Santa Fe County jail. DeVries no longer owns a prestigious art gallery in Santa Fe and now lives in relative obscurity.

At last report, Tony Lorenzo was playing drums in a local band and still dealing in antique Indian goods. He has repeatedly inquired if he could be a paid consultant to the FBI regarding Native American sacred artifacts. His request has not been considered.

Wally Shumaker retired from the FBI and started a private art security and appraisal business.

Peder Sandbakken continued working in a high-level position within the Norwegian Police Administration in Oslo. He retired in 2014.

Several Native Americans, including Alfonso from the Isleta Pueblo, were identified as having stolen and sold sacred objects to Tony Lorenzo. While the penalties varied, most suffered banishment from their respective tribes, which is considered a life sentence of great dishonor.

ACKNOWLEDGMENTS

My greatest thanks are extended to the many Native Americans in the Southwest who crossed cultural boundaries to guide me in an investigation that focused on the recovery of stolen and exploited ceremonial artifacts. I give thanks to Phil Young and other federal agents who took part in this investigation and shared my core belief that Native American spiritual beliefs hold a special place in our world. Thanks too to my husband, Lonnie, who supported me during the long hours, days, and months it took me to complete the manuscript of this book. His patience is unfathomable. Thanks and more thanks to my editor, Erin Turner of Lyons Press, my copyeditor, Ann Marlowe, my project editor, Lauren Brancato, and my fabulous literary agent, Linda Konner, who provided invaluable support and enthusiasm that made this book possible. Special thanks to Diane O'Connell of Write to Sell Your Book, who spent days with me going over the manuscript for this book. She was incredible.

Index

Peruvian funerary figurines, 106
photography, 6, 7, 40, 195–96
Plains Indians, 199
plea bargains, 211
poaching investigations, 32–33,
    95–96, 126
pot cops, 135–36
pots, polychrome Acoma, 43–44,
    93, 228–29
prayer sticks, 57, 80, 191, 200
profiling, criminal, 76–77, 84–85,
    163, 187
protection, divine, 2, 43, 190
provenance, 6, 7, 61–62, 81
Pueblo Indians
    artifact repatriation,
        226–29, 230
    artifacts from, 43–44, 83, 93,
        134, 166, 228–29
    early anthropological collecting
        from, 56
    Isleta Pueblo visits, 166,
        172–75
    Jemez Pueblo visits, 115
    kachinas and significance of
        bird feathers, 87
    land use and traditions, 48

Q
Quinn (Indian dancer), 35–36

R
Raul (illegal worker), 15–16
ravens, 87
recordings, 40, 71–72, 75, 76, 117

red-shafted flickers, 87
red-tailed hawks, 87, 161, 212
repatriation, 212, 217, 218,
    220–29, 230–32
retablos, 126
rez runners, 1–6, 13–14, 37–38, 51.
    See also Lorenzo, Tony
rhinoceros horns, 102
Romero, Marco, 149–56
rugs, Navajo, 59–60, 83, 225

S
Sam (supplier), 144, 175–82
Sandbakken, Peder
    arrival and tour, 111–15
    baggage problem, 159
    corn mother photograph and,
        195–96
    DeVries meetings, 128–40,
        142–45, 144, 175–82, 186–89
    informant partner meeting,
        117–20
    Isleta Pueblo visits, 172–75
    Lorenzo meetings, 144–45,
        159–67, 185–86
    planning and preparation,
        102–4, 105–6, 108–9,
        121–27
    return to Norway, 141–42,
        182, 196
    undeliverable address and
        suspicion, 146
    undercover backstory, 125
    undercover props, 116–17
San Ildefonso Pueblo, 166, 230

ABOUT THE AUTHOR

RHONDA HODGES

Lucinda D. Schroeder worked as special agent for the US Fish and Wildlife Service from 1974 to 2004. One of the first women to work in federal law enforcement, she was charged with investigating wildlife crimes throughout the United States and internationally.

In 1994 she was named one the service's Top Ten Employees, out of an agency of seven thousand, for the work she did in apprehending an international ring of poachers in Alaska. Working undercover, she infiltrated an illegal hunting camp and took it down. This dangerous and exciting investigation is profiled in her first book, *A Hunt for Justice: The True Story of a Woman Undercover Wildlife Agent* (ahuntforjustice.com).

Schroeder has appeared on the Investigation Discovery Channel and the Travel Channel regarding her work to protect wildlife. Today she is a sought-out speaker and enjoys hiking and frequent travels with her husband.